D1298782

(ex•ploring)
SERIES

1. To investigate in a systematic way: examine. 2. To search into or range over for the purpose of discovery.

(ex•ploring)

SERIES

1. To investigate in a systematic way: examine. 2. To search
into or range over for the purpose of discovery.

Microsoft® Office

Publisher 2007

BRIEF

Robert T. Grauer

Cindy P. Stevens

PEARSON

Prentice
Hall

**Upper Saddle River
New Jersey 07458**

Library of Congress Cataloging-in-Publication Data

Grauer, Robert T.
  Microsoft Office Publisher 2007 brief / Robert T. Grauer, Cindy P. Stevens.
      p. cm. — (Exploring series)
  Includes index.
  ISBN-13: 978-0-13-514109-0
  ISBN-10: 0-13-514109-5
  1. Microsoft Publisher. 2. Desktop publishing. I. Stevens, Cindy, 1965- II. Title.
  Z253.532.M53G73 2008
  686.2'2544536—dc22

                                                                2007040199

VP/Publisher: Natalie E. Anderson
Senior Acquisitions Editor, Print: Melissa Sabella
Director, Product Development: Pamela Hersperger
Product Development Manager: Eileen Bien Calabro
Editorial Project Manager: Rebecca Knauer
Editorial Assistant: Melissa Arlio
AVP/Executive Producer: Lisa Strite
Editorial Media Project Manager: Alana Coles
Production Media Project Manager: Lorena Cerisano
Marketing Manager: Scott Davidson
Marketing Assistant: Angela Frey
Senior Managing Editor: Cynthia Zonneveld
Associate Managing Editor: Camille Trentacoste
Production Project Manager: Ruth Ferrera-Kargov
Senior Operations Director: Nick Sklitsis
Senior Art Director: Jonathan Boylan
Art Director: Anthony Gemmellaro
Cover Design: Anthony Gemmellaro
Cover Illustration/Photo: Courtesy of Getty Images/Laurent Hamels
Director, Image Resource Center: Melinda Patelli
Manager, Rights and Permissions: Zina Arabia
Manager, Visual Research: Beth Brenzel
Manager, Cover Visual Research & Permissions: Karen Sanatar
Image Permission Coordinator: Angelique Sharps
Composition: GGS Book Services
Full-Service Project Management: GGS Book Services
Printer/Binder: Banta/Menasha
Typeface: 10/12 Palatino

Microsoft, Windows, Vista, Word, PowerPoint, Outlook, FrontPage, Visual Basic, MSN, The Microsoft Network, and/or other Microsoft products referenced herein are either registered trademarks or registered trademarks of the Microsoft Corporation in the U.S.A. and other countries. Screen shots and icons reprinted with permission from the Microsoft Corporation. This book is not sponsored or endorsed by or affiliated with the Microsoft Corporation.

Copyright © 2008 by Pearson Education, Inc., Upper Saddle River, New Jersey, 07458. Pearson Prentice Hall. All rights reserved. Printed in the United States of America. This publication is protected by Copyright and permission should be obtained from the publisher prior to any prohibited reproduction, storage in a retrieval system, or transmission in any form or by any means, electronic, mechanical, photocopying, recording, or likewise. For information regarding permission(s), write to: Rights and Permissions Department.

Pearson Prentice Hall™ is a trademark of Pearson Education, Inc.
Pearson® is a registered trademark of Pearson plc
Prentice Hall® is a registered trademark of Pearson Education, Inc.

Pearson Education LTD.
Pearson Education Singapore, Pte. Ltd
Pearson Education, Canada, Ltd
Pearson Education–Japan

Pearson Education Australia PTY, Limited
Pearson Education North Asia Ltd
Pearson Educación de Mexico, S.A. de C.V.
Pearson Education Malaysia, Pte. Ltd.

10 9 8 7 6 5 4 3 2 1
ISBN-13: 978-0-13-514109-0
ISBN-10: 0-13-514109-5

Dedications

To Marion—my wife, my lover, and my best friend.

Robert Grauer

I would like to dedicate this book to my strong, beautiful, loving daughter, Alyssa P. Stevens. Thanks also to my parents, Terry and Irene Brown, and my sister, Tracy Hall, who have always been there for me no matter what. Most of all, I would like to thank my best friend, Brian Dowdall, for his endless listening skills and loving support.

Cindy P. Stevens

About the Authors

Dr. Robert T. Grauer

Dr. Robert T. Grauer is an Associate Professor in the Department of Computer Information Systems at the University of Miami, where he has been honored with the Outstanding Teacher Award in the School of Business. He is the vision behind the Exploring Series, which is about to sell its 3 millionth copy.

Dr. Grauer has written more than 50 books on programming and information systems. His work has been translated into three foreign languages and is used in all aspects of higher education at both national and international levels.

Dr. Grauer also has been a consultant to several major corporations including IBM and American Express. He received his Ph.D. in operations research in 1972 from the Polytechnic Institute of Brooklyn.

Dr. Cindy P. Stevens

Dr. Cindy P. Stevens teaches in the Management Department at Wentworth Institute of Technology, Boston, Massachusetts. Dr. Stevens is also an Internet-based Computer instructor for Wayne Community College, Goldsboro, North Carolina.

Dr. Stevens received her Ph.D. in Technology Management-Digital Communication Systems, at Indiana State University, in the fall of 2002. She earned her Masters degree in Technical & Professional Communication from East Carolina University.

Dr. Stevens has written three editions of the Exploring Publisher series books and over 20 instructor manuals for the Exploring series, including test banks, PowerPoint lectures, and online learning exercises.

She has one child. When she isn't teaching or writing she enjoys practicing yoga, reading, spending time with her family and friends, and playing with her dog, Winsten.

Contents

CHAPTER THREE | Accounting Publications: Working with Business Forms

CHAPTER FOUR | Online Publishing: Creating a Web Site

Acknowledgments

The success of the Exploring series is attributed to contributions from numerous individuals. First and foremost, our heartfelt appreciation to Melissa Sabella, senior acquisitions editor, for providing new leadership and direction to capitalize on the strength and tradition of the Exploring series while implementing innovative ideas into the Exploring Office 2007 edition. Scott Davidson, senior marketing manager, was an invaluable addition to the team who believes in the mission of this series passionately and did an amazing job communicating its message.

During the first few months of the project, Eileen Clark, senior editorial project manager, kept the team focused on the vision, pedagogy, and voice that has been the driving force behind the success of the Exploring series. Claire Hunter, market development editor, facilitated communication between the editorial team and the reviewers to ensure that this edition meets the changing needs of computer professors and students at the collegiate level.

Laura Town, developmental editor, provided an objective perspective in reviewing the content and organization of selected chapters. Jenelle Woodrup, editorial project manager, provided valuable assistance in communication among team members and keeping the files moving into production. Eileen Calabro, product development manager, facilitated communication among the editorial team, authors, and production during a transitional stage. Doug Bell and the whole team at GGS worked through software delays, style changes and anything else we threw at them to bring the whole thing together. Art director Blair Brown's conversations with students and professors across the country yielded a design that addressed the realities of today's students with function and style.

The new members of the Exploring author team would like to especially thank Bob Grauer for his vision in developing Exploring and his leadership in creating this highly successful series.

Maryann Barber would like to thank Bob Grauer for a wonderful collaboration and providing the opportunities through which so much of her life has changed.

The Exploring team would like to especially thank the following instructors who drew on their experience in the classroom and their software expertise to give us daily advice on how to improve this book. Their impact can be seen on every page:

Arlene Flerchinger, Chattanooga State

Barbara Stover, Marion Technical College

Bob McCloud, Sacred Heart University

Cassie Georgetti, Florida Technical College

Dana Johnson, North Dakota State University

Jackie Lamoureux, Central New Mexico Community College

Jim Pepe, Bentley College

Judy Brown, The University of Memphis

Lancie Anthony Affonso, College of Charleston

Margaret McManus, Okaloosa-Walton College

Mimi Duncan, University of Missouri – St. Louis

Minnie Proctor, Indian River Community College

Philip Vavalides, Guilford Technical Community College

Richard Albright, Goldey-Beacom College

We also want to acknowledge all the reviewers of the Exploring 2007 series. Their valuable comments and constructive criticism greatly improved this edition:

Aaron Schorr
Fashion Institute of Technology

Alicia Stonesifer
La Salle University

Allen Alexander, Delaware
Tech & Community College

Amy Williams, Abraham
Baldwin Agriculture College

Annie Brown
Hawaii Community College

Barbara Cierny
Harper College

Barbara Hearn
Community College of Philadelphia

Barbara Meguro
University of Hawaii at Hilo

Bette Pitts
South Plains College

Beverly Fite
Amarillo College

Bill Wagner
Villanova

Brandi N. Guidry
University of Louisiana at Lafayette

Brian Powell
West Virginia University – Morgantown
Campus

Carl Farrell
Hawaii Pacific University

Carl Penzuil
Ithaca College

Carole Bagley;
University of St. Thomas

Catherine Hain
Central New Mexico CC

Charles Edwards
University of Texas of the Permian Basin

Christine L. Moore
College of Charleston

David Barnes
Penn State Altoona

David Childress;
Ashland Community College

David Law, Alfred
State College

Dennis Chalupa
Houston Baptist

Diane Stark
Phoenix College

Dianna Patterson
Texarkana College

Dianne Ross
University of Louisiana at Lafayette

Dr. Behrooz Saghafi
Chicago State University

Dr. Gladys Swindler
Fort Hays State University

Dr. Joe Teng
Barry University

Dr. Karen Nantz
Eastern Illinois University.

Duane D. Lintner
Amarillo College

Elizabeth Edmiston
North Carolina Central University

Erhan Uskup
Houston Community College

Fred Hills, McClellan
Community College

Gary R. Armstrong
Shippensburg University of Pennsylvania

Glenna Vanderhoof
Missouri State

Gregg Asher
Minnesota State University, Mankato

Hong K. Sung
University of Central Oklahoma

Hyekyung Clark
Central New Mexico CC

J Patrick Fenton
West Valley College

Jana Carver
Amarillo College

Jane Cheng
Bloomfield College

Janos T. Fustos
Metropolitan State College of Denver

Jeffrey A Hassett
University of Utah

Jennifer Pickle
Amarillo College

Jerry Kolata
New England Institute of Technology

Jesse Day
South Plains College

John Arehart
Longwood University

John Lee Reardon
University of Hawaii, Manoa

Joshua Mindel
San Francisco State University

Karen Wisniewski
County College of Morris

Karl Smart
Central Michigan University

Kathryn L. Hatch
University of Arizona

Krista Terry
Radford University

Laura McManamon
University of Dayton

Laura Reid
University of Western Ontario

Linda Johnsonius
Murray State University

Lori Kelley
Madison Area Technical College

Lucy Parker,
California State University, Northridge

Lynda Henrie
LDS Business College

Malia Young
Utah State University

Margie Martyn
Baldwin Wallace

Marianne Trudgeon
Fanshawe College

Marilyn Hibbert
Salt Lake Community College

Marjean Lake
LDS Business College

Mark Olaveson
Brigham Young University

Nancy Sardone
Seton Hall University

Patricia Joseph
Slippery Rock University.

Patrick Hogan
Cape Fear Community College

Paula F. Bell
Lock Haven University of
Pennsylvania

Paulette Comet
Community College of Baltimore County, Catonsville

Pratap Kotala
North Dakota State University

Richard Blamer
John Carroll University

Richard Herschel
St. Joseph's University

Richard Hewer
Ferris State University

Robert Gordon
Hofstra University

Robert Marmelstein
East Stroudsburg University

Robert Stumbur
Northern Alberta Institute of Technology

Roberta I. Hollen
University of Central Oklahoma

Roland Moreira
South Plains College

Ron Murch
University of Calgary

Rory J. de Simone
University of Florida

Ruth Neal
Navarro College

Sandra M. Brown
Finger Lakes Community College

Sharon Mulroney
Mount Royal College

Stephen E. Lunce
Midwestern State University

Steve Schwarz
Raritan Valley Community College

Steven Choy
University of Calgary

Susan Byrne
St. Clair College

Thomas Setaro
Brookdale Community College

Todd McLeod
Fresno City College

Vickie Pickett
Midland College

Vipul Gupta
St Joseph's University

Vivek Shah
Texas State University - San Marcos

Wei-Lun Chuang
Utah State University

William Dorin
Indiana University Northwest

Finally, we wish to acknowledge reviewers of previous editions of the Exploring series—we wouldn't have made it to the 7th edition without you:

Alan Moltz
Naugatuck Valley Technical Community College

Alok Charturvedi
Purdue University

Antonio Vargas
El Paso Community College

Barbara Sherman
Buffalo State College

Bill Daley
University of Oregon

Bill Morse
DeVry Institute of Technology

Bonnie Homan
San Francisco State University

Carl M. Briggs
Indiana University School of Business

Carlotta Eaton
Radford University

Carolyn DiLeo
Westchester Community College

Cody Copeland
Johnson County Community College

Connie Wells
Georgia State University

Daniela Marghitu
Auburn University

David B. Meinert
Southwest Missouri State University

David Douglas
University of Arkansas

David Langley
University of Oregon

David Rinehard
Lansing Community College

David Weiner
University of San Francisco

Dean Combellick
Scottsdale Community College

Delores Pusins
Hillsborough Community College

Don Belle
Central Piedmont Community College

Douglas Cross
Clackamas Community College

Ernie Ivey
Polk Community College

Gale E. Rand
College Misericordia

Helen Stoloff
Hudson Valley Community College

Herach Safarian
College of the Canyons

Jack Zeller
Kirkwood Community College

James Franck
College of St. Scholastica

James Gips
Boston College

Jane King
Everett Community College

Janis Cox
Tri-County Technical College

Jerry Chin
Southwest Missouri State University

Jill Chapnick
Florida International University

Jim Pruitt
Central Washington University

John Lesson
University of Central Florida

John Shepherd
Duquesne University

Judith M. Fitspatrick
Gulf Coast Community College

Judith Rice
Santa Fe Community College

Judy Dolan
Palomar College

Karen Tracey
Central Connecticut State University

Kevin Pauli
University of Nebraska

Kim Montney
Kellogg Community College

Kimberly Chambers
Scottsdale Community College

Larry S. Corman
Fort Lewis College

Lynn Band
Middlesex Community College

Margaret Thomas
Ohio University

Marguerite Nedreberg
Youngstown State University

Marilyn Salas
Scottsdale Community College

Martin Crossland
Southwest Missouri State University

Mary McKenry Percival
University of Miami

Michael Hassett
Fort Hayes State University

Michael Stewardson
San Jacinto College – North

Midge Gerber
Southwestern Oklahoma State University

Mike Hearn
Community College of Philadelphia

Mike Kelly
Community College of Rhode Island

Mike Thomas
Indiana University School of Business

Paul E. Daurelle
Western Piedmont Community College

Ranette Halverson
Midwestern State University

Raymond Frost
Central Connecticut State University

Robert Spear, Prince
George's Community College

Rose M. Laird
Northern Virginia Community College

Sally Visci
Lorain County Community College

Shawna DePlonty
Sault College of Applied Arts and Technology

Stuart P. Brian
Holy Family College

Susan Fry
Boise State Universtiy

Suzanne Tomlinson
Iowa State University

Vernon Griffin
Austin Community College

Wallace John Whistance-Smith
Ryerson Polytechnic University

Walter Johnson
Community College of Philadelphia

Wanda D. Heller
Seminole Community College

We very much appreciate the following individuals for painstakingly checking every step and every explanation for technical accuracy, while dealing with an entirely new software application:

Barbara Waxer
Bill Daley
Beverly Fite
Dawn Wood
Denise Askew
Elizabeth Lockley

James Reidel
Janet Pickard
Janice Snyder
Jeremy Harris
John Griffin
Joyce Neilsen

LeeAnn Bates
Mara Zebest
Mary E. Pascarella
Michael Meyers
Sue McCrory

Preface

The Exploring Series

Exploring has been Prentice Hall's most successful Office Application series of the past 15 years. For Office 2007 Exploring has undergone the most extensive changes in its history, so that it can truly move today's student "beyond the point and click."

The goal of Exploring has always been to teach more than just the steps to accomplish a task – the series provides the theoretical foundation necessary for a student to understand when and why to apply a skill. This way, students achieve a broader understanding of Office.

Today's students are changing and Exploring has evolved with them. Prentice Hall traveled to college campuses across the country and spoke directly to students to determine how they study and prepare for class. We also spoke with hundreds of professors about the best ways to administer materials to such a diverse body of students.

Here is what we learned

Students go to college now with a different set of skills than they did 5 years ago. The new edition of Exploring moves students beyond the basics of the software at a faster pace, without sacrificing coverage of the fundamental skills that everybody needs to know. This ensures that students will be engaged from Chapter 1 to the end of the book.

Students have diverse career goals. With this in mind, we broadened the examples in the text (and the accompanying Instructor Resources) to include the health sciences, hospitality, urban planning, business and more. Exploring will be relevant to every student in the course.

Students read, prepare and study differently than they used to. Rather than reading a book cover to cover students want to easily identify what they need to know, and then learn it efficiently. We have added key features that will bring students into the content and make the text easy to use such as objective mapping, pull quotes, and key terms in the margins.

Moving students beyond the point and click

All of these additions mean students will be more engaged, achieve a higher level of understanding, and successfully complete this course. In addition to the experience and expertise of the series creator and author Robert T. Grauer we have assembled a tremendously talented team of supporting authors to assist with this critical revision. Each of them is equally dedicated to the Exploring mission of **moving students beyond the point and click.**

- **New** **Office Fundamentals Chapter** efficiently covers skills common among all applications like save, print, and bold to avoid repetition in each Office application's first chapter, along with coverage of problem solving skills to prepare students to apply what they learn in any situation.

- **New** **Moving Beyond the Basics** introduces advanced skills earlier because students are learning basic skills faster.

- **White Pages/Yellow Pages clearly** distinguish the theory (white pages) from the skills covered in the Hands-On exercises (yellow pages) so students always know what they are supposed to be doing.

- **New** **Objective Mapping** enables students to skip the skills and concepts they know, and quickly find those they don't, by scanning the chapter opener page for the page numbers of the material they need.

- **New** **Pull Quotes** entice students into the theory by highlighting the most interesting points.

- **New** **Conceptual Animations** connect the theory with the skills, by illustrating tough to understand concepts with interactive multimedia.

- **New** **More End of Chapter Exercises** offer instructors more options for assessment. Each chapter has approximately 12–15 exercises ranging from Multiple Choice questions to open-ended projects.

- **New** **More Levels of End of Chapter Exercises,** including new Mid-Level Exercises tell students what to do, but not how to do it, and Capstone Exercises cover all of the skills within each chapter.

- **New** **Mini Cases with Rubrics** are open ended exercises that guide both instructors and students to a solution with a specific rubric for each mini case.

Instructor and Student Resources

Instructor Chapter Reference Cards

A four page color card for every chapter that includes a:

- *Concept Summary* that outlines the KEY objectives to cover in class with tips on where students get stuck as well as how to get them un-stuck. It helps bridge the gap between the instructor and student when discussing more difficult topics.

- *Case Study Lecture Demonstration Document* which provides instructors with a lecture sample based on the chapter opening case that will guide students to critically use the skills covered in the chapter, with examples of other ways the skills can be applied.

The Enhanced Instructor's Resource Center on CD-ROM includes:

- **Additional Capstone Production Tests** allow instructors to assess all the skills in a chapter with a single project.

- **Mini Case Rubrics** in Microsoft® Word format enable instructors to customize the assignment for their class.

- **PowerPoint® Presentations** for each chapter with notes included for online students.

- **Lesson Plans** that provide a detailed blueprint for an instructor to achieve chapter learning objectives and outcomes.

- **Student Data Files**

- **Annotated Solution Files**

- **Complete Test Bank**

- **Test Gen Software with QuizMaster**

TestGen is a test generator program that lets you view and easily edit testbank questions, transfer them to tests, and print in a variety of formats suitable to your teaching situation. The program also offers many options for organizing and displaying testbanks and tests. A random number test generator enables you to create multiple versions of an exam.

QuizMaster, also included in this package, allows students to take tests created with TestGen on a local area network. The QuizMaster Utility built into TestGen lets instructors view student records and print a variety of reports. Building tests is easy with Test-Gen, and exams can be easily uploaded into WebCT, BlackBoard, and CourseCompass.

Prentice Hall's Companion Web Site

www.prenhall.com/exploring offers expanded IT resources and downloadable supplements. This site also includes an online study guide for student self-study.

Online Course Cartridges

Flexible, robust and customizable content is available for all major online course platforms that include everything instructors need in one place.
www.prenhall.com/webct
www.prenhall.com/blackboard
www.coursecompass.com

chapter 3 | **Access**

Customize, Analyze, and Summarize Query Data

Creating and Using Queries to Make Decisions

bjectives

After you read this chapter you will be able to:

1. Understand the order of precedence **(page 679)**.
2. Create a calculated field in a query **(page 679)**.
3. Create expressions with the Expression Builder **(page 679)**.
4. Create and edit Access functions **(page 690)**.
5. Perform date arithmetic **(page 694)**.
6. Create and work with data aggregates **(page 704)**.

Hands-On Exercises

Exercises	Skills Covered
1. CALCULATED QUERY FIELDS (PAGE 683) **Open:** chap3_ho1-3_realestate.accdb **Save:** chap3_ho1-3_realestate_solution.accdb **Back up as:** chap3_ho1_realestate_solution.accdb	• Copy a Database and Start the Query • Select the Fields, Save, and Open the Query • Create a Calculated Field and Run the Query • Verify the Calculated Results • Recover from a Common Error
2. EXPRESSION BUILDER, FUNCTIONS, AND DATE ARITHMETIC (page 695) **Open:** chap3_ho1-3_realestate.accdb (from Exercise 1) **Save:** chap3_ho1-3_realestate_solution.accdb (additional modifications) **Back up as:** chap3_ho2_realestate_solution.accdb	• Create a Select Query • Use the Expression Builder • Create Calculations Using Input Stored in a Different Query or Table • Edit Expressions Using the Expression Builder • Use Functions • Work with Date Arithmetic
3. DATA AGGREGATES (page 707) **Open:** chap3_ho1-3_realestate.accdb (from Exercise 2) **Save:** chap3_ho1-3_realestate_solution.accdb (additional modifications)	• Add a Total Row • Create a Totals Query Based on a Select Query • Add Fields to the Design Grid • Add Grouping Options and Specify Summary Statistics

Access 2007 **677**

Objective Mapping

allows students to skip the skills and concepts they know and quickly find those they don't by scanning the chapter opening page for the page numbers of the material they need.

Case Study

begins each chapter to provide an effective overview of what students can accomplish by completing the chapter.

CASE STUDY

West Transylvania College Athletic Department

The athletic department of West Transylvania College has reached a fork in the road. A significant alumni contingent insists that the college upgrade its athletic program from NCAA Division II to Division I. This process will involve adding sports, funding athletic scholarships, expanding staff, and coordinating a variety of fundraising activities.

Tom Hunt, the athletic director, wants to determine if the funding support is available both inside and outside the college to accomplish this goal. You are helping Tom prepare the five-year projected budget based on current budget figures. The plan is to increase revenues at a rate of 10% per year for five years while handling an estimated 8% increase in expenses over the same five-

Case Study

year period. Tom feels that a 10% increase in revenue versus an 8% increase in expenses should make the upgrade viable. Tom wants to examine how increased alumni giving, increases in college fees, and grant monies will increase the revenue flow. The Transylvania College's Athletic Committee and its Alumni Association Board of Directors want Tom to present an analysis of funding and expenses to determine if the move to NCAA Division I is feasible. As Tom's student assistant this year, it is your responsibility to help him with special projects. Tom prepared the basic projected budget spreadsheet and has asked you to finish it for him.

Your Assignment

- Read the chapter carefully and pay close attention to mathematical operations, formulas, and functions.
- Open *chap2_case_athletics*, which contains the partially completed, projected budget spreadsheet.
- Study the structure of the worksheet to determine what type of formulas you need to complete the financial calculations. Identify how you would perform calculations if you were using a calculator and make a list of formulas using regular language to determine if the financial goals will be met. As you read the chapter, identify formulas and functions that will help you complete the financial analysis. You will insert formulas in the revenue and expenditures sections for column C. Use appropriate cell references in formulas. Do not enter constant values within a formula; instead enter the 10% and 8% increases in an input area. Use appropriate functions for column totals in both the revenue and expenditures sections. Insert formulas for the Net Operating Margin and Net Margin rows. Copy the formulas.
- Review the spreadsheet and identify weaknesses in the formatting. Use your knowledge of good formatting design to improve the appearance of the spreadsheet so that it will be attractive to the Athletic Committee and the alumni board. You will format cells as currency with 0 decimals and widen columns as needed. Merge and center the title and use an attractive fill color. Emphasize the totals and margin rows with borders. Enter your name and current date. Create a custom footer that includes a page number and your instructor's name. Print the worksheet as displayed and again with cell formulas displayed. Save the workbook as **chap2_case_athletics_solution**.

Key Terms

are called out in the margins of the chapter so students can more effectively study definitions.

Pull Quotes

entice students into the theory by highlighting the most interesting points.

A **table** is a series of rows and columns that organize data.

A **cell** is the intersection of a row and column in a table.

> The table feature is one of the most powerful in Word and is the basis for an almost limitless variety of documents. It is very easy to create once you understand how a table works.

Tables

A **table** is a series of rows and columns that organize data effectively. The rows and columns in a table intersect to form **cells**. The table feature is one of the most powerful in Word and is an easy way to organize a series of data in a columnar list format such as employee names, inventory lists, and e-mail addresses. The Vacation Planner in Figure 3.1, for example, is actually a 4x9 table (4 columns and 9 rows). The completed table looks impressive, but it is very easy to create once you understand how a table works. In addition to the organizational benefits, tables make an excellent alignment tool. For example, you can create tables to organize data such as employee lists with phone numbers and e-mail addresses. The Exploring series uses tables to provide descriptions for various software commands. Although you can align text with tabs, you have more format control when you create a table. (See the Practice Exercises at the end of the chapter for other examples.)

Vacation Planner			
Item	Number of Days	Amount per Day (est)	Total Amount
Airline Ticket			449.00
Amusement Park Tickets	4	50.00	200.00
Hotel	5	120.00	600.00
Meals	6	50.00	300.00
Rental Car	5	30.00	150.00
Souvenirs	5	20.00	100.00
TOTAL EXPECTED EXPENSES			$1799.00

Figure 3.1 The Vacation Planner

In this section, you insert a table in a document. After inserting the table, you can insert or delete columns and rows if you need to change the structure. Furthermore, you learn how to merge and split cells within the table. Finally, you change the row height and column width to accommodate data in the table.

Inserting a Table

You can create a table from the Insert tab. Click Table in the Tables group on the Insert tab to see a gallery of cells from which you select the number of columns and rows you require in the table, or you can choose the Insert Table command below the gallery to display the Insert Table dialog box and enter the table composition you prefer. When you select the table dimension from the gallery or from the Insert Table dialog box, Word creates a table structure with the number of columns and rows you specify. After you define a table, you can enter text, numbers, or graphics in individual cells. Text

White Pages/
Yellow Pages

clearly distinguishes the theory
(white pages) from the skills
covered in the Hands-On exercises
(yellow pages) so students always
know what they are supposed to
be doing.

Keyword for search

Collections to be searched

Type of clips to be included
in results

CIS 101 Review Session
Test #2

Search results

Monday
7pm
Glass 102

Link to Microsoft Clip
Organizer

Link to more clips online

Figure 3.18 The Clip Art Task Pane

You can access the Microsoft Clip Organizer (to view the various collections) by clicking Organize clips at the bottom of the Clip Art task pane. You also can access the Clip Organizer when you are not using Word: click the Start button on the taskbar, click All Programs, Micros[...] Clip Organizer. Once in the Organi[...] ous collections, reorganize the exi[...] add new clips (with their associate[...] the bottom of the task pane in Figu[...] and tips for finding more relevant c[...]

Insert a Picture

In addition to the collection of clip[...] you also can insert your own pictu[...] ital camera attached to your compu[...] Word. After you save the picture to[...] on the Insert tab to locate and inser[...] opens so that you can navigate to t[...] insert the picture, there are many c[...] mands are discussed in the next sec[...]

Formatting a Grap[...]

When you inse[...]
fined size. For[...]
very large and[...]
resized. Most b[...]
within the d[...]

Remember that graphical elements
should enhance a document, not
overpower it.

220 CHAPTER 3 | Enhancing a Document

Step 2
Move and Resize the
Clip Art Object

Refer to Figure 3.24 as you complete Step 2.

a. Click once on the clip art object to select it. Click **Text Wrapping** in the Arrange group on the Picture Tools Format tab to display the text wrapping options, and then select **Square**, as shown in Figure 3.24.

You must change the layout in order to move and size the object.

b. Click **Position** in the Arrange group, and then click **More Layout Options.** Click the **Picture Position tab** in the Advanced Layout dialog box, if necessary, then click **Alignment** in the *Horizontal* section. Click the **Alignment drop-down arrow** and select **Right.** Deselect the **Allow overlap check box** in the *Options* section. Click **OK.**

c. Click **Crop** in the Size group, then hold your mouse over the sizing handles and notice how the pointer changes to angular shapes. Click the **bottom center handle** and drag it up. Drag the side handles inward to remove excess space surrounding the graphical object.

d. Click the Shape **Height box** in the Size group and type **2.77.**

Notice the width is changed automatically to retain the proportion.

e. Save the document.

Click to select Square Text
Wrapping style

Point to sizing handles

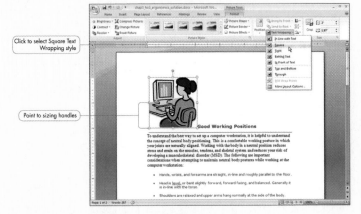

Figure 3.24 Formatting Clip Art

Step 3
Create a WordArt
Object

Refer to Figure 3.25 as you complete Step 3.

a. Press **Ctrl+End** to move to the end of the document. Click the **Insert tab**, and then click **WordArt** in the Text group to display the WordArt gallery.

b. Click **WordArt Style 28** on the bottom row of the gallery.

The Edit WordArt Text dialog box displays, as shown in Figure 3.25.

228 CHAPTER 3 | Enhancing a Document

Summary

1. **Create a presentation using a template.** Using a template saves you a great deal of time and enables you to create a more professional presentation. Templates incorporate a theme, a layout, and content that can be modified. You can use templates that are installed when Microsoft Office is installed, or you can download templates from Microsoft Office Online. Microsoft is constantly adding templates to the online site for your use.

2. **Modify a template.** In addition to changing the content of a template, you can modify the structure and design. The structure is modified by changing the layout of a slide. To change the layout, drag placeholders to new locations or resize placeholders. You can even add placeholders so that elements such as logos can be included.

3. **Create a presentation in Outline view.** When you use a storyboard to determine your content, you create a basic outline. Then you can enter your presentation in Outline view, which enables you to concentrate on the content of the presentation. Using Outline view keeps you from getting buried in design issues at the cost of your content. It also saves you time because you can enter the information without having to move from placeholder to placeholder.

4. **Modify an outline structure.** Because the Outline view gives you a global view of the presentation, it helps you see the underlying structure of the presentation. You are able to see where content needs to be strengthened, or where the flow of information needs to be revised. If you find a slide with content that would be presented better in another location in the slide show, you can use the Collapse and Expand features to easily move it. By collapsing the slide content, you can drag it to a new location and then expand it. To move individual bullet points, cut and paste the bullet point or drag-and-drop it.

5. **Print an outline.** When you present, using the outline version of your slide show as a reference is a boon. No matter how well you know your information, it is easy to forget to present some information when facing an audience. While you would print speaker's notes if you have many details, you can print the outline as a quick reference. The outline can be printed in either the collapsed or the expanded form, giving you far fewer pages to shuffle in front of an audience than printing speaker's notes would.

6. **Import an outline.** You do not need to re-enter information from an outline created in Microsoft Word or another word processor. You can use the Open feature to import any outline that has been saved in a format that PowerPoint can read. In addition to a Word outline, you can use the common generic formats Rich Text Format and Plain Text Format.

7. **Add existing content to a presentation.** After you spend time creating the slides in a slide show, you may find that slides in the slide show would be appropriate in another show at a later date. Any slide you create can be reused in another presentation, thereby saving you considerable time and effort. You simply open the Reuse Slides pane, locate the slide show with the slide you need, and then click on the thumbnail of the slide to insert a copy of it in the new slide show.

8. **Examine slide show design principles.** With a basic understanding of slide show design principles you can create presentations that reflect your personality in a professional way. The goal of applying these principles is to create a slide show that focuses the audience on the message of the slide without being distracted by clutter or unreadable text.

9. **Apply and modify a design theme.** PowerPoint provides you with themes to help you create a clean, professional look for your presentation. Once a theme is applied you can modify the theme by changing the color scheme, the font scheme, the effects scheme, or the background style.

10. **Insert a header or footer.** Identifying information can be included in a header or footer. You may, for example, wish to include the group to whom you are presenting, or the location of the presentation, or a copyright notation for original work. You can apply footers to slides, handouts, and Notes pages. Headers may be applied to handouts and Notes pages.

Summary

links directly back to the objectives so students can more effectively study and locate the concepts that they need to focus on.

More End-of-Chapter Exercises with New Levels of Assessment

offer instructors more options for assessment. Each chapter has approximately 12-15 projects per chapter ranging from multiple choice to open-ended projects.

Practice Exercises

reinforce skills learned in the chapter with specific directions on what to do and how to do it.

New Mid-Level Exercises

assess the skills learned in the chapter by directing the students on what to do but not how to do it.

New Capstone Exercises

cover all of the skills with in each chapter without telling students how to perform the skills.

Mini Cases with Rubrics

are open ended exercises that guide both instructors and students to a solution with a specific rubric for each Mini Case.

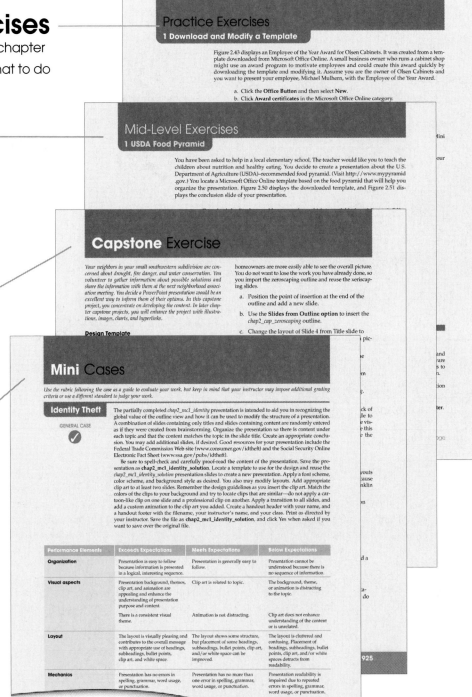

Where Word Processing Ends and Desktop Publishing Begins

Objectives

After you read this chapter, you will be able to:

1. Understand Desktop Publishing **(page 3)**.
2. Learn about the bridge from word processing to Publisher **(page 3)**.
3. Understand typing in text boxes and use the Zoom command **(page 4)**.
4. Know the difference between popular publication types and templates **(page 6)**.
5. Know how to create, save, edit, and print simple publications **(page 13)**.
6. Know how to use the Objects toolbar **(page 24)**.
7. Understand the steps for creating a good publication **(page 37)**.

Hands-On Exercises

Exercises	Skills Covered
1. OUR FIRST PUBLICATION (page 15) **Open:** Flyers Template (A new template from scratch) **Save as:** chap1_ho1_my_first_publication_solution.pub	• Open a Template • Set Template Options • Zoom In or Out of Your Publication • Type in a Publisher Text Box • Type in a Publisher Text Box (Continued) • Modify Text in a Text Box • Change the Clip Art • Save the Publication • Use the Help Feature • Print and Close the Publication • Exit Publisher
2. ADDING OBJECTS TO A PUBLICATION (page 26) **Open:** chap1_ho2_using_objects **Save as:** chap1_ho2_using_objects_solution	• Obtain the Practice Files • Open an Existing Publication • Use the Save As Command • Insert Clip Art • Move and Size the Clip Art • Format the Clip Art Frame • Insert WordArt • Move and Size Objects in Your Publication • Insert a Table • Create the Drawing Objects
3. CHANGING THE DESIGN OF A PUBLICATION (page 40) **Open:** chap1_ho3_price_list_brochure **Save as:** chap1_ho3_price_list_brochure_solution	• Insert the Business Name • Insert Clip Art from the Internet • Move, Size, and Layer the Picture • Choose a Different Logo • Change the Publication Design and Color Scheme

CASE STUDY

Get Your Name Out There

Case Study

For a year now, Joe has owned a small temp agency, specializing only in odd jobs. His temp employees may be contracted to paint or wallpaper interior walls, complete small carpentry projects, complete plumbing projects, and more. All of his temps are licensed and bonded in their specialty areas, and his clientele is increasing. Joe's office consists of an administrative assistant, accounting specialists, and three recruiters.

Joe's wife, Mary, suggested to him that his business cards looked too cartoonish and that he should present his business in a more professional way. Joe decided he would begin using new, professional-looking business cards for himself and each of his employees. Unfortunately, the accountant, Kim, told Joe that there is no room in the budget to have new business cards designed and printed at this time. She explained that although the clientele base is increasing, it is too soon to replace the existing business cards. Kim pointed out that the printing of their existing business cards had not been expensive at all; however, the cost to design the existing card had been very expensive.

Joe decided that if he designed his own business card, it would save him the cost of paying someone else and then the company would only have the expense of printing the new cards. After discussing the idea with Kim, Joe decided to use Microsoft Publisher to design a brand-new business card.

Your Assignment

- Read the chapter, paying special attention to the information pertaining to text boxes, design sets, and design tips.
- Think about how Joe and Kim could create their own business card using Microsoft Publisher.
- Then, design at least three business cards using a Design Set.
- Once you have chosen one of the three cards, print a copy to submit to your instructor.
- In addition, submit several other examples of advertising that Joe could design using Publisher in order to advertise his business and to save money.

Microsoft Office Publisher

Microsoft Office Publisher is a desktop publishing program that allows you to create your own publications from your home or office. The discussion within this chapter focuses on desktop publishing as it is implemented in Microsoft Office Publisher 2007. This version of Publisher incorporates new features that will make your learning process fun! Also, Microsoft has included new tools since the last version of Publisher to get the job done and an easier interface that allows you to design and create publications quickly. You will be shown how to design a publication starting with an existing publication, how to edit an existing publication, and how to insert and import clip art and other objects into a publication. Get ready to have fun while learning to create impressive, professional-looking publications.

Understanding Desktop Publishing

The essence of desktop publishing is the merger of text with graphics to produce a professional-looking publication without reliance on external publication services. Desktop publishing saves you time and money because you are doing the work yourself, as opposed to sending it out to a traditional publishing firm. That is the good news. The bad news is that desktop publishing is not as easy as it sounds, precisely because you are doing work that was done previously by skilled professionals. Nevertheless, with a little practice and a basic understanding of desktop publishing design, which is included in this chapter, you will be able to create effective and attractive publications.

> (Desktop publishing saves you time and money because you are doing the work yourself, as opposed to sending it out to a traditional publishing firm.)

Learning About the Bridge from Word Processing to Publisher

When you move from a word processing program to a desktop publishing program such as Microsoft Publisher, you may be able to quickly grasp your new environment because many of the same commands or options are available in both programs. Publisher is easy to learn because it is a Windows application and follows all of the conventions associated with the common user interface. For instance, commands such as Save, Print, Open, Undo, or Copy function in the same way as they function in other Windows applications. Thus, if you are already familiar with one Windows application, it is easier to learn Publisher because you will be able to apply much of what you already know. If you have used Microsoft PowerPoint, working with Microsoft Publisher may be even easier because you are already familiar with typing in text boxes.

 TIP Help for Microsoft Publisher

Publisher 2007 offers help from a variety of sources. You can pull down the Help menu as you can with any Windows application and/or click the Microsoft Office Publisher Help button on the Standard toolbar. You can also go to the Microsoft Web site to obtain more recent, and often more detailed, information. You will find the answers to frequently asked questions (FAQ), and you can access the same knowledge base used by Microsoft support engineers.

Understanding Typing in Text Boxes and Using the Zoom Command

> The difference between typing within a word processing program and typing in Microsoft Publisher is that when using Publisher, you type the information in a text box.

When typing within a word processing program, you basically position the pointer on the page, click the mouse in order to set the insertion point, and begin typing. In order to type in Publisher, you position the pointer within a text box, click the mouse, and begin typing. The difference between typing within a word processing program and typing in Microsoft Publisher is that when using Publisher, you type the information in a text box. A *text box* is an object used in Publisher to hold text. Once you have set the insertion point within a text box, as shown in Figure 1.1, you can enter new text or edit existing text as you would in any word processing program. You can also resize, move, and rotate the text box.

A *text box* is an object used in Publisher to hold text.

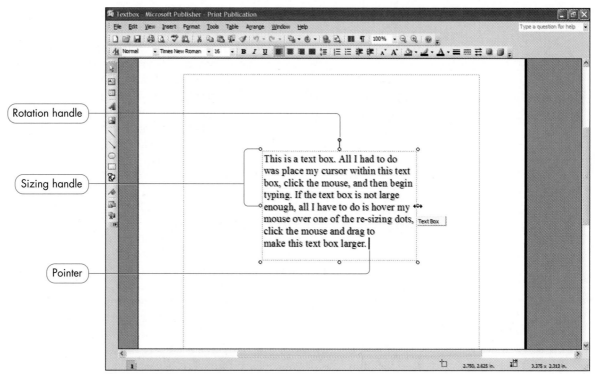

Rotation handle

Sizing handle

Pointer

Figure 1.1 Text Box

Zoom Controls in Publisher

The *Zoom command* displays the publication on the screen at different magnifications.

When you first begin working in Publisher, the publication window may be set to view the whole publication on the screen. To work with the text boxes, you may need to change the display to a different magnification; for example, 75%, 100%, or 200%. The *Zoom command* displays the publication on the screen at different magnifications; however, it does not affect the size of the text on the printed page. You can increase the percentage to 200% to make the text appear larger or decrease the magnification to 75% to see more of the publication at one time. Figure 1.2, for example, displays an unsaved newsletter template at 50% magnification. To work within the text box, you need to change the zoom, as shown in Figure 1.3.

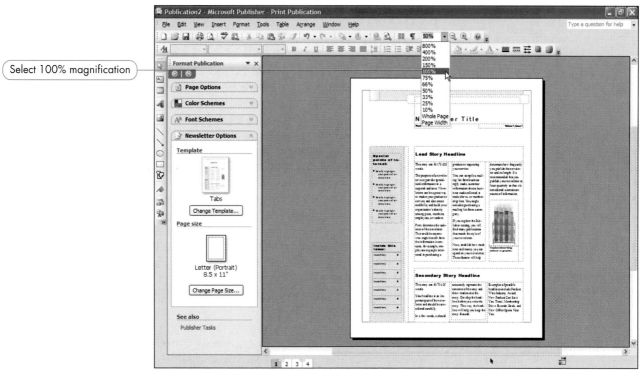

Figure 1.2 Changing Zoom from 50%

Zoom box

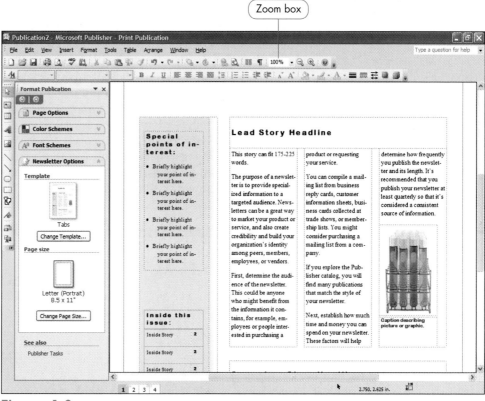

Figure 1.3 Zoom Now 100%

Knowing the Difference Between Popular Publication Types and Templates

The **Publication Types task pane** displays a listing of different publication categories.

The **Popular Publication Types task pane** displays a listing of the most used publications.

The **Recent Publications task pane** displays a listing of your most recently saved publications.

Design sets are a collection of publications with a similar color scheme, font scheme, and more.

As with any Windows application Microsoft Publisher is opened from the Windows Start menu or from a shortcut icon on your destop. The Publisher application window opens with a new Publication Types task pane at the left, Popular Publication Types in the center, and Recent Publications (if any) on the right, as shown in Figure 1.4. The *Publication Types task pane* displays a listing of different publication categories. The *Popular Publication Types task pane* displays a listing of the most used publications. Finally, the *Recent Publications task pane* displays a listing of your most recently saved publications. As displayed at the top of the screen, this Getting Started with Microsoft Office Publisher 2007 window helps you to quickly start a new publication or open publications previously saved. The Publication Types task pane on the left not only displays catagories of different publication types for getting started, but also a link to any saved templates. You will use the Popular Publication Types from the center of this window to create your first publication in this chapter.

In the Publication Types task pane, you can select from different categories, such as Letterhead, and the Popular Publication Types center window will change to that of Figure 1.5, displaying samples of different letterhead design sets. *Design sets* are a collection of publications with a similar color scheme, font scheme, and more. In this window you can also click to view templates from Microsoft Office Online where there are even more design choices. If you cannot find the design that you are looking for by scrolling through all the choices, you can use the Search for templates search box in the upper portion of this screen. You will work with a design publication in the third hands-on exercise in this chapter. Click the Blank Page Sizes category in the Publication Types task pane and the center application window displays a variety of blank page sizes from which to choose, as shown in Figure 1.6. If you scroll down in the center window, you will notice many unique page sizes. You will work with Blank Page sizes in Chapter 2. Finally, click on the Web Sites category and then on the E-mail category from the Publication Types task pane. You will learn about using these items in Chapter 4. The Publication Types task pane offers many publication choices and individual publication options. There are many choices of publication types, including newsletters, brochures, catalogs, and more. In addition, each category offers subcategories. Once you choose a publication type, the Recent Publications task pane changes so that you can select from options such as color schemes, font schemes, and more. The choices in this task pane are similar for all publications; however, the number of available options may vary depending on the publication.

The Publication Types task pane offers many publication choices and individual publication options.

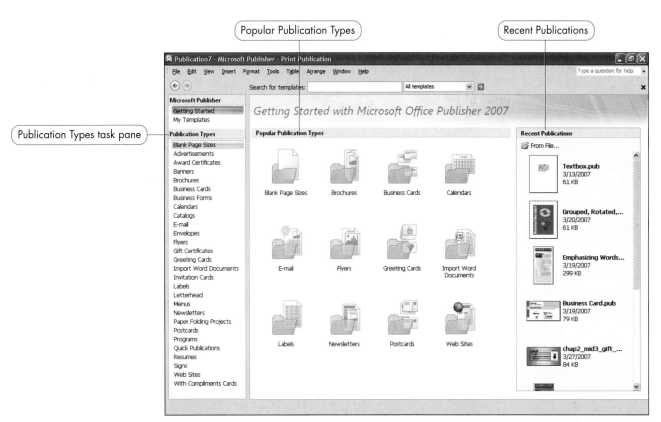

Figure 1.4 Getting Started

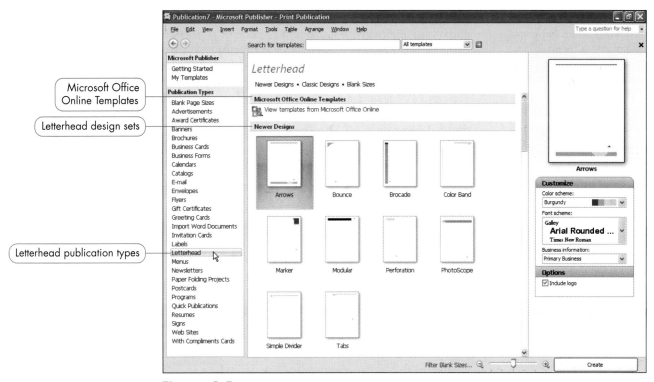

Figure 1.5 Letterhead Design Sets

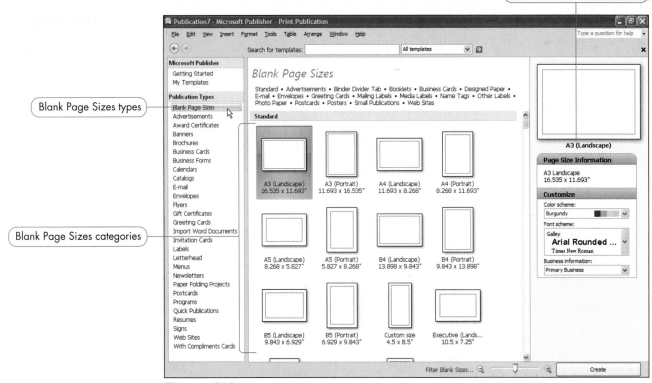

Figure 1.6 Blank Page Sizes

Publication Types

The ***publication gallery*** offers you many different designs.

When you start a new publication from the Publication Types task pane, as in Figure 1.5 above, the ***publication gallery*** in the center of the screen offers you many different designs. We chose the newsletter publication type with the Layers design (scroll down to find the Layers design under Classic Designs) to show as an example. Once you choose a design, the next step is to set up any of the options, as shown in Figures 1.7, 1.8, and 1.9, which includes choices for color schemes, font schemes, and page size. The ***Color Schemes*** drop-down menu allows you to choose a blend of predefined color choices. The ***Font Schemes*** drop-down menu allows you to choose a major and a minor typeface for the title, headings, and paragraph text of the newsletter. The ***Page Size*** drop-down menu allows you to choose the page spread. There is also an option to include business information at this time, such as the primary business address. Once you have made these choices, click the Create button, and then you are ready to add text, headings, and pictures to the newsletter template. A ***template*** is a partially completed publication that contains formatting, text, and/or graphics placeholders (dotted-line boxes that show the position of the objects in a publication's design). A template may be as simple as an envelope or as complex as a newsletter or Web site. All you have to do is replace the template text, headings, or picture placeholders with your own text, headings, and pictures. Each publication template provides a considerable amount of flexibility, as can be inferred from the screens in Figures 1.7, 1.8, and 1.9. (The options vary with the publication type.) The template you create using the task pane choices is an excellent starting point for a newsletter, but you are not restricted to it. You will learn to use commands in Publisher to modify the publication according to your specifications. For instance, you may choose to change the default graphic included in the template or the font size of particular text.

The ***Color Schemes*** drop-down menu allows you to choose a blend of predefined color choices.

The ***Font Schemes*** drop-down menu allows you to choose a major and a minor typeface.

The ***Page Size*** drop-down menu allows you to choose the page spread.

A ***template*** is a partially completed publication that contains formatting, text, and/or graphics placeholders.

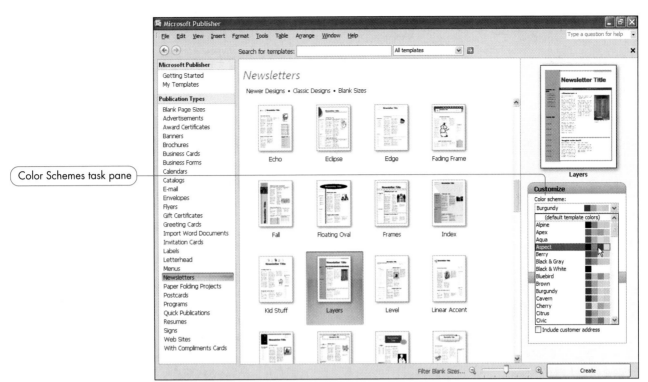

Figure 1.7 Color Schemes

Figure 1.8 Font Schemes

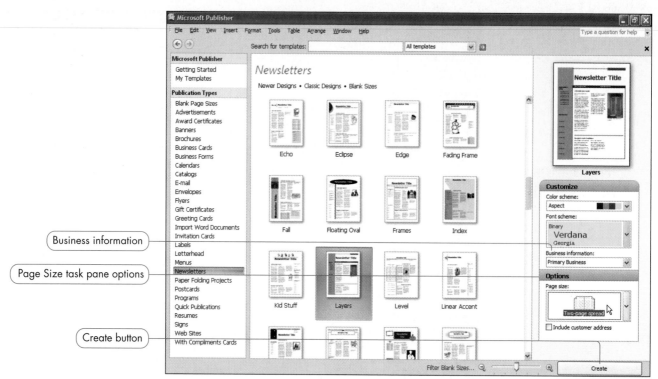

Figure 1.9 Page Size

Customizing Your Own Design Sets

It is very common for a business to use a similar design pattern for items such as business cards, envelopes, and letterheads and apply that same pattern to other company flyers, calendars, and brochure advertising. When you create a publication in Publisher, such as a business card, you can transfer the business information to another publication such as a letterhead. You can also save the design as a template and quickly transfer color schemes, font choices, and other options to new publications. Once you create one publication and then apply the template and business information to the next publication, you will soon see that you are building quickly a core set of publications for your business that you can save to use over and over. For any of the publication choices, you can still make changes from the task pane options; however, when you are finished creating several individual publications, you own a complete set of matching publications, including business cards, fax cover sheets, envelopes, and the like, as shown in Figures 1.10 through 1.13. These customized design sets may provide a valuable resource for your business or personal needs, as shown in the screens from these figures, because these types of publications could be quite costly if you had to purchase them from a print shop.

> When you create a publication in Publisher, such as a business card, you can transfer the business information to another publication such as a letterhead.

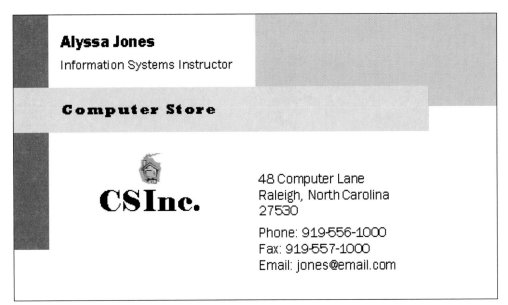

Figure 1.10 Business Card

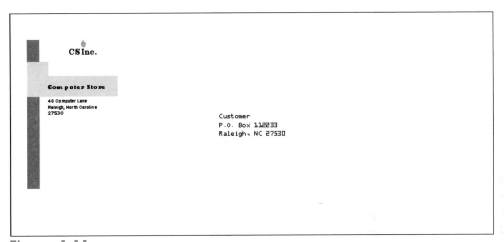

Figure 1.11 Envelope

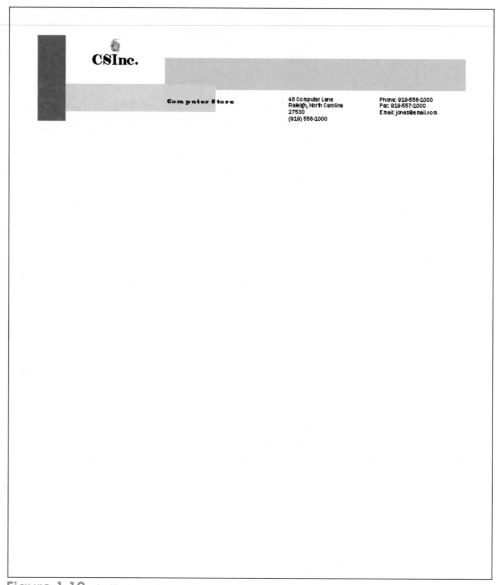

Figure 1.12 Letterhead

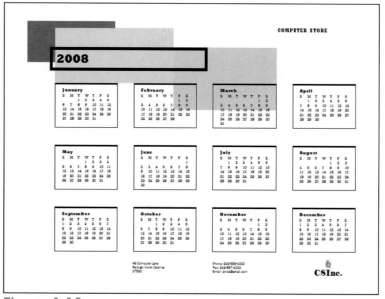

Figure 1.13 Calendar

CHAPTER 1 | Where Word Processing Ends and Desktop Publishing Begins

Knowing How to Create, Save, Edit, and Print Simple Publications

A **title bar** displays the application name.

The **window-sizing buttons** minimize, maximize or restore, or close your application.

The **menu bar** contains drop-down menu items.

The **File menu** contains commands for opening a new file, saving a file, and printing.

The **Print command** prints a publication.

The **Close command** closes the current publication.

The **Save command** copies the publication to disk.

The **Save As command** saves a publication under a different name.

The **Exit** command quits Publisher altogether.

The **Standard toolbar** contains buttons corresponding to the most basic commands.

The **Formatting toolbar** provides access to common formatting operations.

The **Objects toolbar** contains commands to insert text boxes, pictures, WordArt, Shapes, and much more.

Scroll bars are used to move up or down and left or right and appear on the publication window.

The **status bar** shows the position and size of a selected object, as well as page number.

The publication window in Figure 1.14, which shows a calendar publication using the Color Schemes task pane, should look somewhat familiar even if you have never used Publisher because Publisher shares the common user interface that is present in every Windows application. Although most of these items may be familiar to you, the major parts of the Publisher screen should be reviewed because there are a few differences from other Windows applications.

The publication window has a **title bar** displaying the application (Microsoft Publisher), the name of the publication with which you are working (Publication 1), and the standard **window-sizing buttons**, which will minimize, maximize or restore, or close your application. A **menu bar** appears immediately below the title bar, containing drop-down menu items, such as the File menu. The **File menu** contains commands for opening a new file, saving a file, printing, changing your page setup, and much more. It is a critically important menu in every Windows application. The File menu also contains the **Print command** to print a publication, the **Close command** to close the current publication, the **Save command** to copy the publication that is currently being edited to disk, the **Save As command** to save a publication under a different name, and the **Exit command** to quit Publisher altogether.

The **Standard toolbar**, which contains buttons corresponding to the most basic commands in Publisher, such as saving files or opening a new file, appears below the menu bar. The **Formatting toolbar**, which also appears below the menu bar, provides access to common formatting operations such as boldface, italics, or underlining. Formatting buttons become active (i.e., able to be used) when you select an object on which they can operate. Most of the buttons apply to text boxes and so also become active when a text box is selected. When another object is selected, only the buttons appropriate to it become active. The appearance/disappearance of buttons may become confusing at first; however, there is no need to memorize when they will appear. We do suggest that you will have a better appreciation for the various buttons if you consider them in groups, according to their general function, as shown in Figures 1.15, 1.16, and 1.17.

The Objects toolbar, discussed later in this chapter, appears to the left of the task pane, a side pane that appears when you begin any of several tasks in Publisher. The **Objects toolbar** contains commands to insert text boxes, pictures, WordArt, Shapes, and much more. **Scroll bars**, to move up or down and left or right, appear at the right and bottom of the publication window, and the status bar at the bottom of the publication window contains Page Navigation buttons for moving between pages in the publication. The **status bar** indicates which page is displayed presently on the screen and shows the position and size of a selected object.

Learning by Doing

Every chapter contains a series of hands-on exercises that enable you to use the computer to apply what you learn. In the first hands-on exercise in this chapter, you create a simple publication using the New Publication task pane's Publication for Print commands; in the second and third hands-on exercises, you open and modify an existing publication.

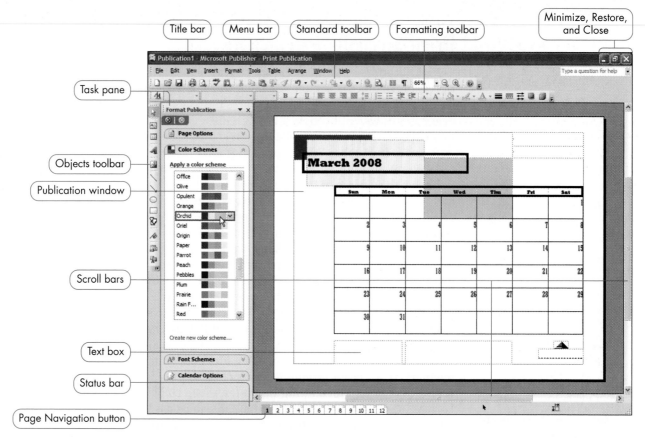

Figure 1.14 Publisher Screen

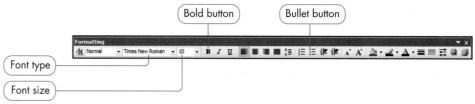

Figure 1.15 Standard Toolbar

Figure 1.16 Formatting Toolbar

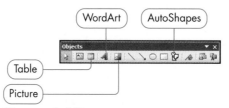

Figure 1.17 Objects Toolbar

Hands-On Exercises

1 | Our First Publication

Skills Covered: 1. Open a Template **2.** Set Template Options **3.** Zoom In or Out of Your Publication **4.** Type in a Publisher Text Box **5.** Type in a Publisher Text Box (Continued) **6.** Modify Text in a Text Box **7.** Change the Clip Art **8**. Save the Publication **9.** Use the Help Feature **10.** Print and Close the Publication **11.** Exit Publisher

---

Step 1
Open a Template

Refer to Figure 1.18 as you complete Step 1.

a. Start Publisher.

The application window opens with a new Publication Types task pane at the left, Popular Publication Types in the center, and Recent Publications (if any) on the right.

b. Click the **Flyers category** in the Publications Types task pane on the left of the screen, as shown in Figure 1.18.

The category expands to show types of flyers available in the center pane.

c. Scroll down, if necessary, in the publication gallery and select (click once) the **Blocks informational flyer** found under the Classic Designs choices.

TROUBLESHOOTING: If this is the first time you have worked in Publisher, a box may appear after you select the Blocks Informational Flyer asking you to add personal information such as your name and address so that you do not have to do this for every publication you create. Once you click OK, the Personal Information dialog box opens, where you supply this information. Click Update or click Cancel to close the dialog box and begin choosing options for your flyer. If this box does not appear, we will add this information later.

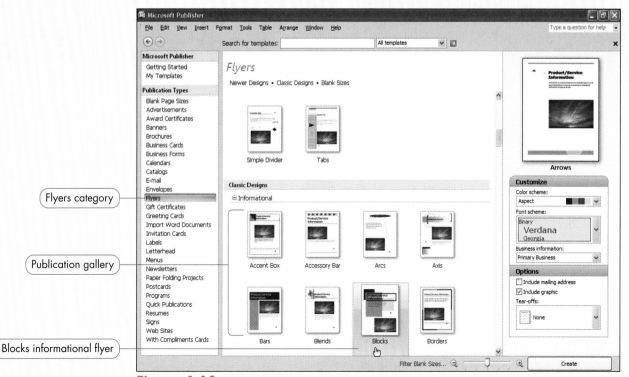

Figure 1.18 Open Blocks Flyer Template

Refer to Figure 1.19 as you complete Step 2.

a. Click the **Color Scheme drop-down arrow** under Customize to select the **Burgundy Color Scheme**.

b. Click the **Font Scheme drop-down arrow** to select **Arial Rounded** (Galley category) with the subcategory Times New Roman for the Font Scheme.

Leave the Business Information option alone for now. We will type that information into the text boxes in upcoming steps.

c. Under Options, in the Tear-offs section, click the **Contact Information command** to include tear-offs at the bottom of your flyer.

The template in the publication windows changes to display the tear-offs.

d. Click the **Create button** in the lower right corner of the Publisher window, as shown in Figure 1.19.

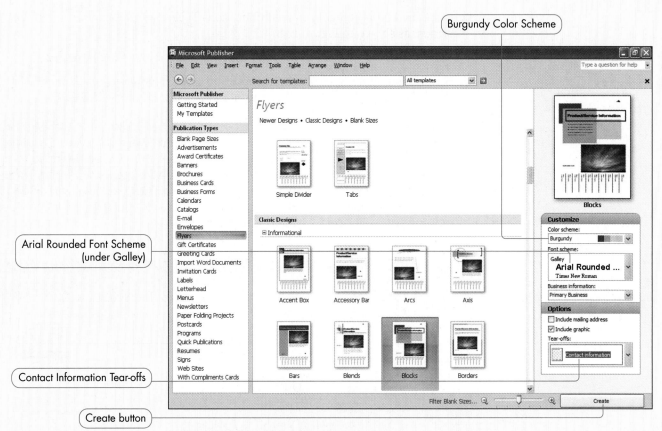

Burgundy Color Scheme

Arial Rounded Font Scheme (under Galley)

Contact Information Tear-offs

Create button

Figure 1.19 Set Template Options

Refer to Figure 1.20 as you complete Step 3.

a. Click the **Close button** on the Format Publication task pane so that the publication window takes up the entire desktop.

b. Click the **Zoom box drop-down arrow** found on the Standard toolbar to select **75%** or **100%** magnification, as shown in Figure 1.20.

TROUBLESHOOTING: If you have trouble seeing the text boxes, you may need to select a higher percentage.

You can also use the F9 key to toggle back and forth between the current zoom and 100%.

c. Scroll up or down and left or right to view the top of your flyer template.

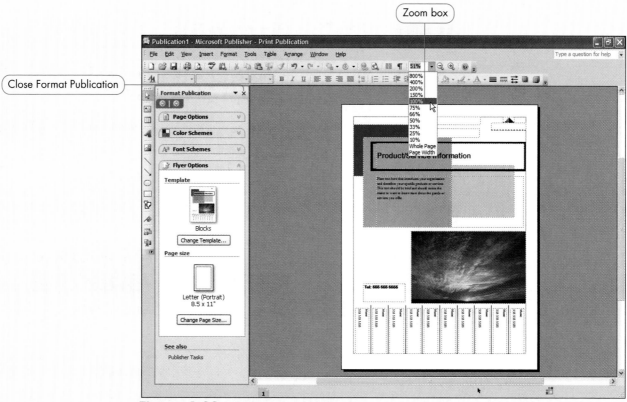

Figure 1.20 Zooming In or Out

Refer to Figure 1.21 as you complete Step 4.

a. Click on the **Business Name text box** to select it, as shown in Figure 1.21. (Sizing handles appear around it.) Here is where you enter the name of your business.

b. Type the name of your business, which automatically replaces the selected text.

We chose the fictitious business name Computer Shop. You may type the same text to follow along exactly, or you may choose any other business name.

c. Click outside the text box to deselect it.

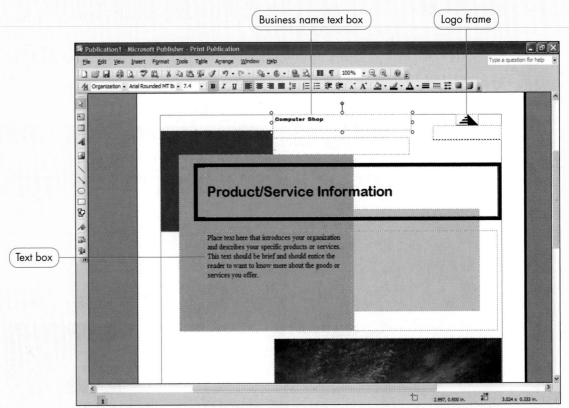

Business name text box — Logo frame

Text box

Figure 1.21 Type in a Text Box

TIP Pick Up the Mouse

It seems that you always run out of room on your real desk just when you need to move the mouse a little further. The solution is to pick up the mouse and move it closer to you—the pointer will stay in its present position on the screen, but when you put the mouse down, you will have more room on your desk in which to work.

Step 5
Type in a Publisher Text Box (Continued)

Refer to Figure 1.22 as you complete Step 5.

a. Click in the **Logo text box** to enter the logo text for your business, as shown in Figure 1.22.

b. Type **CSInc.** for the Organization logo text, or type any other text of your choice.

c. Click in the **Tag Line text box**, as shown in Figure 1.22, and type **Computer Supplies and Services**, or enter your choice of text.

d. Enter text in the **information paragraph text box**, **telephone number text box**, and the **tear-offs text box**, as shown in Figure 1.22, or enter your own business information just as in the preceding steps.

The tear-offs text boxes will automatically update all tear-offs after you have entered the text for the first one.

TROUBLESHOOTING: Type all information in the first tear-off text box without hitting Enter, and then use your space bar to move any information down to the second line.

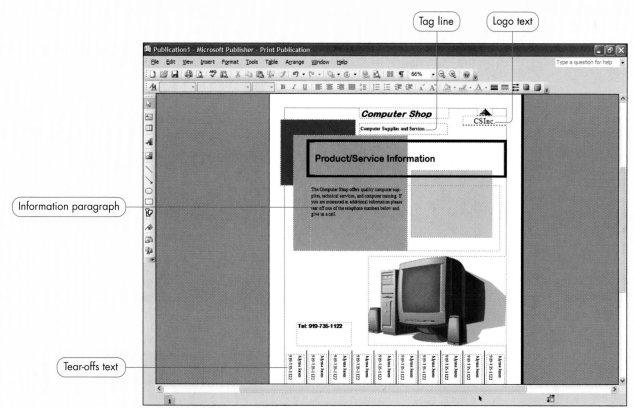

Figure 1.22 Add More Text

Step 6
Modify Text in a Text Box

a. Click and drag to select the business name **Computer Shop**.

b. Click the **Italic button** on the Formatting toolbar to italicize the selected text.

c. Click the **Font Size drop-down arrow** on the Formatting toolbar, then select **20** to increase the size of the selected text.

d. Click outside the text area to deselect the text and see the results.

Step 7
Change the Clip Art

Refer to Figure 1.23 as you complete Step 7.

a. Select (click) the **default picture** on your flyer publication, and then press the **Delete key** on your keyboard.

TROUBLESHOOTING: If a message box asks whether you want to change to a design without a graphic placeholder, click No.

Please keep in mind that there are a few different ways to add clip art to your publications. For this exercise, we are using the Main Menu bar.

b. Pull down the **Insert menu**, point to **Picture**, and click **Clip Art**.

The Insert Clip Art task pane opens on the left of your screen.

c. Click the **Results should be drop-down arrow** to be sure the Clip art toggle box is checked.

d. Type **computers** in the Search for text box, then click the **Go button**, as shown in Figure 1.23.

TROUBLESHOOTING: If a message box asks whether you want to search Microsoft Online, click Yes if you have an Internet connection.

The Media Gallery will search for images of computers and display them in the task pane. If you have an active Internet connection, it will show images from the Microsoft Web site as well as those on your computer's hard disk drive.

e. Select (click) any computer image or the same one as we have shown in Figure 1.23.

The clip art should appear on the publication page.

f. Close the **Clip Art task pane** by clicking its **Close button**.

g. Click to move and size the clip art.

TROUBLESHOOTING: Point your mouse at the computer image, click and drag it to move the image, and then point to one of the corner sizing dots and drag to resize it.

You will learn more about this in the next hands-on exercise.

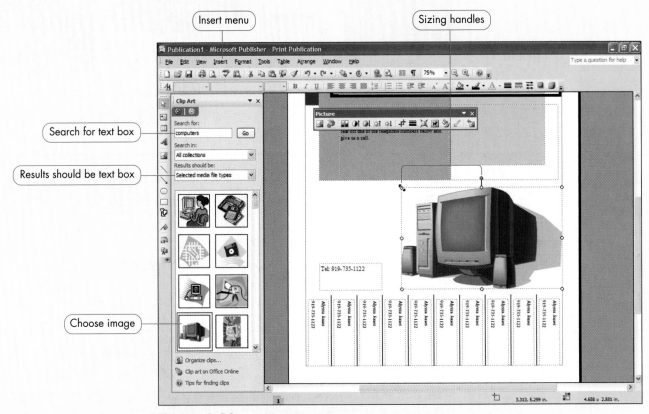

Figure 1.23 Change the Clip Art

Refer to Figure 1.24 as you complete Step 8.

a. Pull down the **File menu** and click **Save** (or click the **Save button** on the Standard toolbar) to open the Save As dialog box, as shown in Figure 1.24.

b. Click the drop-down arrow on the **Save In list box**.

c. Click the appropriate drive, e.g., drive C, depending on where you want to save this file.

You may want to create a new folder for this file or place it in your My Documents folder. If you are working at school and cannot save your files on the school's computers, you may want to use a flash drive to store your files or burn your files to a CD.

d. Click in the **File Name text box**, drag across the default file name, *Publication1*, and enter **chap1_ho1_my_first_publication_solution** as the name of the publication.

e. Click **Save** (or press **Enter**) to save your publication.

TROUBLESHOOTING: If a dialog box appears asking you to save the new logo, CSInc., click Yes or No depending on whether you want to keep your new logo for future publications.

The title bar changes to reflect the publication name.

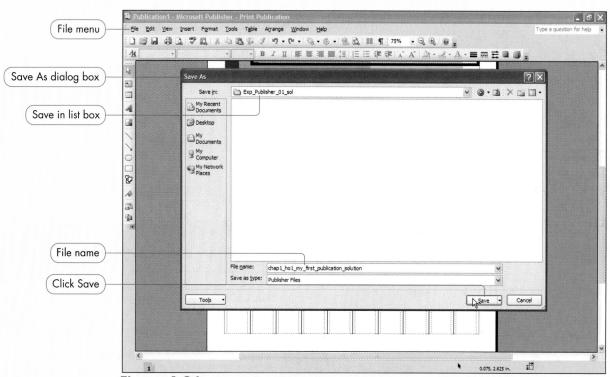

Figure 1.24 Save the Publication

TIP   Find the Right Clip Art

The Clip Organizer is available to all of the Office applications, and you can open it from the Windows Start menu. Click Start, then Programs, then Microsoft Office, then Microsoft Office Tools, then Microsoft Clip Organizer. When you open the organizer, the left pane displays the Collection List, a tree diagram of the gallery's collections. Click the plus sign next to Office Collections to see the main categories and click the plus sign next to a category to see its subcategories. When you click a category, the right pane of the organizer window displays its contents.

Refer to Figure 1.25 as you complete Step 9.

a. Pull down the **Help menu** and click **Microsoft Office Publisher Help**.

> **TROUBLESHOOTING:** You may see a slightly different screen if you have recently used the help menu before this exercise.

b. Type **Print a Publication**, as shown in Figure 1.25, and then click the **Search button** to look for the answer.

The task pane changes to provide several topics that may be appropriate to choose.

c. Click the topic **Print a publication on a desktop printer**.

A Help window that contains links to various topics, each with detailed information, appears.

d. Click any of the links in the **Help window** to read the information or scroll down to read the information provided.

You can print the contents of any topic by clicking the Print button in the Help window.

e. Close the Help window when you are finished.

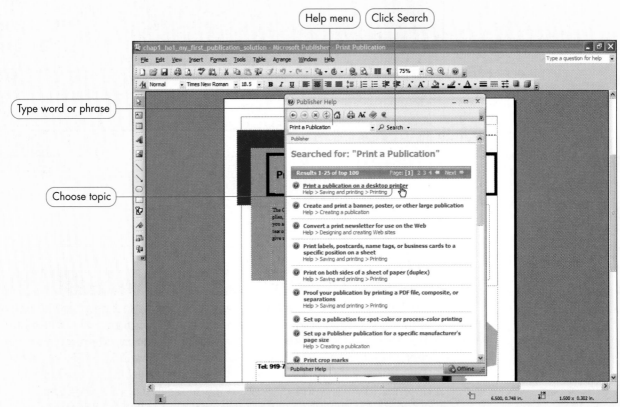

Figure 1.25 Help Feature

Step 10
Print and Close the Publication

Refer to Figure 1.26 as you complete Step 10.

a. Pull down the **File menu**. Click **Print** to display the dialog box shown in Figure 1.26.

b. Click the **Print button** to print the publication.

You can also click the Print button on the Standard toolbar to print the publication immediately without displaying the Print dialog box.

c. Pull down the **File menu**. Click **Close** to close this publication but remain in Publisher.

TROUBLESHOOTING: Click Yes if prompted to save the publication again.

Print button

Click Print to print the publication

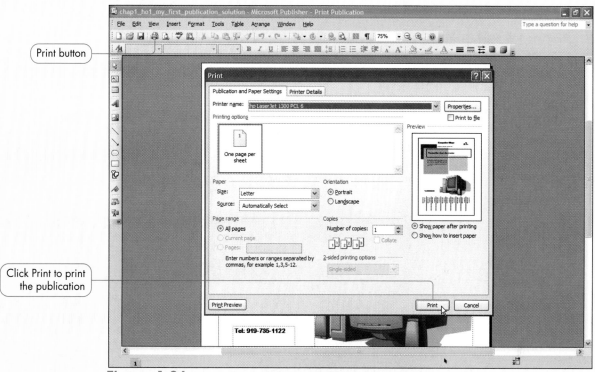

Figure 1.26 Print and Close the Publication

Step 11
Exit Publisher

a. Pull down the **File menu**.

b. Click **Exit** to exit Publisher if you do not want to continue with the next exercise at this time.

You can also exit Publisher by clicking the Close button on the Publisher title bar to exit Publisher.

TIP   Twenty Levels of Undo

The Undo command is present in Publisher, as it is in every Windows application. Publisher enables you to undo the last 20 changes to a publication. After the last 20 changes, the Undo command is no longer available. You can undo an action by clicking the Undo button on the Standard toolbar or you can choose the Undo command from the Edit menu. Keep in mind that some actions cannot be undone, and your last action may have been one of them.

Beyond the Default Publication

We trust you have completed the hands-on exercise without difficulty and that you were able to duplicate the flyer publication. Creating a publication using task pane options, however, is the easy part of using Microsoft Publisher. The more difficult aspect is to add elements to the default design. With that said, other skills are necessary, and so we continue with a brief introduction to the Objects toolbar, which contains commands to add objects to your publications.

Knowing How to Use the Objects Toolbar

The Objects toolbar contains commands to add objects to your publications. Some objects appear in the publication when you click the tool on the Objects toolbar. With others, you click the tool, click in the publication where you want the object to appear, and drag diagonally, as shown for a text box in Figure 1.27. With still others, clicking the tool opens a dialog box or a task pane where you provide added information.

> The Objects toolbar contains commands to add objects to your publications.

A ***canvas*** is a container that can be selected, deleted, moved, rotated, and sized.

Many objects in Publisher are placed on a canvas. A ***canvas*** frame is a container that can be selected, deleted, moved, rotated, and sized. When you insert a new picture into a publication, for instance, you drag the pointer to set the size of the canvas frame that will hold the picture. Table frames work the same way. A frame is not visible in the printed publication unless you add a border. You will learn about this in the next hands-on exercise.

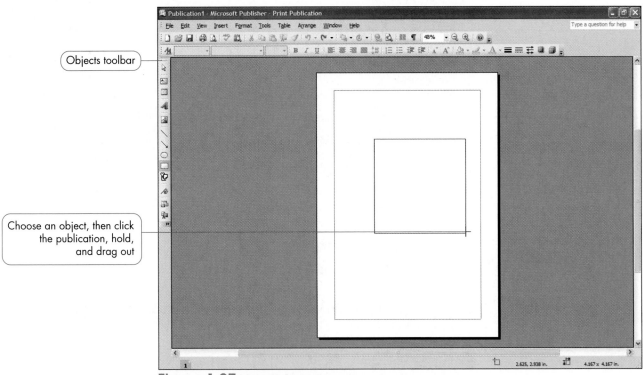

Objects toolbar

Choose an object, then click the publication, hold, and drag out

Figure 1.27 Drawing an Object

Additional Objects

The Objects toolbar contains all the tools necessary to add text boxes, pictures, clip art, tables, drawing objects, and more to your publications. If you have worked with Microsoft Word or PowerPoint before, you are probably already familiar with most of these objects. Consider, for example, the objects shown in Figure 1.28, which were created in Publisher using the Objects toolbar. The clip art (a graphic as opposed to a photograph) was taken from the ***Clip art on Office Online***, which is a site provided by Microsoft that contains extra clip art, photos, sounds, and more. The title of the publication was created using Microsoft ***WordArt***, which is a uniquely designed text object. The publication also illustrates several drawings within a table and a text box.

Clip art on Office Online is a site provided by Microsoft that contains extra clip art, photos, sounds, and more.

WordArt is a uniquely designed text object.

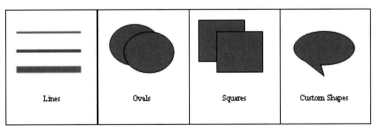

Figure 1.28 Using Objects

Hands-On Exercises

2 | Adding Objects to a Publication

Skills Covered: 1. Obtain the Practice Files **2.** Open an Existing Publication **3.** Use the Save As Command **4.** Insert Clip Art **5.** Move and Size the Clip Art **6.** Format the Clip Art Frame **7.** Insert WordArt **8.** Move and Size Objects in Your Publication **9.** Insert a Table **10.** Create the Drawing Objects

---

Step 1
Obtain the Practice Files

Refer to Figure 1.29 as you complete Step 1.

We have created a series of practice files (also called a "data disk") for you to use throughout the rest of this text. Your instructor may have made the files available to you on a network drive, in which case you need to use My Computer to copy the files from the network to your storage device.

> **TROUBLESHOOTING:** You can also download the files from our Web site, provided you have an Internet connection. Start Internet Explorer, and then go to the Exploring Series home page at www.prenhall.com/exploring.

a. Click the **Student Resources link**, as shown in Figure 1.29.

b. Follow the links for downloading the Microsoft Office Publisher 2007 files to your computer.

> **TROUBLESHOOTING:** You will see the File Download dialog box asking what you want to do. The option button to save this program to disk is selected. Click OK. The Save As dialog box appears. If a yellow bar appears at the top of the browser indicating that the pop-up window has been blocked, click the yellow bar, and then choose download.

c. Click the down arrow in the **Save In list box** to enter the drive and folder where you want to save the file.

> **TROUBLESHOOTING:** It is best to save the file to the Windows desktop or to a temporary folder on drive C. If you are working at school and cannot save your files on the school's computers, you may want to use a flash drive to store your files or burn your files to a CD.

When the download is complete, you can exit from Internet Explorer.

d. Locate the file on your computer and double-click the **file name**, then follow the onscreen instructions to decompress the folder.

Check with your instructor for additional information.

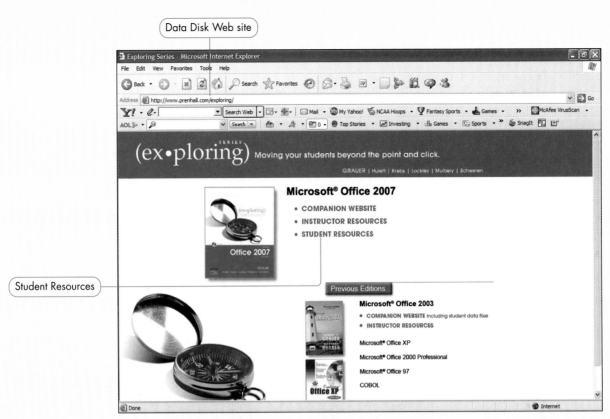

Figure 1.29 Obtain the Practice Files

Refer to Figure 1.30 as you complete Step 2.

a. If it is not already open, start Microsoft Publisher.

b. Pull down the **File menu** and click **Open** or click the **Open button** on the Standard toolbar.

> **TROUBLESHOOTING:** Your Open dialog box may be slightly different from ours. Our Views drop-down button, as shown in Figure 1.30, is set to show Icon view. Yours may be set for list or thumbnails, or other.

c. Click the drop-down arrow on the **Look In list box**, as shown in Figure 1.30.

d. Click the appropriate drive, for example, drive C.

e. Double-click the **Exploring Publisher Student Practice Files folder** to make it the active folder.

This is the folder you downloaded and installed in the previous step, from which you will open the publication.

f. Click the *chap1_ho2_using_objects* file name.

g. Click the **Open command button** to open the publication.

Alternately, you can double-click the *chapt1_ho2_using_objects* file to skip clicking the Open button.

h. The publication should appear on the screen. Take a look at it; at present, it consists of a single text box with text already typed up for you.

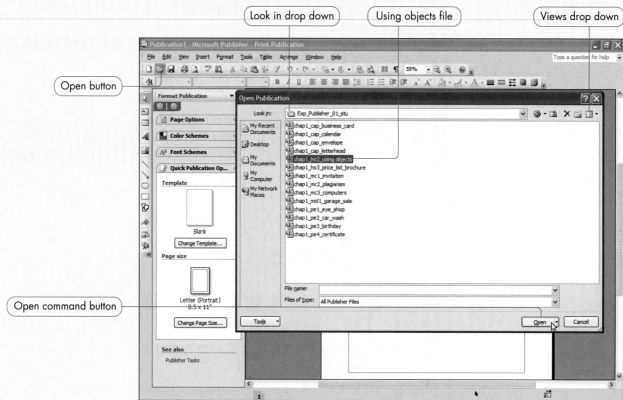

Figure 1.30 Open an Existing Publication

TIP Replace New from Existing Publication

You can open an existing publication using the File menu's Open command and save it with a new name using the Save As command. Publisher 2007 also provides a recent publications list when you first start Publisher.

Step 3
Use the Save As Command

Refer to Figure 1.31 as you complete Step 3.

a. Pull down the **File menu**. Click **Save As** to produce the dialog box in Figure 1.31.

b. Enter **chap1_ho2_using_objects_solution** as the name of the new publication.

TROUBLESHOOTING: A file name may contain up to 255 characters, and blanks are permitted.

c. Click the **Save command button**.

There are now two identical copies of the publication on disk: *chap1_ho2_using_ objects*, which we supplied, and *chap1_ho2_using_objects_solution*, which you just created.

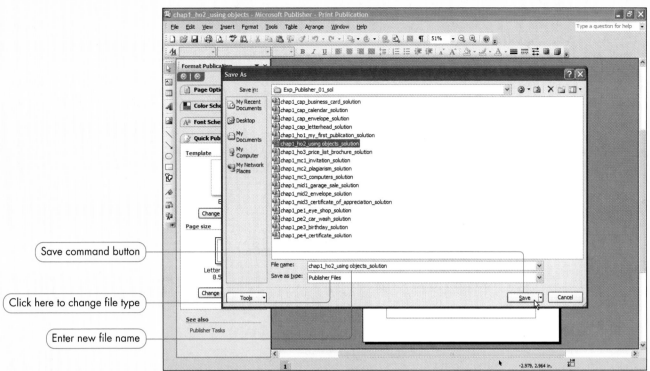

Figure 1.31 Use the Save As Command

Labels on figure:
- Save command button
- Click here to change file type
- Enter new file name

TIP   File Formats That Publisher Converts

Publisher can convert many file formats, including older versions of Publisher as well as other programs. If you look up "file formats" in the Publisher Help files, you will discover that in most cases Publisher can preserve the character and paragraph formatting of the text. In a nutshell, Publisher can convert older Publisher files, plain text files, rich text format, Word for Windows and Macintosh files, WordPerfect, and Microsoft Excel files. Also, with a plug-in, you can now save Publisher files as PDF versions.

Step 4
Insert Clip Art

Refer to Figure 1.32 as you complete Step 4.

a. If necessary, use the **Zoom command** to increase the size of the publication in the window.

b. Click the **Picture Frame tool** on the Objects toolbar and choose **Clip Art**. Your task pane should change to the Insert Clip Art screen, as shown in Figure 1.32.

c. Type **computers** in the Search For text box, then click the **Go button**.

The organizer will search for images of computers and display them in the Results list box. If you have an active Internet connection, it will show images from the Microsoft Web site as well as those on your computer's hard disk drive.

d. Click any image and the clip art should appear on the publication page, where it can be moved and sized as described in the next several steps.

We chose the last one showing up in the organizer in the first row. Your image may be in a different spot, so please see the next step to determine which clip art image we chose.

e. Click outside the clip art to deselect the picture so that you can continue working on the publication.

f. Close the Insert Clip Art task pane.

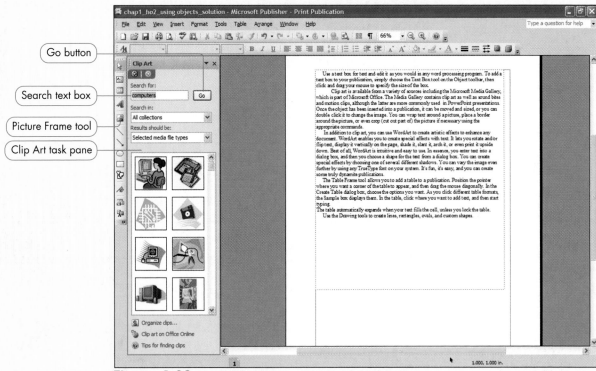

Figure 1.32 Insert Clip Art

TIP Pictures, Pictures, Pictures

Do not feel that you have to use only Clip Organizer pictures. There are many pictures available on the Internet and in other picture packages that you can buy. If you choose to buy a package of pictures, you generally do not need to ask for copyright permission. However, if you find any clip art on the Internet, even if it says it is free, you should make sure you understand the copyright permissions that are generally posted at the site. Search for free clip art on any search engine and you will find many hits from which to choose. Or go to one of our favorite clip art directories at http://www.clipart.com and search from there.

Step 5
Move and Size the Clip Art

Refer to Figure 1.33 as you complete Step 5.

TROUBLESHOOTING: The clip art may be initially too large or too small and thus may force the bottom of the publication text into the overflow area of the text box (described in Chapter 2). To overcome this problem, you can move and size the clip art just as you can any Windows object.

a. Click anywhere within the clip art object to display the sizing handles, as shown in Figure 1.33.

b. Drag a corner handle to change the length and width of the picture simultaneously.

Dragging simultaneously from a corner keeps the graphic in proportion as it is resized.

c. To move an object, click it to display the sizing handles.

d. Point to any part of the image except a sizing handle, and then click and drag to move the clip art to the upper left corner, as shown in Figure 1.33.

e. Save the publication.

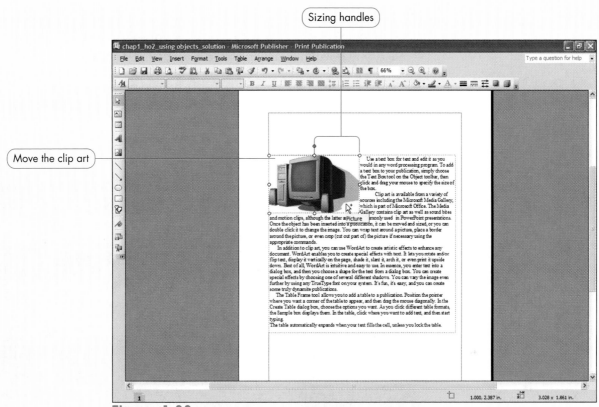

Figure 1.33 Move and Size the Clip Art

 TIP The Picture Toolbar

The Picture toolbar offers the easiest way to execute various commands associated with a picture or clip art image. It is displayed automatically when a picture is selected and it is hidden otherwise.

Step 6

Format the Clip Art Frame

Refer to Figure 1.34 as you complete Step 6.

a. Be sure the clip art is still selected, then pull down the **Format menu** and click **Picture** to display the Format Picture dialog box, as shown in Figure 1.34.

b. Click the **Layout tab** and make sure the Square Wrapping Style is selected.

c. Change the Distance from text setting by clicking to remove the check mark next to Automatic and then change the Top, Bottom, Left, and Right settings from **0.04** to **0.06**.

This moves the image slightly farther away from the text.

d. Click the **Colors and Lines tab**.

e. Click the **Fill Color drop-down arrow**, and then select a fill color.

We chose a bright pink color under the More colors link.

f. Click the **Line Color drop-down arrow** on the same tab, and then select a black border (or a different border if you prefer).

g. Click **OK** to accept the changes.

You can also change the border using the Picture toolbar. If the toolbar is not visible, pull down the View menu, click Toolbars, and click Picture. On the toolbar click the Line/Border Style button to select a different border thickness. (If a tip appears suggesting you use the color scheme commands, just ignore the tip for now, as you will learn about color schemes in the next section.)

h. Save the publication.

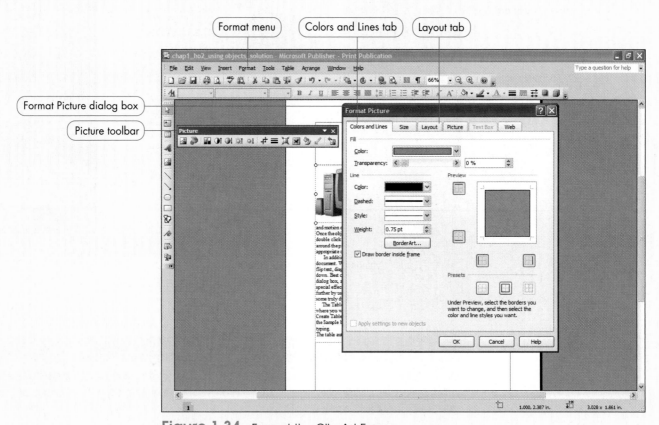

Figure 1.34 Format the Clip Art Frame

Refer to Figure 1.35 as you complete Step 7.

a. Click the **Insert WordArt tool** on the Objects toolbar.

b. In the WordArt Gallery that opens, select a style you like and click **OK**.

Look at the next step to see which WordArt style we chose if you are following along with our publication exactly.

c. In the Edit WordArt Text dialog box that opens, replace the default text by typing **Using Objects**.

d. Click the down arrow in the **Font box** and choose **Arial Rounded MT Bold** or any other font that you prefer; leave the font size as 36 pt, as shown in Figure 1.35.

e. Click **OK** to close the dialog box, insert the WordArt text into the publication, and display the WordArt toolbar.

f. Click the **Format WordArt button** on the WordArt toolbar to open the Format WordArt dialog box.

g. On the **Colors and Lines tab** on the Format WordArt dialog box, change the fill color to any of the choices offered in the drop-down list.

We chose Blue, if you are following along with our publication exactly.

h. Click the **Layout tab** and change the Wrapping Style to **Square**, then click **OK** to apply the changes.

i. Click anywhere outside the WordArt frame to deselect it.

j. Save the publication.

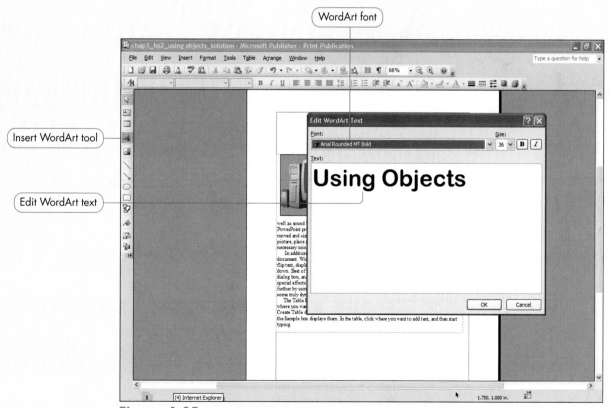

Figure 1.35 Insert WordArt

Refer to Figure 1.36 as you complete Step 8.

a. To move the objects around in the publication to match Figure 1.36, point to each object until the Move pointer appears.

b. Click and drag the text box to move it down lower on the publication window.

c. Click and drag the clip art image to move it lower down on the publication window.

d. Click and drag the WordArt object frame to move it to the top of the publication window.

e. To size the WordArt, click anywhere within the object to display the sizing handles.

f. Drag a corner handle (the mouse pointer changes to a double arrow) to change the length and width of the picture simultaneously; this keeps the object in proportion as it is resized.

g. Save the publication.

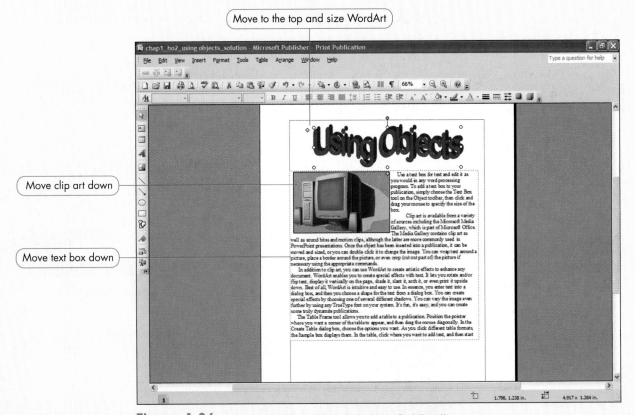

Move to the top and size WordArt

Move clip art down

Move text box down

Figure 1.36 Move and Size Objects in Your Publication

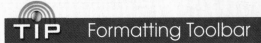

TIP   Formatting Toolbar

The Formatting toolbar offers the easiest way to execute various commands associated with many Publisher objects. Depending on which type of object is selected, various buttons become active. You will find buttons, for instance, to add fill color and line color to a WordArt frame and to choose a shadow and 3-D style. For text boxes and tables, many more buttons are active. Using the toolbar instead of the drop-down menus or dialog boxes can save you time.

Refer to Figure 1.37 as you complete Step 9.

a. If necessary, scroll down to the bottom of your publication window.

b. Click the **Insert Table tool** on the Objects toolbar.

c. To create the table frame object, point, click, and hold the mouse to draw out a table at the bottom of your publication window just under the text box.

TROUBLESHOOTING: If necessary, you can size and move the table later.

d. In the Create Table dialog box, enter **1** as the number of rows. Enter **4** as the number of columns, as shown in Figure 1.37.

e. Leave the Default Table format selected, as shown in Figure 1.37.

f. Click **OK** and the table will be inserted into the publication.

g. To create a border around the table cells, select the table, then pull down the **Table menu**, point to **Select**, and click **Table**.

h. Click the **Line/Border Style button** on the Formatting toolbar and choose **More Lines** to open the Format Table dialog box to the Colors and Lines tab.

i. Select **Black** from the Line Color options and **Grid** from the Presets options.

j. Change the Weight option to **2 pt**.

k. Click **OK** to apply the new border grid, and then click outside of the table to deselect the row.

l. Save the publication.

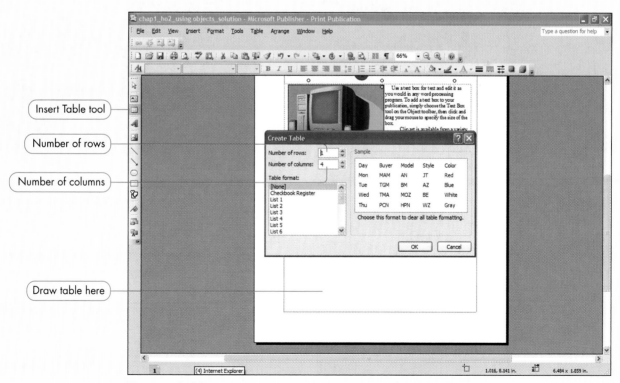

Figure 1.37 Insert a Table

Refer to Figure 1.38 as you complete Step 10.

a. To create each of the drawing objects shown in Figure 1.38, click the **Line tool** on the Objects toolbar.

b. Point, click, and hold the mouse within the first cell to draw out the first line, as shown in Figure 1.38.

c. Draw out the remaining two lines.

d. Select the first line within the first cell, and then select **More Lines** from the Line/Border Style button on the Formatting toolbar to choose a different line color in the Format AutoShape dialog box.

e. Click **OK** to close the dialog box.

f. Change both the line thickness and the color of the remaining two lines to match the figure or choose a different thickness or color, if you prefer.

g. Click the **Oval tool** on the Objects toolbar.

h. Draw out each of the ovals, as shown in Figure 1.38.

i. Select each oval, and then click the **Fill Color button** on the Formatting toolbar to change the fill color to match Figure 1.38.

j. Draw out the remaining objects using the AutoShapes button on the Objects toolbar, as shown in Figure 1.38. Change the fill color and borders to match the shapes in the figure.

k. If necessary, size and move any of the drawing objects.

l. Save the publication a final time. Print the completed publication and submit it to your instructor as proof you completed this exercise. Congratulations on a job well done!

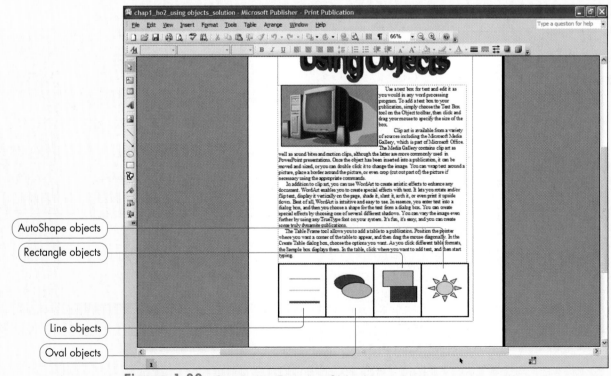

Figure 1.38 Create the Drawing Objects

Considering Good Publication Design

What is wrong with the front cover of the brochure shown in Figure 1.39? Would you pick up this brochure in a doctor's office to read all about this wonderful vacation spot? If you said, "Not likely," you are only one of many who would not even consider looking at a publication as poorly designed as this one. The text suggests not only that you would be sleeping on the ocean but that your room would be filled with sand as well. The picture of the hotel is too small, the butterfly border just does not work for this publication, and many of the boxes are not placed appropriately on the page. If you think we went a little overboard to get our point across, just start looking around and you will soon see that there are many publications that are poorly designed.

Figure 1.39 Example of Bad Design

Understanding the Steps for Creating a Good Publication

Good design makes it easy for the reader to determine what is important. Emphasis can be achieved through appropriate text, object formatting and layering, and paying attention to the message you are trying to deliver. Even if your message does not come across quite as you want it to, the way you position objects on the page can make all the difference. When objects overlap on the page, they are stacked in layers, one in front of another. One characteristic of professional publications is the use of uniform layering for each element on the publication page. Notice, for instance, the way the name of the hotel, The Uptom, shown in Figure 1.39 above, does not look stacked (i.e., layered) appropriately on the front of the brochure cover, but awkwardly overlaps the butterfly border. The butterfly border, even though it is a bad choice for this type of brochure, may have worked just a little better if it had been layered appropriately. If you are like most people, you will change your mind several times before arriving at a satisfactory design, after which you will want to check consistent layering for each element in the publication. *Layering* means positioning each object on the publication in such a way as to achieve an uncluttered look.

> One characteristic of professional publications is the use of uniform layering for each element on the publication page.

Layering means positioning each object on the publication.

Use Publisher's Templates for Good Design

The best way to create a publication with good design is to use the templates provided by Publisher. The templates provide a considerable amount of flexibility, and all you have to do is add the text, any clip art, and/or any other objects for your publication. Once you have chosen a publication type and design or design set, the task pane options allow for experimenting with your publication by offering various Font Scheme and Color Scheme choices to match the tone of your publication. You also have the flexibility to easily add clip art, photos, and sound and motion files from the Office Online site. You should work until you are satisfied with the look of your publication, and one design, color scheme, or clip art image may look better than others. Consider, for instance, the front covers on the brochures shown in Figures 1.40 and 1.41. The wording and the graphic are exactly the same, but the design choice and color scheme are different.

Figure 1.40 Good Publication Design Sample 1

Figure 1.41 Good Publication Design Sample 2

Tips for Creating Good Publications

The mere availability of a desktop publishing program does not guarantee an effective publication. Many aspects need to be taken into consideration during the publication design process. These aspects include, but are not limited to, the following items:

- Determine your audience and the message you want to deliver to the reader.
- Offer enough information to the reader, but try to keep the overall design simple and consistent.
- Choose a design template that matches the message you wish to deliver.
- Pay attention to layering objects.
- Make sure graphical images are not too small, too large, or incorrectly layered on the publication page.
- Become an architect; draw out your publication on paper first.
- Never give up! Keep experimenting with your publication until you are satisfied with the design.

Hands-On Exercises

3 | Changing the Design of a Publication

Skills Covered: 1. Insert the Business Name **2.** Insert Clip Art from the Internet **3.** Move, Size, and Layer the Picture **4.** Choose a Different Logo **5.** Change the Publication Design and Color Scheme

---

Step 1
Insert the Business Name

Refer to Figure 1.42 as you complete Step 1.

a. Start Publisher. Open the *chap1_ho3_price_list_brochure* publication in the Exploring Publisher folder. Save the publication as **chap1_ho3_price_list_ brochure_solution**.

This publication is based on the Accents Box Price List Brochure template. It is a two-page brochure with three panels on each page. When printed on both sides of a sheet of paper and folded, it makes six pages.

b. Scroll through the brochure and become familiar with its content.

c. If necessary, change the zoom to **75%** or **100%**, whichever you prefer.

d. Click the **Page Navigation buttons** on the status bar to move between pages.

e. If necessary, move to page 1, then scroll to the front cover of the brochure (the third panel on the right) and select the **Business Name text box** at the top of the brochure to enter the business name **Serenity Spa**, as shown in Figure 1.42.

f. Click outside the text box.

The new business name should appear automatically in two other locations: in the middle panel of page 1 and in the third panel of page 2. When you update an element in a publication template, all instances are automatically updated. (You saw this earlier with the tear-off text in Hands-On Exercise 1.)

g. Save the publication.

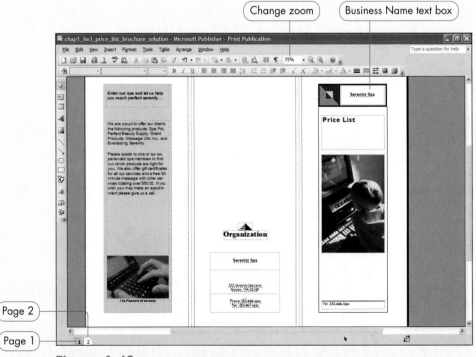

Figure 1.42 Insert the Business Name

TIP First Impressions

A reader's first impressions are important. People will judge your business when looking at your publications. Using the design templates, you can create great-looking brochures to show that your business is professional. Be careful when choosing a design and color scheme. You want to make sure both match the tone of your business. After choosing a template, feel free to experiment by adding your own content, designing a new logo, and/or designing your own color scheme.

Step 2

Insert Clip Art from the Internet

Refer to Figure 1.43 as you complete Step 2.

a. Click the **default template graphic** on the front cover of the brochure.

b. Pull down the **Insert menu**, point to **Picture**, and click **Clip Art** to display the Insert Clip Art task pane.

c. Click **Clip art on Office Online** at the bottom of the task pane, as shown in Figure 1.43.

> **TROUBLESHOOTING:** You need access to the Internet to complete this step. If it does not work for you, you can choose clip art from the existing selections in the Clip Organizer instead, as you did in Hands-On Exercise 1.

> **TROUBLESHOOTING:** The Microsoft Office Online site opens in a browser window. Accept the terms and conditions, if this screen appears.

You can limit the search in several ways. You can search by keyword or browse by category. You can limit the results by media type. Click the drop-down arrow on the Search button to investigate the possibilities near the top of the screen.

d. Enter **sunset** as a keyword in the Search all Media Types text box.

e. Choose **Photos** from the Search drop-down arrow to search for photos in the gallery.

f. When you find a clip you like, click in the check box next to the picture to add the picture to the Selection basket at the left of the screen, and then click the **Red download arrow** to download.

g. Follow the next screens' prompts to download the image.

A download screen will appear to save the image to your computer.

> **TROUBLESHOOTING:** If a dialog box appears for you, click Open to go ahead.

h. Once saved, close all of the browser windows unless you want to download more clips.

After saving the new picture, you can now search for the new picture from the task pane to insert the picture.

i. Type **Sunset** in the Search for box.

j. Scroll down, if necessary, to find your image.

k. Click the image to replace the default image on your price list brochure.

l. Search to replace the image in the first panel on page 1 with a nature image, as shown in Figure 1.43.

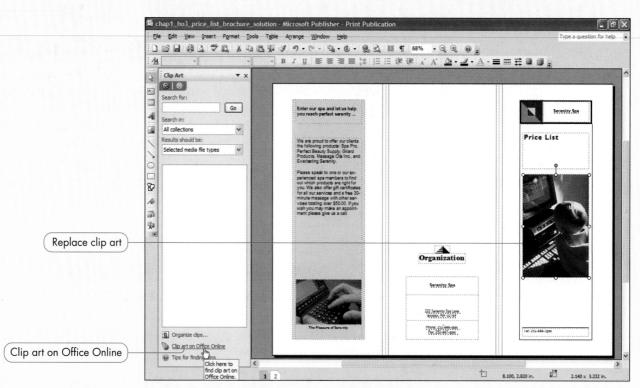

Figure 1.43 Insert the Clip Art from the Internet

Step 3
Move, Size, and Layer the Picture

Refer to Figure 1.44 as you complete Step 3.

a. Click and drag the clip art image on the main panel to move it up on the publication window, as shown in Figure 1.44.

b. Click a corner sizing handle and drag out to resize the picture.

c. Point and click to drag the picture to fit evenly within the brochure guides.

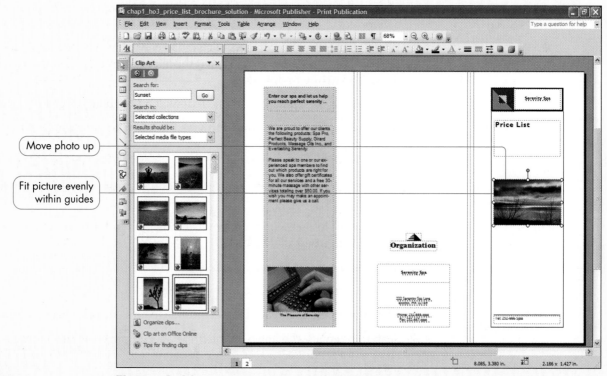

Figure 1.44 Move, Size, and Layer the Picture

Refer to Figure 1.45 as you complete Step 4.

a. If necessary, use the Zoom command to enlarge the publication in the window.

b. Select **page 1** of your brochure.

c. Click the **Organization logo**, and then hit **Delete** on your keyboard.

d. Click **Design Gallery Object** from the Insert Menu.

e. Click the **Logos option**, as shown in Figure 1.45, and choose a design from the Logo Gallery in the middle of the window.

We chose the Perpendicular logo design, but you may choose to keep the same logo, or pick a different logo.

f. In the middle panel, select the **Organization Logo text box**, and then type **Serenity** in the text box to replace the default text.

g. Click to drag the logo back to where the one you deleted was positioned.

h. Close the task pane, and then click outside the logo to deselect it.

i. Save the publication.

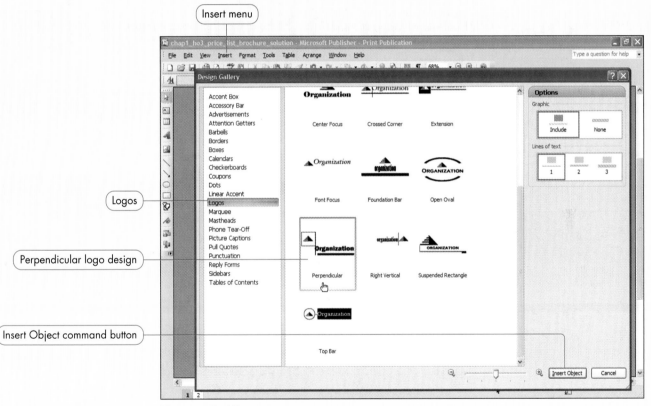

Figure 1.45 Choose a Different Logo

Refer to Figure 1.46 as you complete Step 5.

a. Change the Zoom to **Whole Page** to see the entire brochure in the publication window.

b. Open the task pane from the View menu, click the drop-down arrow next to the **Clip Art task pane**, as shown in Figure 1.46, and choose **Format Publication**.

c. Experiment by choosing the **Accessory Bar design** from the Change Template button.

TROUBLESHOOTING: A dialog box will appear asking if you want to apply the template to the existing publication or a new publication. Be sure to apply to the current publication and click OK.

d. Change the design back by clicking the **Undo button** on the Standard toolbar or by choosing **Accent Box** from the design list.

e. Click the **Color Schemes link** in the task pane and experiment by choosing the **Mahogany color scheme**.

f. Change the color scheme back by clicking the **Undo button** or by choosing the **Waterfall color scheme** from the list.

g. Save the publication a final time.

h. Print the completed publication and submit it to your instructor as proof that you completed this exercise.

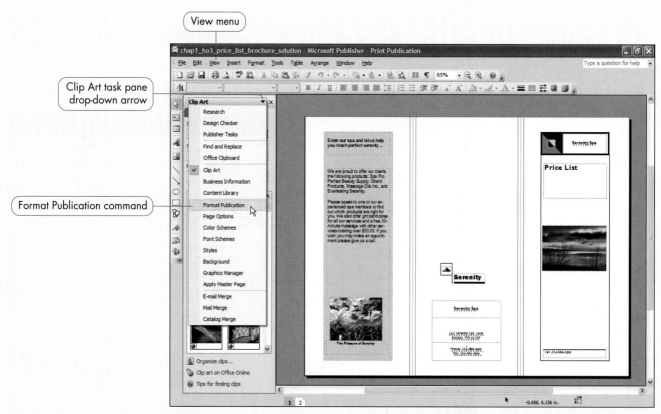

Figure 1.46 Change the Publication Design and Color Scheme

TIP The Undo and Redo Commands

Click the drop-down arrow next to the Undo button to display a list of your previous actions, and then click the action you want to undo, which also undoes all of the commands listed above it. Undoing the fifth command in the list, for example, will also undo the top four commands. The Redo command works in reverse and cancels the last Undo command.

Summary

1. **Understand desktop publishing.** The essence of desktop publishing is the merger of text with graphics to produce an effective publication. Proficiency in desktop publishing requires knowledge of the associated commands in Microsoft Publisher, as well as familiarity with the basics of graphic design.

2. **Learn about the bridge from word processing to Publisher.** If you are already familiar with word processor software such as Microsoft Word or presentation software such as Microsoft PowerPoint, then you may already be familiar with basic Windows commands.

3. **Understand typing in text boxes and use the Zoom command.** The Zoom command on the Standard toolbar allows you to see objects clearly or see the whole publication when necessary.

4. **Know the difference between popular publication types and templates.** The templates provided in Publisher help you to design some of the most common publications. They can be selected by Publication Type or by Popular Publication Types.

5. **Know how to create, save, edit, and print simple publications.** To create a publication, you would start with Publication Types or Popular Publication Types. The templates in Publisher allow you to easily create a great publication without having to start from scratch. You will want to save your publications often using the save commands from the File menu or Standard toolbar so that you do not lose any of your hard work. The templates allow you to edit basic template options such as graphics, business names, addresses, and much more. To print publications, use the Print command from the File menu or the Standard toolbar.

6. **Know how to use the Objects toolbar.** Clip art, WordArt, and drawing objects, used in moderation, will catch the reader's attention and enhance almost any publication. Clip art and photos are available from a variety of sources including Microsoft Office Online, which is accessed most easily through the Insert Picture command on the menu bar. Once clip art, WordArt, and/or drawing objects have been inserted into a publication, they can be moved and sized just like any other Windows object.

7. **Understand the steps for creating a good publication.** Choosing an appropriate template and making sure objects are layered appropriately on the page are two major elements to consider when designing a desktop publication. Emphasis can be achieved in several ways. One of the easiest ways to achieve emphasis includes varying the design and color scheme of the publication and adding objects to the publication, such as WordArt, tables, text boxes, and/or drawing objects.

Key Terms

Multiple Choice

1. A text box is:

    (a) An object that is available on the Objects toolbar

    (b) Where you type your text in Microsoft Publisher

    (c) Both (a) and (b)

    (d) Neither (a) nor (b)

2. How do you save changes to a Publisher presentation?

    (a) Pull down the File menu and click the Save command.

    (b) Click the Save button on the Standard toolbar.

    (c) Both (a) and (b).

    (d) Neither (a) nor (b).

3. Which of the following are common publication design sets for many businesses?

    (a) Letterhead

    (b) Envelope

    (c) Business Card

    (d) All of the above

4. What is the effect of dragging one of the four corner handles on a selected object?

    (a) The length of the object is changed but the width remains constant.

    (b) The width of the object is changed but the length remains constant.

    (c) The length and width of the object are changed in proportion to one another.

    (d) Neither the length nor width of the object is changed.

5. How would you increase the size of the text in the publication window to an easily readable size?

    (a) Use the Zoom command to change the magnification to 25%.

    (b) Use the Zoom command to change the magnification to 100%.

    (c) Use the Zoom command to change the magnification to 10%.

    (d) Use the Zoom command to change the magnification to 400%.

6. What is the first screen that appears after starting the Publisher program?

    (a) A window showing Publication Types

    (b) A Recent Publications window

    (c) A window showing Popular Publication Types

    (d) All of the above

7. How do you change the font for existing text within a text box?

    (a) Select the text, and then choose the new font.

    (b) Choose the new font, and then select the text.

    (c) Either (a) or (b).

    (d) Neither (a) nor (b).

8. Which of the following can be inserted from the Clip Art task pane?

    (a) Clip art

    (b) Photographs

    (c) Sounds

    (d) All of the above

9. Which of the following can be downloaded and inserted from the Clip art on Microsoft Online?

    (a) Clip art

    (b) Photos

    (c) Sounds

    (d) All of the above

10. Which of the following is true related to the use of graphics in a publication?

    (a) Use large graphics to dominate the publication page.

    (b) Use a lot of graphics to catch the reader's eye.

    (c) Do not use any graphics, because it takes away from your message.

    (d) None of the above.

11. Which of the following is true regarding templates?

    (a) A template cannot be changed once created.

    (b) A template may be changed once created.

    (c) Both (a) and (b).

    (d) Neither (a) nor (b).

12. What happens if you double-click a picture in a publication?

   (a) A dialog box will appear with available commands to format the picture.

   (b) The Insert Clip Art task pane opens.

   (c) The WordArt dialog box appears.

   (d) Nothing will happen when you double-click a picture.

13. What does it mean to layer the objects correctly on a publication page?

   (a) Layering objects means to ensure objects are stacked on top of one another without regard to readability.

   (b) Layering objects means to stack clip art randomly on top of text.

   (c) Layering objects means to stack text randomly on top of clip art.

   (d) None of the above.

14. Which of the following is available on the Objects toolbar?

   (a) Text box tool

   (b) Insert Table tool

   (c) Insert WordArt tool

   (d) All of the above

15. Which of the following formatting options are available from the Formatting toolbar?

   (a) Fill color

   (b) Line color

   (c) Line/Border style

   (d) All of the above

16. What do you need to consider in designing a publication?

   (a) Your audience

   (b) Keeping the design simple

   (c) Offering enough information

   (d) All of the above

17. What is one major difference between desktop publishing and word processing programs?

   (a) The ability to add clip art

   (b) Greater control over the placement of text and objects

   (c) Typing in text boxes

   (d) Automatic spell check

18. How many levels of undo are present in Microsoft Publisher?

   (a) 10

   (b) 20

   (c) 50

   (d) None

Chapter 1 introduced you to many of the basic features and abilities of a desktop publisher. In the following steps, you use those tools to make modifications and enhancements to a brochure that will be sent to potential customers. In this case, you will edit text in a text box, format text, change clip art, and layer the clip art and other objects in the publication to enhance the design.

a. Start Publisher, if necessary, and open the *chap1_pe1_eye_shop* publication. Save the file as **chap1_pe1_eye_shop_solution**.

b. Change the text box business name, as shown in Figure 1.47, to **The Eye Shop**.

c. Change the business name font to **14 pt**, and then resize the text box to fit the business name all on one line.

d. Change the default clip art on the brochure cover to something more appropriate.

e. Move and/or size the new clip art to layer appropriately on the brochure cover.

f. Redesign the Organization logo object on the back cover of the brochure. Double-click to change the default logo graphic to something more appropriate, and then change the Organization text to **EyesRUs**.

g. Change the remaining graphics on pages 1 and 2, as shown in Figure 1.48 of the brochure, to something more appropriate.

h. Move and/or size the new clip art to layer it appropriately in its pane.

i. Change the caption text boxes to match the graphic.

j. Experiment with different color schemes.

k. Save the publication and close Publisher.

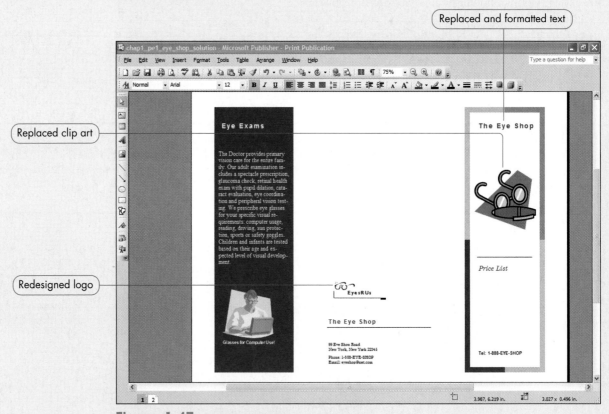

Figure 1.47 Designing a Brochure Page 1

...continued on Next Page

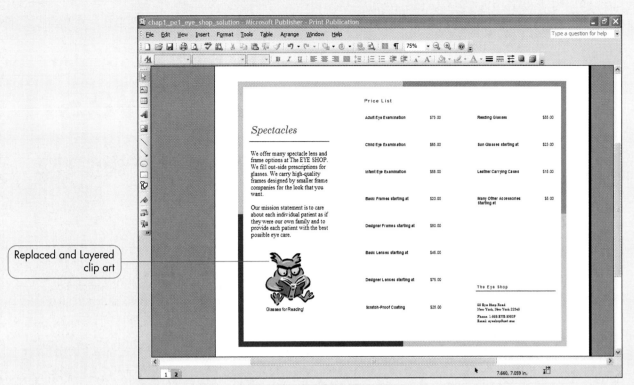

Replaced and Layered clip art

Figure 1.48 Designing a Brochure Page 2

2 Designing a Flyer

The boys and girls club of Boston has decided to set up a car wash for this year's fundraiser. Last year, one of the parents paid out of pocket to have flyers designed and printed at a local print shop. This year, one of the parents volunteered to design a flyer herself because she just purchased Microsoft Office Publisher 2007. It is important to design a flyer that will be eye-catching and free of errors. There is enough money this year to print color flyers. Your job is to open last year's flyer provided to you from the previous parent and redesign the old flyer to add color, graphics, and more.

a. Start Publisher, if necessary, open the *chap1_pe2_car_wash* flyer publication, and save it as **chap1_pe2_car_wash_solution**.

b. Open the task pane from the View menu, if necessary, and click the drop-down arrow to select **Format Publication**.

c. Click the **Change Template button** and choose the **Car Wash 2 template** to apply to the current publication.

d. Select the text **Date and the date** and change the text to **Car Wash**.

e. Edit the Time text and change it to **Date**, and then enter the current date of the event, as shown in Figure 1.49.

f. Change the current time of the event, as shown in Figure 1.49.

g. Add the text to describe your location in the lower right text box, as shown in Figure 1.49.

h. Change the Color Scheme to **Marine**.

i. Change the Font Scheme to **Arial bold** under the Basis scheme.

j. Save the publication.

...continued on Next Page

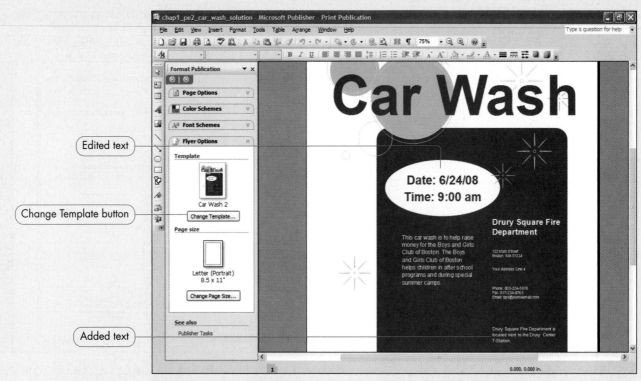

Edited text

Change Template button

Added text

Figure 1.49 Designing a Flyer

3 Birthday Surprise

Your mom has decided that she wants to have a surprise 50th birthday party for her sister and has asked you to design the perfect invitation. She has provided you with the following information:

- **Date: October 18, 2008**
- **Time: 4:00pm until 9:00pm**
- **Place: Knights of Columbus on Oak Avenue**

Be sure to consider the overall age group of the people attending the party, and do not forget to mention that this is a SURPRISE party. We started the invitation for you, but you will need to finish it using the above information.

a. Start Publisher, if necessary, open the *chap1_pe3_birthday* file, and save it as **chap1_pe3_birthday_solution**.

b. On page 2, scroll down to change the party details using the information above and add the text, as shown in Figure 1.50.

c. Using the Insert Picture and Clip Art Command, search for birthday images and insert the two birthday cake pictures, as shown in Figure 1.50.

   TROUBLESHOOTING: Be sure that the Search In Everywhere toggle box is checked to also include any Web collections.

d. Move, size, and layer the images, as shown in Figure 1.50.

e. Select the party details text and use the Formatting toolbar to change the **font size** to **16 pt**, and then use the Center button to center the text, as shown in Figure 1.50.

f. Select the location text and change the font to **14 pt**.

g. Print out and start folding!

h. Save the publication.

...continued on Next Page

Figure 1.50 Birthday Surprise

4 Certificate of Completion

You have done such a great job of learning Microsoft Office Publisher 2007 that your teacher has asked you to design a Certificate of Completion that she would use to give out to other students. We have started the certificate for you, but your teacher does not like the template, colors, or font. She would also like you to add her name to the certificate for now so that she can see a completed sample.

a. Open Publisher, if necessary, and then open the *chap1_pe4_certificate* file. Save the publication as **chap1_pe4_certificate_solution**.

b. Open the task pane from the View menu, and then choose **Format Publication** from the drop-down arrow.

c. Using the Change Template button, change the template to the **Star design** and apply it to the current publication.

d. Edit the name of the recipient, as shown in Figure 1.51.

e. Edit the business name, as shown in Figure 1.51.

f. Select the logo and hit **Delete**.

g. Using the Insert menu and Design Gallery Object, insert the Perpendicular logo choice.

h. Click to drag the logo object to the previous logo location, as shown in Figure 1.51, and edit the logo text as well.

i. In the task pane, select **Clip Art** from the drop-down arrow task pane and search for **computers**.

j. Select the default clip art on the certificate, and then select the clip art from the search gallery to replace the default image.

TROUBLESHOOTING: Move the picture over just a bit if it is too close to your text, as shown in our figure.

...continued on Next Page

k. Save the publication.

l. Submit your sample for approval to your instructor.

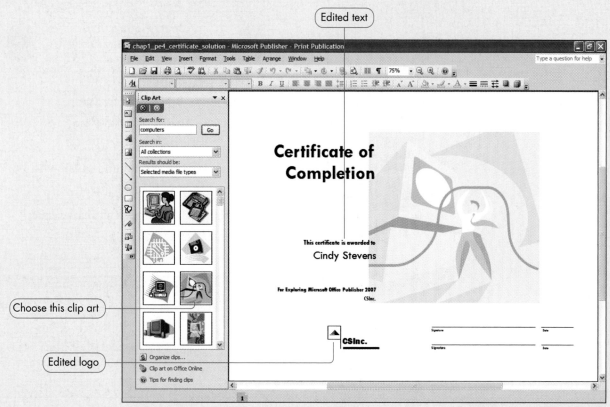

Figure 1.51 Certificate of Completion

Mid-Level Exercises

1 Garage Sale Flyer

Kim, your best friend, has sold her house and she has begun to pack up for the move. She is overwhelmed by the amount of "stuff" she has collected over the past 20 years living in this home. She has decided to have a garage sale on June 15, 2008, at 7:00 a.m. to get rid of many items and to make a little money to boot. She lives at 40 West Street near the Old Theatre. Her daughter agreed to create a one-page flyer that she could post all over the neighborhood but gave up after her boyfriend called. Kim decided to finish the flyer herself.

a. Open Publisher, if necessary, and then open the *chap1_mid1_garage_sale* file. Save the file as **chap1_mid1_garage_sale_solution**.

b. Delete the Garage Sale Flyer's default text box announcing *Garage Sale*, and then use the Objects toolbar to draw out and insert WordArt instead. Use the fourth WordArt choice in the top row.

c. Using the WordArt toolbar, change the WordArt font color to **bright orange** (or any color of your choice) and change the font size to **80 pt**.

d. Replace the default clip art and insert a garage sale clip art picture.

e. Move and size the new clip art as necessary so that it will fit at the top of the flyer.

f. Use the Formatting toolbar to add yellow fill color to all the informational text boxes on the flyer.

g. Add the garage sale details such as date, time, and location to the top two text boxes.

h. Save and close the publication.

2 Customized Envelope

You have just graduated from college with a degree in Interior Design. Since you already worked three co-op positions in the last two years for other companies and got a feel for what it was like to work for someone else, you have decided to start your own business. You are ready to send out information to potential clients and need a business envelope for your new company: Alyssa's Designs located at 15 Downtown Street, Boston, MA 02222. Instead of contacting a costly printing service, you have decided to use your new Microsoft Office Publisher 2007 program to get the job done. All the letters are ready to go because you already typed them in Microsoft Word.

a. Start Publisher, if necessary, and select **Envelopes** on the Publication Types task pane.

b. Select the **Bounce category** under Newer Designs. Uncheck the logo toggle box.

c. Choose the **#10 page size envelope**.

d. Save the publication as **chap1_mid2_envelope_solution**.

e. Edit the text to include your business name and your address (provided above) and add your first potential customer's address (make up the information).

f. Change the Color Scheme to **Glacier**.

g. Change the Font Scheme to **Impact**.

h. Save and close the publication.

...continued on Next Page

The Quincy Homeless society wants to give volunteers a token of their appreciation. One of the board members suggested giving volunteers a paper certificate of appreciation and decided to create it himself. Use your skills to design this certificate using the steps listed below.

a. Start Publisher, if necessary, and choose **Certificate of Appreciation 4** from the Award Certificates preview gallery. Save the publication as **chap1_mid3_certificate_of_ appreciation_solution**.

b. Click to select the text **Name of Recipient** and type **Alyssa Stevens**.

c. Add to the second text box the text **In recognition of valuable contributions at the Quincy Homeless Society**.

d. Apply the **Waterfall Color Scheme**.

e. Apply the **Georgia Bold (under Archival) Font Scheme**.

f. Select the text box **this certificate is awarded to**.

g. Click on the **Fill Color button arrow**, and then select **More Fill Colors**. Choose a **medium purple color**.

h. Click on the **Fill Color button arrow**, and then choose **Fill Effects**. Under Colors, select **Two colors** and a **diagonal down shading style**.

i. Select the text box for the recipient's name. Change the fill color and fill effects to match those in steps g and h.

j. Change the clip art to a picture of a hand holding a ribbon.

k. Adjust the size to make the picture larger, as shown in the figure.

l. Save and close the publication.

Capstone Exercise

You have recently accepted a new job in an architecture firm, called Burke Architecture, owned by Michael Burke. The logo text is MBArch. The firm is in need of new stationary, and because you have some experience in graphic design, you volunteered to create the stationary. They need designs for a business card, letterhead on which to print their important documents, envelopes to use with the letterhead, and a company calendar for both personal use and as gifts to clients. All four items need to have the same design. Luckily, the projects were started before you were hired so the design graphic that matches with the company's signs has already been inserted into each of these items. Your job is to finish each part of the design set.

Create the Business Card

a. Open the file *chap1_cap_business_card*, found in the Exploring Publisher folder. Save the publication as **chap1_cap_business_card_solution**.

b. Insert the logo text name and choose the black-and-white arcs image (search for arcs clip art) from the Clip Art task pane to replace the default image for the logo.

c. Include the name of your organization.

d. Insert the owner's name in the appropriate areas.

e. Enter your address information, your phone and fax numbers, and your e-mail address.

f. Save and close the publication.

Create the Envelope

a. Open the file *chap1_cap_envelope*, found in the Exploring Publisher folder. Save the publication as **chap1_cap_envelope_solution**.

b. Enter the appropriate information for the logo and organization.

c. Insert the logo text name and choose the black-and-white arcs image (search for arcs clip art) from the Clip Art task pane to replace the default image for the logo.

d. Provide the rest of the information for a customer.

e. Save and close the publication.

Create the Letterhead

a. Open the file *chap1_letterhead*, found in the Exploring Publisher folder. Save the publication as **chap1_cap_letterhead_solution**.

b. Enter the appropriate information for the logo and organization.

c. Insert the logo text name and choose the black-and-white arcs image (search for arcs clip art) from the Clip Art task pane to replace the default image for the logo.

d. Enter your contact information from the business card.

e. Save and close the publication.

Create the Calendar

a. Open the file *chap1_cap_calendar*, found in the Exploring Publisher folder. Save the publication as **chap1_cap_calendar_solution**.

b. Enter the appropriate information for the logo and organization.

c. Insert the logo text name and choose the black-and-white arcs image (search for arcs clip art) from the Clip Art task pane to replace the default image for the logo.

d. Enter your contact information.

e. Save and close the publication.

Mini Cases

Use the rubric following the case as a guide to evaluate your work, but keep in mind that your instructor may impose additional grading criteria or use a different standard to judge your work.

Invitation

GENERAL CASE

You are throwing a surprise party for Michael Burke's 21st birthday by taking him to one of his favorite restaurants, the No Name Restaurant in Boston. (Yes, that really is the name of the restaurant.) You have written a simple invitation, but you do not like the graphic. Open the *chap1_mc1_invitation* publication. Replace the current graphic with a photo of a birthday cake that you locate on Office Online. Use your knowledge of searching for images online to modify this invitation, and then save your invitation as **chap1_mc1_invitation_solution**.

Performance Elements	Exceeds Expectations	Meets Expectations	Below Expectations
Change Graphic	Graphic is a photo	Graphic remains clip art	No change in graphic
Text	Some text is added; format changed to match picture	All text remains untouched	Some text is deleted

Computer Power

RESEARCH CASE

Publisher is a very powerful program when it comes to graphic design; therefore, it requires a computer with enough power to use the program efficiently. Using http://www.google.com, research the computer itself, portable storage devices like the CD-ROM, the Internet, and e-mail. Open the poster publication *chap1_mc3_computers* that is provided; include at least five different graphic images and a text box next to each image describing each of the following: computers, diskettes, CDs, the Internet, and finally e-mail. The poster is 20" by 30" and will be presented to a group of senior citizens who do not know much about computers; format the poster appropriately. Keep in mind that the poster will look small on the screen but will be much larger if printed. Your finished document should be saved as **chap1_mc3_computers_solution**.

Performance Elements	Exceeds Expectations	Meets Expectations	Below Expectations
Format of poster	Use of text boxes; very organized	Clear, concise layout; organized	Information is not organized; messy design
Graphics	Good use of graphics	Graphics for most text	Few graphics
Font	Font is readable everywhere (above 36 pt)	Font is readable from the standard of 10 feet (24–36 pt)	Too small, not readable from a distance (below 18 pt)
Computer Information	More than five topics	Five topics	Fewer than five topics

Plagiarism

DISASTER RECOVERY

You see a presentation by a classmate on plagiarism, and you notice that some of his information is incorrect. The student doesn't seem to notice that anything is wrong and won't redo the presentation. You decide to change his presentation to a flyer and hand it out to the class. You notice that he has quoted the Wikipedia Web site without using any citations. Open the *chap1_mc2_plagiarism* publication, hold down the Ctrl key and click the words "desktop publishing." (If you have an Internet connection, the Wikipedia site will open in your browser so that you can obtain the proper source information.) Properly cite that quote. His definition of plagiarism is also wrong; write your own definition. Also include some information on copyrighting and at least one graphic related to copyright, and then save the flyer as **chap1_mc2_plagiarism_solution**.

Performance Elements	Exceeds Expectations	Meets Expectations	Below Expectations
Citations	Cited quote perfectly	Cited quote, but not a correct citation	Did not cite quote
Definition	Includes lots of information	Includes some information	Includes very little information

Becoming Your Own Designer

Creating a Publication from Scratch

Objectives

After you read this chapter, you will be able to:

1. Work with Blank Page Sizes **(page 59)**.

2. Understand layout guides **(page 61)**.

3. Understand the master page **(page 65)**.

4. Emphasize words **(page 68)**.

5. Make objects transparent **(page 77)**.

6. Group, rotate, and flip objects **(page 78)**.

7. Troubleshoot layout guides **(page 79)**.

Hands-On Exercises

Exercises	Skills Covered
1. ADVERTISING PUBLICATION (page 71). **Open:** chap2_ho1_advertising **Save as:** chap2_ho1_advertising_solution	• Adjust the Layout Guides • Layer Text Boxes Using the Layout Guides • Format the Publication's Text • Create the Color Reverses and Apply a Line/Border Style • Create a Drop Cap and a Numbered List
2. COMPLETE THE ADVERTISING PUBLICATION (page 80) **Open:** chap2_ho2_modified_advertising **Save as:** chap2_ho2_modified_advertising_solution	• Insert a Picture into the Master Page • Layer the Picture Along the Layout Guides • Format the Picture • Make a Text Box Transparent • Design a Logo

CASE STUDY

Get Motivated!

Penny participated in last year's Deagan 5K run to help raise money for the local fire department. The donations help families left homeless due to home fires. When Penny ran last year, she noticed that many of her friends did not participate. When she asked them later, she found out that most of her friends did not know about the race and wished they had. After speaking with about 12 of her friends, she realized that the fire department is not doing enough advertising to potential volunteers.

Case Study

Penny decided that she would like to volunteer to help get the word out to the community. She spoke with the chief of the fire department to ask if she could help. Jim, the chief, was very happy and said yes. All that he asked of Penny was to see any written documents before they go out to the general public. The city must inspect all ads before they are released.

Penny decided to use Microsoft Publisher to create an advertisement to get the word out to the community. She could pass out the ad herself, plus the city said it would print large quantities and have other volunteers pass them out to the community and to local businesses.

Your Assignment

- Read the chapter.
- Pay special attention to the information on layout guides, master pages, and typography.
- Think about how Penny could create a professional-looking, yet simple one-page advertisement to promote the 5K race.
- Design the publication, print out a copy, and submit it to your instructor.

Introduction

This chapter significantly extends your capabilities by showing you how to create a new publication from scratch and how to use a variety of commands to change the appearance of your publications.

The previous chapter taught you the basics of Microsoft Publisher and enabled you to create and print simple publications using the built-in templates. This chapter significantly extends your capabilities by showing you how to create a new publication from scratch and how to use a variety of commands to change the appearance of your publications. Publisher's built-in templates, presented in Chapter 1, provide a considerable amount of flexibility. However, as the publication designer, you must often edit templates. For instance, what if you want to include two graphics rather than the single one provided in the default template or want the graphic in a different position? As you saw in Chapter 1, you can insert additional graphics or move the graphic frame to a different position within the publication. You will find, however, that it is just as easy to create publications from scratch, and that doing so gives you greater control over your publications. You will finish with a publication that is what you need. In this chapter you will learn how to use the task pane's Blank Page Sizes link to create a simple publication from scratch and how to use the nonprinting layout guides to ensure consistency throughout your publications. You will also learn the basics of working with the master page of your publications, advanced layering techniques, and various Publisher commands to enhance the quality of your publications.

As you read the chapter, realize that there are many different ways to accomplish the same task and that it would be impossible to cover them all. Our approach is to present the overall concept and suggest ways we think are most appropriate at the time we introduce the material.

As always, the hands-on exercises are essential to our learn-by-doing philosophy, because they enable you to apply the conceptual material at the computer. As you do the exercises, you may recognize many commands from other Windows applications, all of which share a common user interface and consistent command structure. In addition, you already know, for example, how to insert objects, move and size objects, and format objects. The same concepts apply within this chapter. As you read the chapter, look for these similarities to apply your existing knowledge to new material. There are, of course, additional commands that you will need to learn, but all commands are executed from within Publisher through pull-down menus, toolbars, short-cut menus, or the task panes. Do not worry about memorizing the new commands presented in this chapter, because you can always find instructions within the Publisher Help files, if necessary.

Working with Blank Page Sizes

In addition, the Blank Page Sizes gallery contains some very unique page sizes, such as booklets, mailing labels, and name tags.

The *Blank Page Sizes task pane* to the right of the screen, shown in Figure 2.1, includes page size information, color and font scheme options, and business information options.

The *Blank Page Sizes task pane* to the right of the screen, shown in Figure 2.1, includes page size information, color and font scheme options, and business information options.

The Blank Page Sizes option in the Publication Types task pane, shown in Figure 2.2, is where you start to create a publication from scratch. When you click the link, Publisher displays the Blank Page Sizes gallery. The *Blank Page Sizes* is a gallery of different page size options. This gallery contains common page layouts. In addition, the Blank Page Sizes gallery contains some very unique page sizes, such as booklets, mailing labels, and name tags.

The *Blank Page Sizes* is a gallery of different page size options.

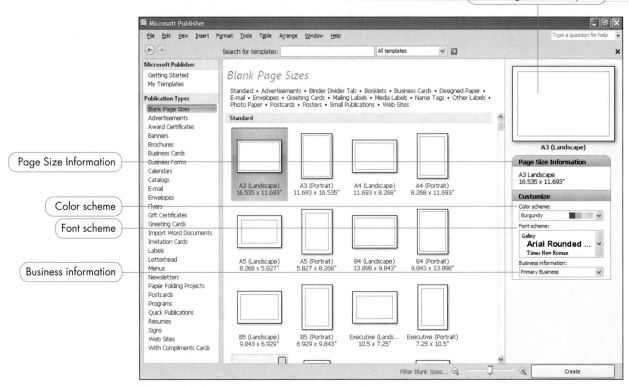

Figure 2.1 Blank Page Sizes Task Pane

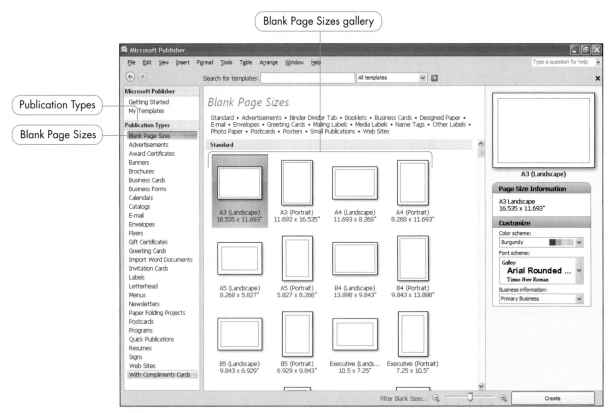

Figure 2.2 Blank Page Sizes

Understanding Layout Guides

Layout guides are an underlying, but nonprinting, set of blue and green horizontal and vertical lines.

The design of a publication is developed using layout guides. **Layout guides** are an underlying, but nonprinting, set of blue and green horizontal and vertical lines that determine the placement of the major elements. These guides repeat on each page of a publication, establishing its overall structure by indicating the number of columns, the space between columns, the size of the margins, the placement of objects, and so on. The guides do not appear in the printed publication but help you organize the publication's objects into appropriately layered rows and columns. The layout guides can be toggled on or off at any time from the Boundaries and Guides command on the View menu.

Layout guides may be simple or complex, but the type of publication you are working on always determines the guides. For example, the blank publication guides of Figures 2.3 and 2.4 are among the most common and utilitarian designs. Each shows the basic margin and grid guides on the publication. Figure 2.5 shows a two-column design for a blank publication, with unequal column widths to provide interest. Many other designs are possible as well. For example, a one-column guide may be used for flyers, signs, and business forms. A two-column, wide and narrow format may be appropriate for textbooks and manuals. Two- and three-column formats are used for newsletters and magazines.

The simple concept of layout guides should make the underlying design of any publication obvious, which in turn gives you an immediate understanding of page layout. Moreover, the conscious use of guides will help you organize your material and result in a more polished and professional-looking publication. It will also help you to achieve consistency from page to page within a publication (or from issue to issue of a newsletter). Indeed, much of what goes wrong in desktop publishing stems from failing to follow or use the underlying margin and grid guides.

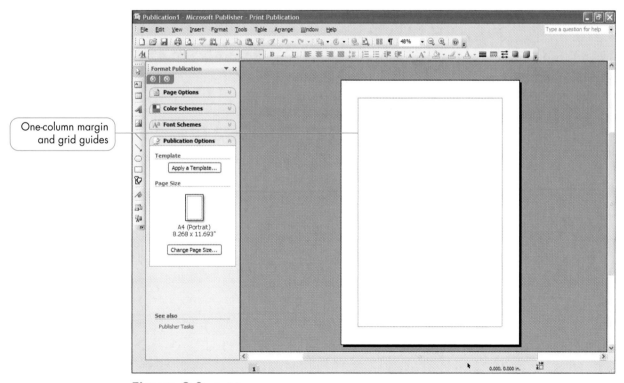

One-column margin and grid guides

Figure 2.3 Full Page

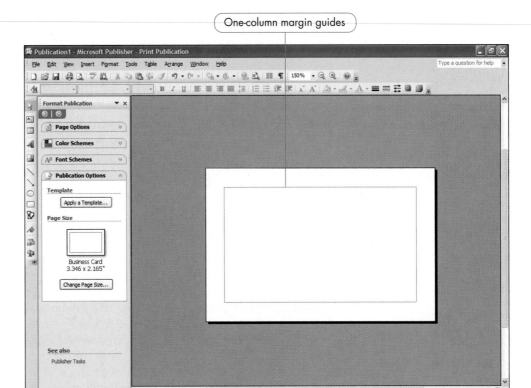

Figure 2.4 Business Card

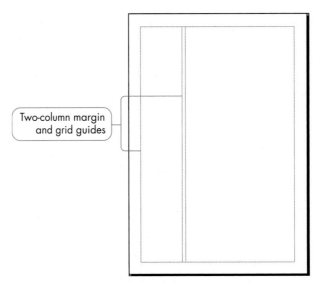

Figure 2.5 Two-column

Working with Layout Guides

(Publisher provides a default layout for each publication type.)

A **default layout** is a predefined template.

The **Layout Guides dialog box** enables you to change the position of the margin guides, the number of column or row grid guides, and whether you want to create mirrored guides.

The **Layout Guides command** allows you to change margin guides, grid guides, and baseline guides.

Publisher provides a default layout for each publication type. A **default layout** is a predefined template that contains grid guides, picture placeholders, color and font schemes, and more. A blank publication generally only contains layout guides. To make basic changes in the default layout guides for a blank publication, simply select the Layout Guides command from the Arrange menu. The **Layout Guides dialog box** appears, which enables you to change the position of the margin guides, the number of column or row grid guides, and whether you want to create mirrored guides (for publications printed on facing pages), as shown in Figure 2.6. The **Layout Guides command** allows you to change margin guides, grid guides, and baseline guides. **Margin guides** define the top, bottom, left, and right margins. **Grid guides** help to align columns and rows. **Baseline guides** help to align text. The changes you make apply to all pages of the publication.

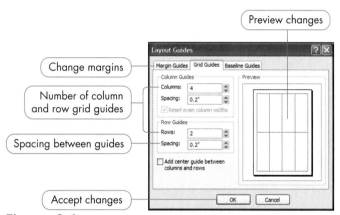

Figure 2.6 Working with Layout Guides

Layout and Ruler Guides

Margin guides define the top, bottom, left, and right margins.

Grid guides help to align columns and rows.

Baseline guides help to align text.

The **master page** contains items that you want to show up on every page.

The **ruler guides** can be used to position objects that are not repeated on every page.

(You can also add guides to an individual page of the publication.)

The row and column guides you specify in the Layout Guides dialog box are distributed evenly on the publication page. You can easily move them by selecting the Master Page command on the View menu. The **master page** contains items that you want to show up on every page such as margin guides, clip art, text, and more. Once you have toggled on the Master Page command, position the mouse pointer over the grid guide (the pointer changes to an Adjust pointer) and click to drag the guide to a new position on the publication window, as shown in Figure 2.7. Then toggle off the Master Page command by clicking the Master Page command again or click the Close Master View button on the Master View toolbar. The new guide position will appear on all pages of your publication. You will learn about the Master Page command in the next section.

You can also add guides to an individual page of the publication. The **ruler guides** can be used to position objects that are not repeated on every page. To add a ruler guide, pull down the Arrange menu, click Ruler Guides, and choose Add Horizontal Ruler Guide or Add Vertical Ruler Guide. You can also add ruler guides directly from the publication page's horizontal and vertical rulers. Make sure the Master Page command is toggled off, point to the horizontal or vertical ruler, and when the pointer changes to the Adjust pointer, drag it onto the publication, as shown in Figure 2.8. Ruler guides are green. Once you add a green ruler guide to a page, you can move it around just like the grid guides described above.

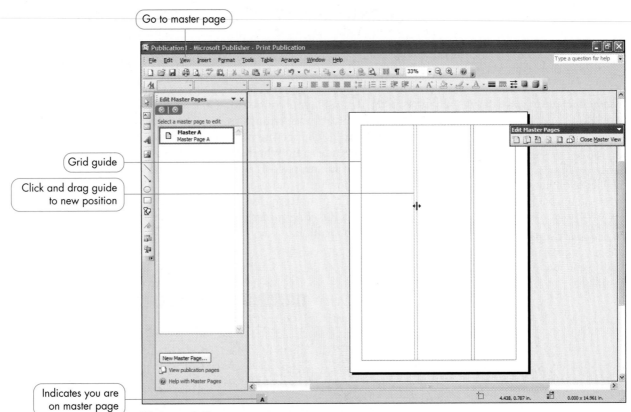

Go to master page

Grid guide

Click and drag guide to new position

Indicates you are on master page

Figure 2.7 Changing Column Guides

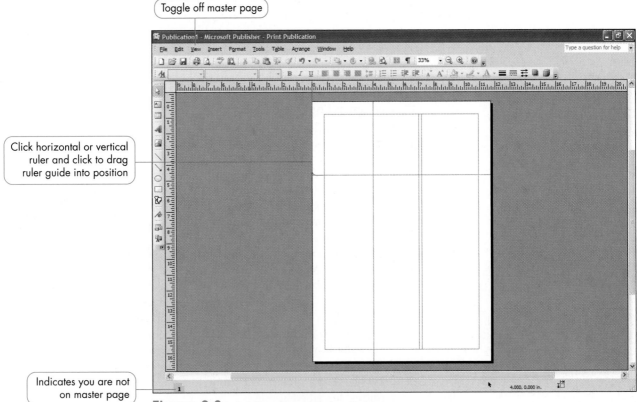

Toggle off master page

Click horizontal or vertical ruler and click to drag ruler guide into position

Indicates you are not on master page

Figure 2.8 Adding Green Ruler Guides

TIP   Learn More About Desktop Publishing

Use your favorite Web search engine to look for additional information about desktop publishing. A keyword search for desktop publishing tips and tricks, desktop publishing guides, desktop publishing tutorials, and/or desktop publishing will result in a number of hits. The Microsoft site located at www.microsoft.com will usually have many feature articles related to Microsoft Publisher and desktop publishing in general, as well.

Understanding the Master Page

When designing a publication from scratch, you need to have an understanding of working with the publication master page. As mentioned earlier, the master page of your publication is a background page on which you can place objects that are repeated on every page of your publication, such as logos, page numbers, WordArt, and/or other objects. As you saw in the preceding section, the master page is also where you adjust the position of the row and column grid guides. Any change you make to the master page applies to the whole publication. The master page background includes objects on the foreground of all other pages in the publication. Working with the publication master page is a lot like working with Microsoft Word header and footer controls.

> (Any change you make to the master page applies to the whole publication.)

Working with the Master Page

The *foreground* contains all objects and text that will appear on that page only, as opposed to the background master page.

To create business cards for all of the salespersons in your organization, you could use the master page of a business card publication for all of the common elements (the logo, the business name and address, and so forth) on the card and put the individual salesperson's name, office phone, etc. on a publication page. You would have one page for each salesperson. To work with the master page, pull down the View menu and click Master Page to toggle it on. When you are working with the master page of a publication, you will not be able to see any objects on the foreground, as can be inferred from the screens shown in Figures 2.9 through 2.12. The *foreground* contains all objects and text that will appear on that page only, as opposed to the background master page. Figure 2.9 shows a business card with all objects on the foreground. Figure 2.10 shows the master page of the business card before any objects have been placed on it. To add an object such as a text box, drawing object, or picture to the master page, toggle the page on and perform the commands described in Chapter 1. Size, move, and format it as you would an object placed on the foreground. Figure 2.11 shows an object that has been added to the master page of the business card. Figure 2.12 shows the foreground of the business card with the added master page object. To send an object from the foreground to the master page, pull down the Arrange menu and click Send to Master Page.

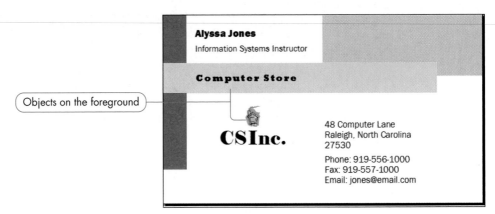

Alyssa Jones
Information Systems Instructor

Computer Store

CSInc.

48 Computer Lane
Raleigh, North Carolina
27530

Phone: 919-556-1000
Fax: 919-557-1000
Email: jones@email.com

Objects on the foreground

Figure 2.9 Objects Visible on Foreground

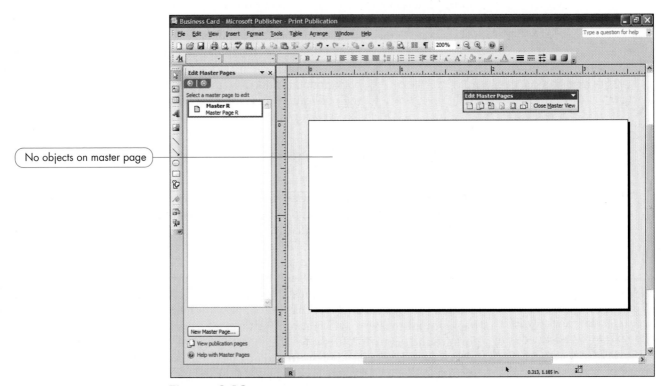

No objects on master page

Figure 2.10 Master Page of Business Card

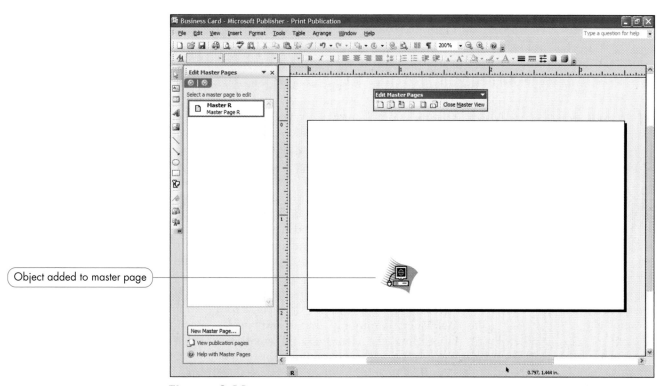

Object added to master page

Figure 2.11 Altered Master Page

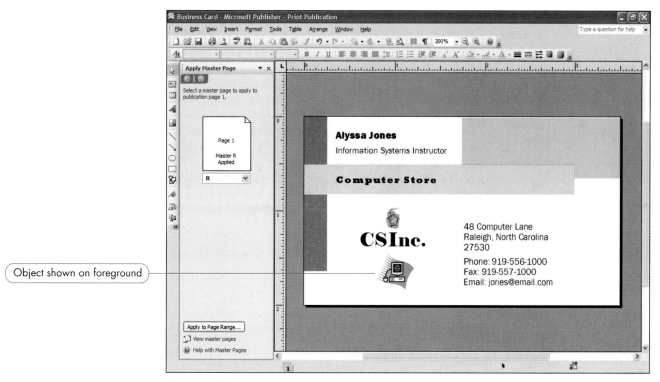

Object shown on foreground

Figure 2.12 Altered Foreground

Emphasizing Words

Now that you understand how to work with the guides and the master page of your publications, it is a good time to review the formatting techniques for emphasizing the words in your publications. The hands-on exercises in this chapter are built around the advertising publication shown in Figure 2.13 on the next page. These formatting techniques are presented conceptually, after which you will implement them in the first hands-on exercise, which includes working with the layout guides and the master page of this particular publication. The second hands-on exercise will implement advanced layering techniques and troubleshooting guidelines, which are described later in this chapter. To create great-looking publications from scratch, you need to understand many techniques that can be implemented in your publications through basic commands in Publisher to emphasize typography. Many of the techniques may not be new if you have worked with Microsoft Word or PowerPoint; however, because words can make or break a publication, we define them briefly in the next few paragraphs.

> A **pull quote** is a phrase or sentence taken from a publication to emphasize a key point. It is typically set in larger type, often in a different typeface and/or italics, and may be offset with a border surrounding it.

A **reverse** is light text on a dark background and is a favorite technique of desktop publishers, commonly used to emphasize a specific element. It is sometimes used in the heading (the identifying information) at the top of a newsletter or flyer and provides a distinctive look to the publication.

A **pull quote** is a phrase or sentence taken from a publication to emphasize a key point. It is typically set in larger type, often in a different typeface and/or italics, and may be offset with a border surrounding it.

A **dropped-capital letter** (also called a drop cap) is a large capital letter at the beginning of a paragraph. It, too, catches the reader's eye and calls attention to the associated text.

Line/Border Style and Fill Color are effective individually, or in combination with one another, to emphasize important objects within a publication. **Lines and borders** are boxes around objects, text, and tables. **Fill Color** adds a choice of different colors to text boxes, objects, and more. The techniques are especially useful in the absence of clip art or other graphics and are a favorite of desktop publishers.

Lists, whether bulleted or numbered, help to organize information by emphasizing important topics. A **bulleted list** emphasizes (and separates) the items. A **numbered list** sequences (and prioritizes) the items. Publisher automatically updates numbered lists to accommodate additions or deletions.

All of these techniques can be implemented with commands you already know, as you will see in the first hands-on exercise.

A **reverse** is light text on a dark background.

A **pull quote** is a phrase or sentence taken from a publication to emphasize a key point.

A **dropped-capital letter** (also called a drop cap) is a large capital letter at the beginning of a paragraph.

Lines and borders are boxes around objects, text, and tables.

Fill Color adds a choice of different colors to text boxes, objects, and more.

A **bulleted list** emphasizes (and separates) the items.

A **numbered list** sequences (and prioritizes) the items.

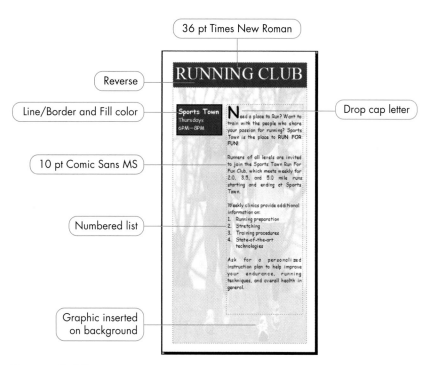

Figure 2.13 Emphasizing Words

TIP Adding Interest

Boxes, shading, and reverses (light text on a dark background) add interest to a publication. Horizontal and/or vertical lines are also effective in separating one topic from another, emphasizing a subhead, or calling attention to a pull quote (a phrase or sentence taken from the publication to emphasize a key point). Clip art, used in moderation, may catch the reader's eye and can enhance almost any publication. A dropped-capital letter is another way to add interest to your document.

Typography

Typography is the process of selecting typefaces, type styles, and type sizes.

A **typeface** (or font) is a complete set of characters.

A **serif typeface** has tiny cross lines at the ends of the characters to help the eye connect one letter with the next.

A **sans serif typeface** (sans from the French for without) does not have these cross lines.

Type size is a vertical measurement and is specified in points.

Typography is the process of selecting typefaces, type styles, and type sizes, and it is a critical, often subtle, element in the success of a publication. Good typography goes almost unnoticed; whereas poor typography calls attention to itself and detracts from a publication. Our discussion uses basic terminology, which we review below.

A **typeface** (or font) is a complete set of characters (upper and lowercase letters, numbers, punctuation marks, and special symbols). Typefaces are divided into two general categories, serif and sans serif. A **serif typeface** has tiny cross lines at the ends of the characters to help the eye connect one letter with the next. A **sans serif typeface** (sans from the French for without) does not have these lines. A commonly accepted practice is to use serif typefaces with large amounts of text and sans serif typefaces for smaller amounts. The brochure cover in Figure 2.13 uses Times New Roman (a serif typeface) for the heading and Comic Sans MS (a sans serif typeface) for the text. **Type size** is a vertical measurement and is specified in points (pts). One pt is equal to 1/72 of an inch. The text in most publications is set in 10 or 12 pt type, whereas headings are usually set much larger. Different elements in the same publication are often set in different type sizes to provide suitable emphasis. A variation of at least two points, however, is necessary for the difference to be noticeable. The title in the brochure, for example, was set in 36 pt type, whereas the text of the brochure is in 10 pt type.

We reiterate that there are no hard and fast rules for the selection of formatting techniques and typeface, only guidelines and common sense. You will find that the design that worked so well in one publication may not work at all in a different publication. Indeed, good typography is often the result of trial and error, and we encourage you to experiment freely.

Learning by Doing

The first hands-on exercise in this chapter has you open an existing file that contains text for an advertising publication. Even though this chapter is about creating publications from scratch, we thought you might enjoy the exercises more if you did not have to type a large amount of text. After completing this first hands-on exercise, keep in mind that your publication will not be complete. That is, we will only be halfway through with its design. You will complete the design of the publication in the second hands-on exercise, once you are introduced to advanced layering concepts and some basic troubleshooting techniques.

Hands-On Exercises

1 | Advertising Publication

Skills Covered: 1. Adjust the Layout Guides **2.** Layer Text Boxes Using the Layout Guides **3.** Format the Publication's Text **4.** Create the Color Reverses and Apply a Line/Border Style **5.** Create a Drop Cap and a Numbered List

Step 1 **Adjust the Layout Guides**	Refer to Figure 2.14 as you complete Step 1. **a.** Start Publisher, if necessary, and open the *chap2_ho1_advertising* file in the Exploring Publisher student data folder. Save the publication as **chap2_ho1_advertising_solution** so that you can return to the original publication, if necessary. **b.** Close the Format Publication task pane. **c.** Pull down the **View menu** and click **Master Page** (or press **Ctrl+M**) to display the background of the publication. **d.** Point your mouse at the top layout guide, hold down the mouse, and drag the guide up to the top of the publication page to match ours shown in Figure 2.14. **TROUBLESHOOTING:** Do not worry if your layout guides are slightly different from ours because you can always adjust them again later. **e.** Use the same procedure to adjust the remaining layout guides on the publication page. **f.** Pull down the **View menu** and click the **Master Page command** again (or press **Ctrl+M**) to toggle off the master page and display the foreground of the publication. **g.** Save the publication.

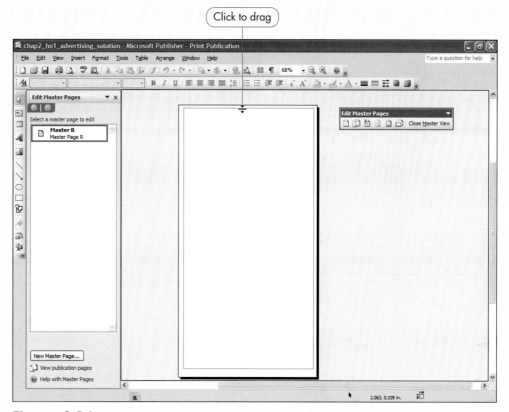

Figure 2.14 Adjust the Layout Guides

Refer to Figure 2.15 as you complete Step 2.

a. Zoom to a larger magnification, if necessary.

b. Adjust the text boxes on the publication page to layer appropriately within the layout guides by clicking the **Running Club text box border** once to activate the sizing handles.

c. Point at the text box border, press and hold the mouse, and then drag the text box slightly up, and position the box within the top layout guides, as shown in Figure 2.15.

You will see the Move pointer (a four-headed arrow) when you point at the text box border.

d. With the Running Club text box still selected, click and hold the mouse pointer on the middle left sizing handle, and then drag to increase the size of the text box, as shown in Figure 2.15.

e. Click to resize the right side as well, as shown in Figure 2.15.

f. Click the **informational text box** to activate the sizing handles. Move the pointer over any border of the text box, and when the Move pointer appears, drag to position the text box within the right layout guide as shown in the figure.

g. With the informational text box still selected, click and hold the mouse pointer on the middle left sizing handle, and then drag to decrease the size of the text box, as shown in Figure 2.15, so that it does not overlap the Sports Town text box.

h. Save the publication.

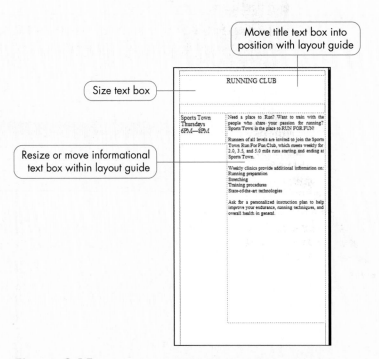

Figure 2.15 Layer Text Boxes Using the Layout Guides

TIP Snapping Objects into Place

Sometimes when you are trying to align objects along the layout guides, they just do not quite align as close to the guides as you want them to. One way to move any object closer to a guide is to turn on the snap command from the Arrange menu. When the snap command is toggled on, any object will snap into place when you move it close to the guide. When using the Snap commands on the Arrange menu, you can set rulers, guides, or objects to act like magnets that pull on the object. When all three Snap commands are toggled on, Publisher will first try to snap to a nearby guide. If no guide is nearby, Publisher snaps to the nearest object. If there is no object, Publisher snaps to the closest ruler mark.

Step 3
Format the Publication's Text

Refer to Figure 2.16 as you complete Step 3.

a. Click and drag to select the title, **Running Club,** at the beginning of the publication.

b. Click the drop-down arrow on the **Font Size box** on the Formatting toolbar and change the font size to **36 pt**, as shown in Figure 2.16.

c. Select all of the text in the informational text frame.

You can click and drag or click once in the text box and press Ctrl+A.

d. Click the drop-down arrow in the **Font box** and change the font to **Comic Sans MS**. (Leave the font size at 10 pt.)

e. Select the phrase **RUN FOR FUN** within the informational text.

f. Click the **Bold button** to make the selected text bold, as shown in Figure 2.16.

g. Select the running club's name, **Sports Town,** and the day and time of the runs, **Thursdays 6PM–8PM**.

h. Change the font to **Comic Sans MS**.

i. Change the font size of the name *Sports Town* to **14 pt** and also make the text bold, as shown in Figure 2.16.

TROUBLESHOOTING: You may have to resize the text frame after changing the point size.

j. Select **Thursdays 6PM–8PM**.

k. Change the font size to **11 pt**, as shown in Figure 2.16.

l. Save the publication.

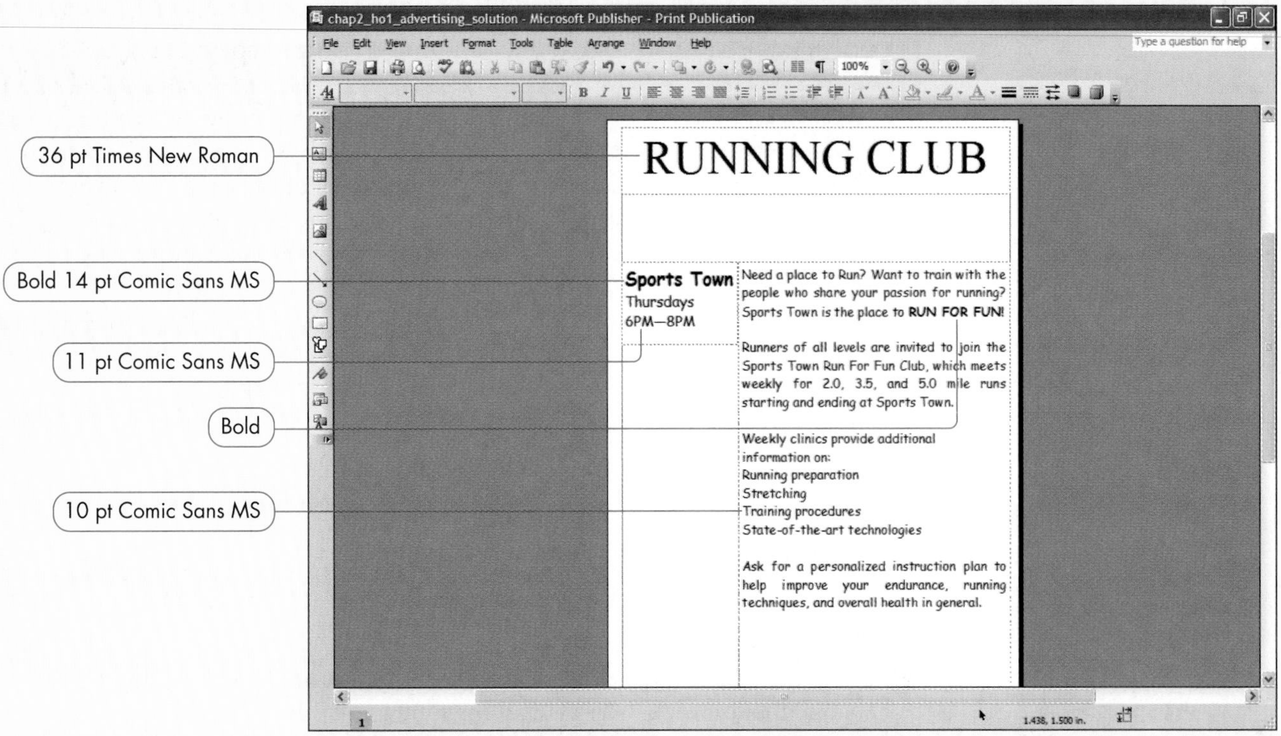
36 pt Times New Roman
Bold 14 pt Comic Sans MS
11 pt Comic Sans MS
Bold
10 pt Comic Sans MS
RUNNING CLUB
Sports Town
Thursdays
6PM—8PM
Need a place to Run? Want to train with the people who share your passion for running? Sports Town is the place to RUN FOR FUN!
Runners of all levels are invited to join the Sports Town Run For Fun Club, which meets weekly for 2.0, 3.5, and 5.0 mile runs starting and ending at Sports Town.
Weekly clinics provide additional information on:
Running preparation
Stretching
Training procedures
State-of-the-art technologies
Ask for a personalized instruction plan to help improve your endurance, running techniques, and overall health in general.

Figure 2.16 Format the Publication's Text

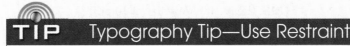

TIP Typography Tip—Use Restraint

More is not better, especially in the case of too many typefaces and styles, which produce cluttered publications that impress no one. Try to limit yourself to a maximum of two typefaces per publication but choose multiple sizes and/or styles within those typefaces. Use boldface or italics for emphasis but do so in moderation, because if you emphasize too many elements, the effect is lost.

Step 4
Create the Color Reverses and Apply a Line/Border Style

Refer to Figure 2.17 as you complete Step 4.

a. To create a reverse for the advertising publication, as shown in Figure 2.17, click anywhere within the title *Running Club* at the top of the publication.

b. Click the down arrow on the **Fill Color button** on the Formatting toolbar. In the palette that drops down, click **More Fill Colors**.

   The Colors dialog box opens.

c. Click a **dark red** color, and then click **OK** to close the dialog box and to change the fill color of the text box, as shown in Figure 2.17.

d. Select the text **Running Club**.

e. Click the down arrow on the **Font Color button** on the Formatting toolbar and choose **White** to complete the reverse for the title of the advertisement.

   You can also pull down the Format menu, click Font, and change the color in the Font dialog box.

f. Create the same type of reverse for the text box that contains the name of the club *Sports Town* and the day and time of the runs, as shown in Figure 2.17.

TROUBLESHOOTING: You may need to resize these two text boxes to layer appropriately. After adding the fill color it will be obvious where this needs to occur, if necessary.

g. Make sure the Sports Town text box is still selected.

h. Click the **Line/Border Style button** on the Formatting toolbar to select a **1/4 pt border**.

TROUBLESHOOTING: If necessary, size this text box so that it is not layered on top of the informational text frame, as shown in Figure 2.17.

i. Save the publication.

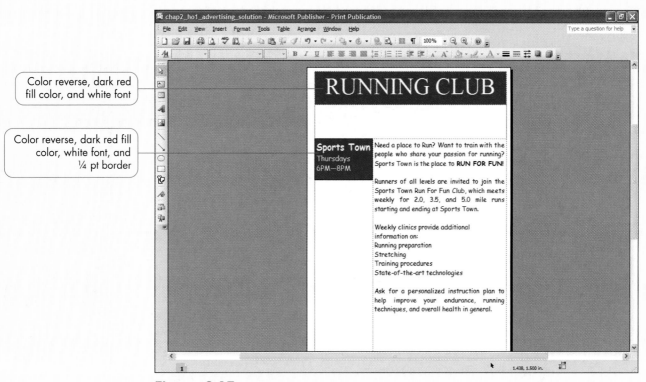

Color reverse, dark red fill color, and white font

Color reverse, dark red fill color, white font, and ¼ pt border

Figure 2.17 Create the Color Reverses and Apply a Line/Border Style

Refer to Figure 2.18 as you complete Step 5.

a. To create a drop cap and a numbered list, as shown in Figure 2.18, select the **N** at the beginning of the informational text box.

b. Choose **Drop Cap** from the Format menu.

The Drop Cap dialog box will appear.

c. Select the second drop cap style in the second column (or any other style), and then click **OK** to apply the new drop cap style, as shown in Figure 2.18.

d. Select the text within the informational text box starting with *Running preparation* and ending with *State-of the-art technologies*.

e. Click the **Numbering button** on the Formatting toolbar to apply a numbered list to the selected text.

f. Save the publication.

g. Print the completed publication and submit it to your instructor as proof you completed this exercise.

Remember that we are not finished with the publication design. We will complete the design in the second hands-on exercise.

h. Exit Publisher, unless you plan to continue working on the second hands-on exercise.

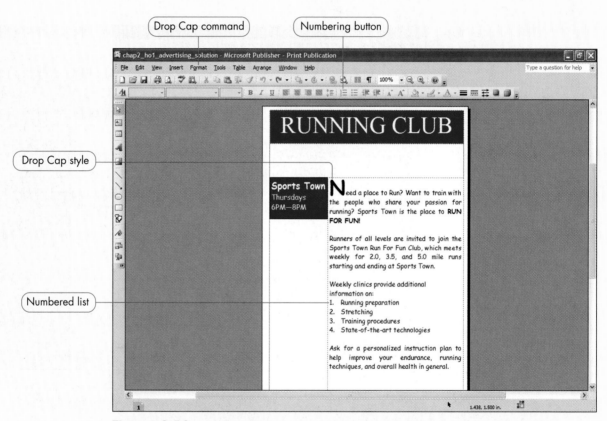

Figure 2.18 Create a Drop Cap and a Numbered List

TIP   Quit Without Saving

There will be times when you do not want to save the changes to a publication, such as when you have edited it beyond recognition and wish you had never started. Pull down the File menu and click the close command, and then click No in response to the message asking whether you want to save the changes to the publication. Pull down the File menu and reopen the file (it should be the first file in the list of most recently edited publications). Then start over from the beginning.

(Publisher has several advanced layering techniques for working with objects (i.e., text boxes, clip art, or WordArt on the publication page.))

Advanced Layering Concepts

Publisher has several advanced layering techniques for working with objects (i.e., text boxes, clip art, or WordArt on the publication page.) These techniques include: making objects transparent, grouping objects, rotating objects, and flipping objects. *Transparent objects* enables you to see other text or objects stacked behind or on the master page. *Grouping objects* makes separate objects become one grouped set of objects. *Rotating objects* enables you to rotate an object 90 degrees left or right. And finally, *flipping objects* enables you to flip the object horizontally or vertically. If you have worked with the Drawing toolbar in Word or PowerPoint, you are already familiar with these techniques. However, even though the concepts are similar, the commands to accomplish these tasks are somewhat different in Publisher.

Transparent objects enables you to see other text or objects stacked behind or on the master page.

Grouping objects makes separate objects become one grouped set of objects.

Rotating objects enables you to rotate 90 degrees left or right.

Flipping objects enables you to flip the object horizontally or vertically.

Making Objects Transparent

One of the more useful techniques in Publisher is to make an object transparent. The idea is to be able to layer objects on top of one another, and then make the top layer transparent so that you can see the layer beneath it. To make an object transparent, select the object and press Ctrl+T. To reverse the effect, press Ctrl+T again. Look at Figure 2.19, the advertising publication you are working on in the hands-on exercises. The informational text box in Figure 2.19 has been made transparent so that you can see the layer underneath it. When the text frame is not transparent, as in Figure 2.20, you cannot see the layer underneath. The graphic with the two runners has been added to the master page (discussed in the previous section) of this publication and the shading of this graphic has been adjusted to grayscale. You will use both of these techniques in the second hands-on exercise.

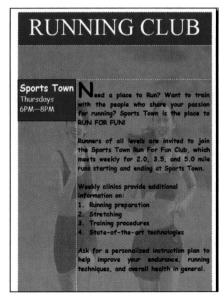

Figure 2.19 Top Layer Transparent

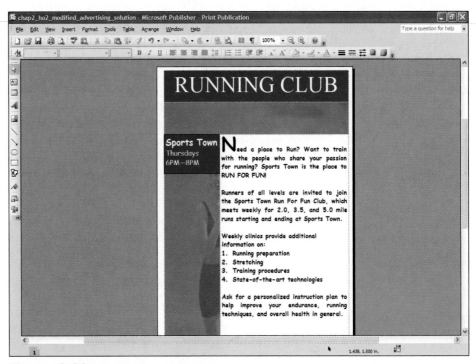

Figure 2.20 Text Box Opaque

Grouping, Rotating, and Flipping Objects

Other advanced layering techniques include grouping, rotating, and flipping objects on the publication page. These techniques can add a nice touch to your publications, but we suggest you use good judgment in implementing these features in the design of your publications. With commands on the Arrange menu, any object can be grouped with another object on the publication page, rotated, and/or flipped. Figure 2.21 shows examples of objects that have been grouped, rotated, and/or flipped. (The more practice you get with these techniques, the more sophisticated your designs should look.) In the second hands-on exercise, you will use these techniques to create a design logo for the advertising publication.

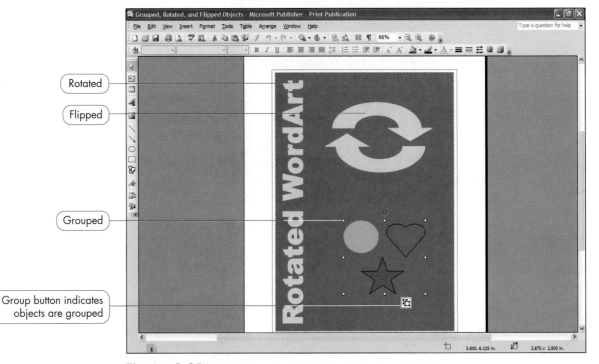

Figure 2.21 Grouping, Rotating, and Flipping Objects

Troubleshooting Layout Guides

When working with Publisher's layout guides and when layering objects on the publication page, there are several troubleshooting tips you should keep in mind:

- If you cannot see your layout guides, you may have objects stacked on top of them or you may have to turn on the guides using the Boundaries and Guides command on the View menu.

- If you want to see how your publication will look when printed, you can toggle off the layout guides using the Boundaries and Guides command on the View menu.

- If you want to stop snapping objects to your layout guides, turn this feature off by toggling off the Snap command on the Arrange menu.

- When you click on an object, you can tell that it is grouped if you only see one set of sizing handles.

- To ungroup objects, select the grouped objects, and then click the Ungroup button.

Hands-On Exercises

2 | Complete the Advertising Publication

Skills Covered: 1. Insert a Picture into the Master Page **2.** Layer the Picture Along the Layout Guides **3.** Format the Picture **4.** Make a Text Box Transparent **5.** Design a Logo

<table>
<tr>
<td>

Step 1
Insert a Picture into the Master Page

</td>
<td>

Refer to Figure 2.22 as you complete Step 1.

a. Open the *chap2_ho2_modified_advertising* publication and save the publication as **chap2_ho2_modified_advertising_solution**.

b. Pull down the **View menu** and click **Master Page**.

c. Pull down the **Insert menu**, point to the **Picture command**, and click **Clip Art** to display the Clip Art task pane.

d. Click the down arrow on the **Results should be list box** and clear the check marks from all media except Photographs.

e. Type **joggers** in the Search text box, and then click the **Go button**.

f. Look for the picture shown in Figure 2.22 (two women running in the woods).

TROUBLESHOOTING: If you cannot find this picture, then choose any similar picture. Be sure to insert a similar portrait layout (tall and narrow) since we will change the size of the picture. If you choose a landscape layout (short and wide), the picture will be to distorted to work with when you size the picture.

g. Click the **down arrow** next to the picture and select **Insert** from the menu that opens.

You can also simply click on the picture to insert it.

h. Close the task pane.

i. Save the publication.

</td>
</tr>
</table>

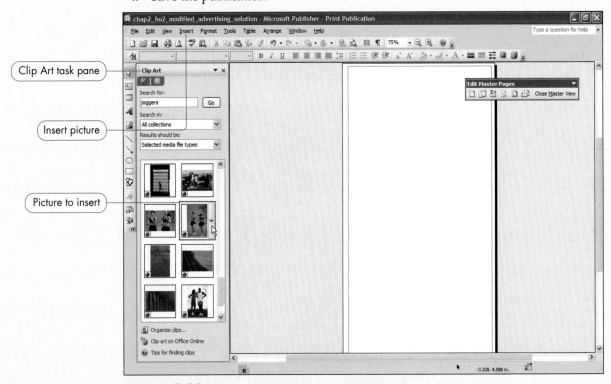

Figure 2.22 Insert a Picture into the Master Page

Refer to Figure 2.23 as you complete Step 2.

a. If necessary, use the **Zoom command** to adjust your viewing area.

b. To layer the picture along the layout guides, click the photo to display the sizing handles.

c. Point to any part of the image except a sizing handle, and then click and drag to move the image to the center of the advertising page.

The mouse pointer changes to a four-sided arrow.

d. Drag a corner handle to change the length and width of the picture simultaneously.

The mouse pointer changes to a Resize double arrow.

e. Drag a top, bottom, left, or right middle sizing handle toward the layout guides, as shown in Figure 2.23.

TROUBLESHOOTING: Do not worry if dragging the middle sizing handles distorts the image slightly, because in the next step, you will format the image to grayscale, and this effect works nicely for the design of your publication.

f. Continue working with the sizing handles until your publication matches ours shown in Figure 2.23.

g. Press **Ctrl+M** to toggle to the foreground and make sure you have properly layered the image along the layout guides.

If you have not layered the image appropriately, return to the master page and move or size again.

h. Save the publication.

Figure 2.23 Layer the Picture Along the Layout Guides

Refer to Figure 2.24 as you complete Step 3.

a. Go back to the master page of your publication.

b. To format the picture to grayscale, click the photo to display the sizing handles.

c. From the **Color button** on the Picture toolbar, toggle on the **Grayscale command**, as shown in Figure 2.24.

TROUBLESHOOTING: Right-click any toolbar and click to activate the Picture toolbar if it did not appear when you clicked on the picture.

d. On the Picture toolbar, click the **Less Contrast button** several times to lighten the picture.

e. Pull down the **View menu** and click **Master Page** to go to the foreground of your publication.

f. Save the publication.

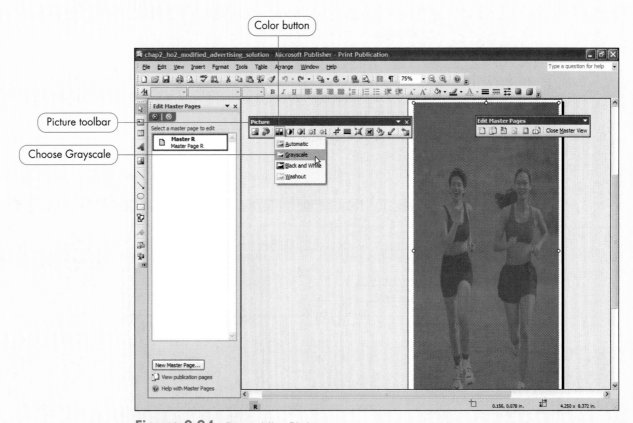

Figure 2.24 Format the Picture

TIP   Picture File Formats

You can import a variety of pictures into your publications. Some of the most common file formats include .bmp, .jpg, and .gif. The Publisher Help files list about fifteen different file formats that you can import into Publisher. Click on Microsoft Publisher Help from the Help menu and type Picture File Format. Follow the links to Graphic File Formats and Filters.

Refer to Figure 2.25 as you complete Step 4.

a. Make sure you are on the foreground, not the master page, of your publication. One way to make sure you are on the foreground of your publication is to look at the page number reference on the status bar. When you are on the master page, it reads A instead of a number.

b. To make the informational text box transparent, as shown Figure 2.25, click the **informational text box** to select it.

c. Press **Ctrl+T** to make the text box transparent.

d. Select the information text to change the font to white and bold.

e. Click outside the informational text box to view your change.

f. Save the publication.

Press Ctrl+T to toggle between transparent and opaque

Figure 2.25 Make a Text Box Transparent

TIP   Connect Those Text Boxes

Publisher has a wonderful feature that allows you to connect text boxes in different parts of a publication. Once you have connected the boxes, you can type text in the first box and keep typing when the box fills up. The next text you type flows automatically to the connected text box. This feature allows you to start a story on page 1 of a newsletter, for instance, and connect the continued story in another place on the same page or a different page within the publication. If you do not connect text boxes, the text you type after the box is full goes into the overflow area of that box. When text goes into an overflow area, you cannot see it. You can enlarge the text box to reveal it or connect the box to another empty box. To connect one text box to another existing empty text box, click the box that has the overflow text, click the Create Text Box Link button on the Connect Text Boxes toolbar, and move the pointer into the publication. The pointer changes to a pitcher. Now click the empty text box to connect it to the first, and the overflow text flows into it. You can connect as many text boxes as you wish, starting a "chain" of connected text boxes.

Refer to Figure 2.26 as you complete Step 5.

a. Change your viewing area to 75% or higher and scroll down to the bottom of the advertising publication.

b. Click the **AutoShapes button** on the Objects toolbar, and then point to the **Basic Shapes command**.

c. Click the **Lightning Bolt** shape and draw out a lightning bolt to match the one shown in Figure 2.26.

d. Click the down arrow on the **Fill Color button** on the Formatting toolbar and click the **dark red color** you used for the Running Club text box.

e. Click the **Copy button** on the Standard toolbar.

f. Click next to the lightning bolt, and then click the **Paste button** on the Standard toolbar.

A second lightning bolt will appear stacked on top of the first one.

g. Click to drag the newly pasted lightning bolt a little to the right to line it up next to the first lightning bolt.

h. While the second lightning bolt is still selected, pull down the **Arrange menu**, point to **Rotate or Flip**, and click **Flip Horizontal**.

i. Drag to move either of the lightning bolts up, down, or closer together to match ours.

j. Hold down **Shift**, select each of the lightning bolts, and then click the **Group Objects button** that appears just below the grouped objects to group these two objects together.

k. Click the **Text box tool** on the Objects toolbar, and then draw out a small text box underneath the lightning bolts.

l. Click the **Center button** on the Formatting toolbar, and then type **Just Run!** inside the text box and format the text to white and bold.

m. Select the grouped lightning bolts and the **Just Run! text box** and combine them into one group.

n. Save the publication a final time. Congratulations on a job well done!

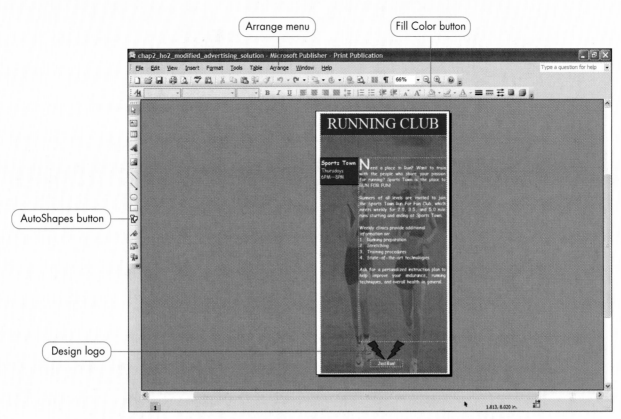

Arrange menu

Fill Color button

AutoShapes button

Design logo

Figure 2.26 Design a Logo

Summary

1. **Work with Blank Page Sizes.** Starting with Publisher's Blank Page Sizes publication command, you can choose from many publication Page Size types. From there you can choose page size, color and font schemes, and more. Once you choose your desired Blank Page Size publication, you can add text, objects, and clip art and then save and print the publication.

2. **Understand layout guides.** In this chapter, you learned how to create a simple publication starting with a new blank publication and how to use the nonprinting layout guides to ensure consistency throughout your publications. The design of a publication is developed on layout guides, an underlying, but nonprinting, set of blue and green horizontal and vertical lines that determine the placement of the major elements.

3. **Understand the master page.** You also learned the basics of working with the master page of your publications, advanced layering techniques, and various Publisher commands to enhance the quality of your publications. You can easily move layout guides by selecting the Master Page command on the View menu. Once you have switched to the master page, click to drag the guide to a new position in the publication window.

4. **Emphasize words.** To produce great looking publications the designer should have a basic understanding of typography. A typeface is a complete set of characters. Typefaces are divided into two general categories, serif and sans serif. A serif typeface has tiny cross lines at the ends of the characters to help the eye connect one letter with the next. A sans serif typeface does not have these lines.

5. **Make objects transparent.** Making objects transparent in Publisher is a great desktop publishing technique. Once you layer an object on top of another object, you can make the top object transparent. This technique allows you to see the layered object beneath it.

6. **Group, rotate, and flip objects.** You learned how to use advanced layering techniques within your publications. Publisher has several advanced layering techniques for working with objects (e.g., text boxes, clip art, or WordArt) on the publication page. These techniques include making objects transparent, grouping objects, rotating objects, and flipping objects.

7. **Troubleshoot layout guides.** Working with layer guidelines, the master page, and objects is pretty easy. When mistakes happen, there are basic troubleshooting fixes to help solve the problem.

Key Terms

Multiple Choice

1. The Blank Publication option enables you to create:

   (a) A publication based on a predefined set

   (b) A publication based on a series of questions

   (c) A publication from scratch

   (d) None of the above

2. Which of the following publication types can you pick from the Blank Page Sizes task pane?

   (a) Full page

   (b) Web page

   (c) Business card

   (d) All of the above

3. Layout guides are applicable to the design of:

   (a) Publications with one, two, or three columns and moderate clip art

   (b) Publications with four or more columns and no clip art

   (c) Both (a) and (b)

   (d) Neither (a) nor (b)

4. Which menu contains the command to toggle on/off the layout guides?

   (a) Edit menu

   (b) View menu

   (c) Format menu

   (d) Arrange menu

5. Which menu contains the command to change the number of layout guides?

   (a) Edit menu

   (b) View menu

   (c) Format menu

   (d) Arrange menu

6. Which layout guide(s) appear on all pages?

   (a) Blue and green

   (b) Yellow and pink

   (c) Red and pink

   (d) Green

7. Which ruler guide(s) appear only on a single page?

   (a) Blue and pink

   (b) Yellow and pink

   (c) Red and pink

   (d) Green

8. Which types of objects might you want to put on the master page of your publication to show up on every page?

   (a) Company logo

   (b) Page numbers

   (c) Border

   (d) All of the above

9. Which of the following can be used to add emphasis to a publication?

   (a) Borders and fill color

   (b) Pull quotes and reverses

   (c) Both (a) and (b)

   (d) Neither (a) nor (b)

10. A reverse is implemented:

    (a) By selecting dark fill color

    (b) By changing the font color to a light color

    (c) Both (a) and (b)

    (d) Neither (a) nor (b)

11. Which of the following is a commonly accepted guideline in typography?

    (a) Use a serif typeface for headings and a sans serif typeface for text.

    (b) Use a sans serif typeface for headings and a serif typeface for text.

    (c) Use a sans serif typeface for both headings and text.

    (d) Use a serif typeface for both headings and text.

12. Which of the following describes the Comic Sans MS and Times New Roman fonts?

    (a) Comic Sans MS is a sans serif font; Times New Roman is a serif font.

    (b) Comic Sans MS is a serif font; Times New Roman is a sans serif font.

    (c) Both are serif fonts.

    (d) Both are sans serif fonts.

13. Which command acts like a magnet that pulls objects as close as possible to the layout guides?

    (a) Snap to Ruler Marks

    (b) Snap to Objects

    (c) Snap to Guides

    (d) None of the above

14. How do you select more than one object at a time?

(a) Click the Select Objects tool on the Objects toolbar, and then click the mouse to drag out a square around the objects you want to select.

(b) Hold down the Shift key while selecting each object.

(c) Both (a) and (b).

(d) Neither (a) nor (b).

15. Which of the following is a recommended guideline in the design of a publication?

(a) Use at least three different clip art images in every publication.

(b) Use at least three different typefaces in a publication to maintain interest.

(c) Use the same type size for the heading and text of an article.

(d) None of the above.

16. What is the definition of a pull quote?

(a) A phrase or sentence taken from a publication to emphasize a key point

(b) Light text on a dark background

(c) A large capital letter at the beginning of a paragraph

(d) The absence of clip art or graphics

17. Which of the following are advanced layering techniques?

(a) Grouping

(b) Rotating

(c) Flipping objects

(d) All of the above

18. In the picture toolbar, which button will change the photograph to grayscale?

(a) Set Transparent Color

(b) More Brightness

(c) Line/Border Style

(d) None of the above

Practice Exercises

1 Business Card

Sports Town, the running club used in the hands-on exercises in this chapter, wants to create new business cards just like the one shown in Figure 2.27 for its employees using a style similar to the flyer you just created. Irene Brown, the owner, does not like any of the templates she looked at in Publisher. She has asked you to start from scratch to create a design that matches the flyer.

a. Open a new blank page sizes publication and select the **business card type**, as shown in Figure 2.27. Save the publication as **chap2_pe1_business_card_solution**.

b. On the Master Page, reposition the layout guides to make more room on the business card design area.

c. On the Master Page, insert the same photo as shown in Figure 2.27.

   TROUBLESHOOTING: Search for *success* as the key word.

d. On the Master Page, design the same logo used in the hands-on exercise and shown in Figure 2.27.

e. On the Master Page, insert **Sports Town** in a text box using a reverse and the same dark red.

f. Change the font to **Comic Sans MS, 16 pt** and center the text.

g. On the Master Page, insert a text box that includes the address and telephone number for the running club, as shown in Figure 2.27.

h. Change the font to **Comic Sans MS, 8 pt**.

i. From the Paragraph command on the Format menu, change the Line Spacing after Paragraphs to **0 pt**.

j. Switch to the foreground using **Ctrl+M**.

k. Insert a text box with the employee's name in 10 pt, Comic Sans MS font and his/her position in 8 pt Comic Sans MS font. Center the text.

   TROUBLESHOOTING: You may need to go back to the master page to lay out objects and text appropriate on the business card. You can switch back and forth from the master page to the foreground by using Ctrl+M on your keyboard.

l. Save the publication.

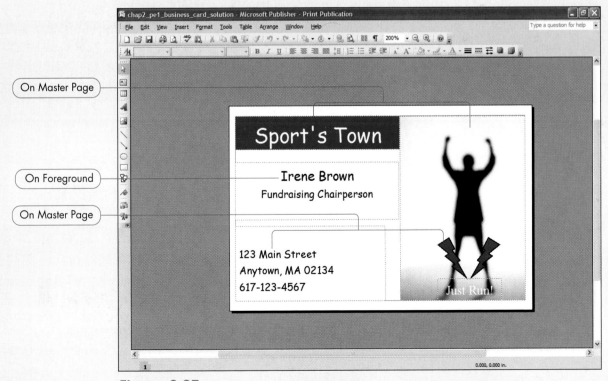

Figure 2.27 Sport's Town Business Card

...continued on Next Page

Did you know that Publisher allows you to make and print index cards? So the next time you have to give a speech or are putting together a report and need to use index cards, there is a way for you to make them easier to read. In this exercise, you will create a small set of index cards starting from Blank Page Sizes for a training session that you volunteered to give at a nursing home on the topic of computers. This particular nursing home likes to provide training sessions on many different topics for their residents. They do not expect anything fancy, but you think it is a good idea to be prepared. Using index cards can help to organize your thoughts, especially when notes are typed instead of handwritten. You will use a previously prepared publication to help you create the index cards. Open the *chap1_mc3_computers_solution* file to obtain the poster that you designed for Chapter 1 Mid-Level Exercise 3. Using the information provided on this poster, you will create a set of index cards to use while you are giving the training session at the nursing home.

a. Open Publisher a second time and under Blank Page Sizes, search for *Index Cards* on your computer.
   You now have two Publisher sessions open, one for the poster and one to search for the index cards.
b. Choose the standard 5 x 3 index card and save the publication as **chap2_pe2_computer_presentation_solution**.
c. From the **Page command** on the **Insert menu**, insert 5 more pages to create a total of 6 index cards.
d. Click back on the first index card.
e. Switch to the master page and from the **Page Numbers command** on the **Insert menu**, insert page numbers in the lower right-hand corner of the index card.
f. Switch back to the foreground of the index cards.
g. Using the poster as a guide, insert the same clip art on each of the six index cards just like the first index card in Figure 2.28.
h. Resize each clip art image and reposition each image to the right of the index card.
   You can either search for the same clip art or you can copy and paste the clip art images from the poster to the index card publication.
i. On the first index card, draw out a text box.
j. Create a bulleted list using 12 pt font for each of the sentences using the poster information, as shown in Figure 2.28, for the first index card.
k. Save the publication.

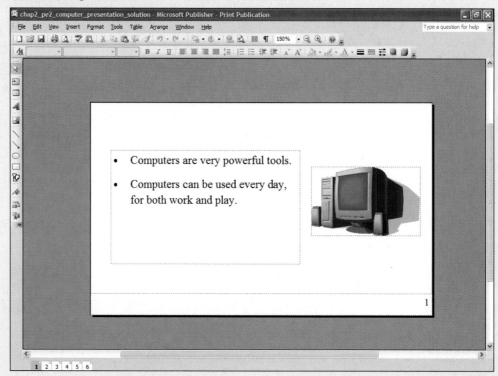

Figure 2.28 Computer Presentation

...continued on Next Page

As mentioned in the chapter, too much text, too many images, and items layered incorrectly on the publication will distract readers from the message that the publication is trying to convey. Jennifer owns a photography shop that specializes in black-and-white photography. Her business card contains too many images and the wrong type of images. The card also contains inappropriately layered objects, improper font type size, and too much informational text on the card. This exercise emphasizes the fact that not all designs are good designs and that with a little extra thought a design can easily be changed to reflect the style of a business.

a. Open the *chap2_pe3_photography* publication and save it as **chap2_pe3_photography_solution**.

b. Remove the left side image from the master page.

c. Insert a more appropriate image on the left side of the card, as shown in Figure 2.29. We searched *photography*.

d. Resize, move, and layer the figure on the left side of the card.

e. Select the figure and, using the Picture toolbar **Color command**, change the image to black and white.

f. Lower the brightness by clicking the **Less brightness command** several times on the picture toolbar.

g. Copy the image, paste it twice, and then layer the copied images appropriately on the left side of the card, as shown in Figure 2.29.

h. Click on the second image on the right side of the card and change the **Color** to **Grayscale**.

i. On the foreground of the card, remove each of the heart images from the card.

j. Change the font of the business name to **Antique Olive Compact**, **11 pt** (or other) font and bold.

k. Change the font of the business subtitle to **Antique Olive Compact**, **6 pt** (or other) font and bold.

l. Insert a table and change the photography to a bulleted list item, as shown in Figure 2.29.

m. Change the font of the bulleted items to **Antique Olive Compact**, **5 pt** (or other) font and bold.

n. Save the publication.

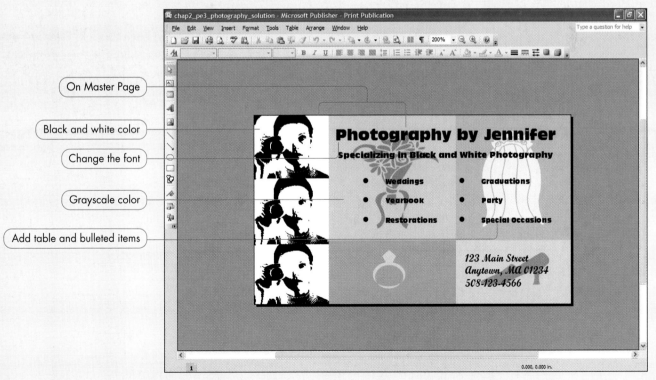

Figure 2.29 Photography

...continued on Next Page

The photographer that had you redesign her business cards was very happy with the results and has now asked you to design letterhead and envelopes for her business. Using the same clip art and font that you used on the business cards, design these two publications for her. Open the *chap2_pe3_photography_solution* publication. Use this publication as a guide to help you create the letterhead and envelope.

a. Open a second Publisher program.

b. Select the **full page letter (portrait) design type** from the Blank Page Sizes gallery.

c. Save the publication as **chap2_pe4_photography_letterhead_solution**.

d. On the master page, expand the layout guides to make better use of the letter space.

e. While on the master page, insert the photo clip art as shown in Figure 2.30.

f. Copy and paste the photo twice and reposition the images as shown in Figure 2.30.

g. Select each image and click the **Group button**.

   You can search for the clip art and then apply grayscale or you can copy and paste the image from the *chap2_pe3_photography_solution* file.

h. While on the master page, insert the business name and subtitle text boxes and reposition the text boxes as shown in Figure 2.30.

i. Change the font for the business name to **16 pt** and to **12 pt** for the subtitle.

j. Insert the business address and telephone numbers at the bottom of the master page. Adjust the layout as shown in Figure 2.30.

k. From the **Paragraph command** on the **Format menu**, adjust the **Line Spacing** to **0 pt**.

l. Change the address and phone number font to **12 pt**.

m. Save the finished letterhead.

n. From the **Blank Page Sizes Envelopes category**, choose a standard number 10, landscape envelope.

o. Save the publication as **chap2_pe3_photography_envelope_solution**.

p. Insert the same clip art and text that you used on the letterhead, except for the telephone numbers, as shown in Figure 2.31.

q. Include a fictional customer mailing address, as shown in Figure 2.31.

r. Save the envelope.

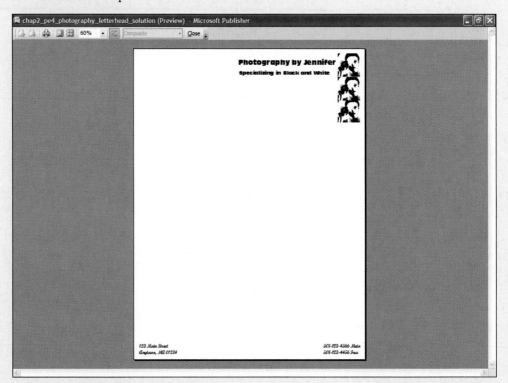

Figure 2.30 Photography Letterhead

...continued on Next Page

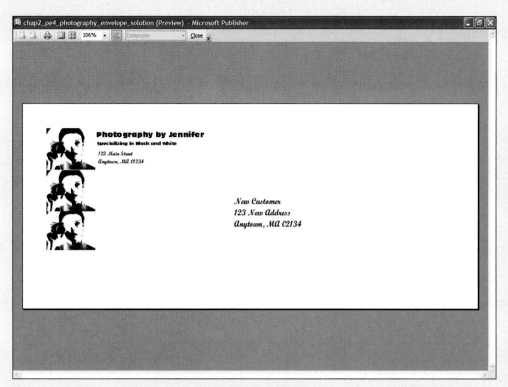

Figure 2.31 Photography Envelope

Tracy Brown needs a new résumé for an upcoming job interview. She is an interior design major, but this particular company has asked for a simple one-page résumé. She has most of the information typed in Microsoft Word. However, she has decided to use Publisher instead because, if she gets a job interview with another company, she wants to spruce up the design of the résumé at a later date. She remembers that there is a way to insert text typed in Word into Publisher. Using the text provided in the *chap2_mid1_resume* document, design a simple résumé for this soon-to-be college graduate.

a. Open Publisher and open a new 8.5 × 11 portrait blank page size.

b. From the **Import Word Document command** on the **File menu**, browse for the *chap2_mid1_resume* document from the Exploring Publisher folder. Select the file and click **OK**.

c. Save the publication as **chap2_mid1_resume_solution**.

d. On the master page, adjust the layout guides to make more use of the page area.

e. On the foreground, select the name, address, telephone number, and e-mail address, and then click the **Center button** on the Formatting toolbar and adjust the font size to **14 pt**.

f. Select the name on the résumé and click the **Bold button** on the Formatting toolbar.

g. On the foreground, move the bottom text box sizing handle up to just below the bottom of the text to make room at the bottom of the page.

h. Insert a table that consists of five rows and two columns at the bottom of the page.

i. Add the text for each of the five left table cells, as shown in Figure 2.32.

j. Select the appropriate text for each table category from the imported Word document, and then drag and drop the text into each cell on the right, as shown in Figure 2.32.

You can also select the text, and then click Cut and Paste on the Formatting toolbar.

k. Select the table and click to move the entire table up on the publication page, as shown in Figure 2.32. Resize and adjust the table as necessary.

l. Select all the text in the second column, choose **0 First Line Indent** from the **Paragraph command** on the **Format menu**, and change the left indent here also to **0**.

m. Resize column two on the table, as shown in Figure 2.32.

n. Add bulleted lists for the work experience items and for the honors information, as shown in Figure 2.32.

o. Add some blank links under *Experience*, if necessary.

p. Select the table, right-click, and then from the **Format Table command** change the **Cell Margins** to **.14** from the **Cell Properties tab**.

q. Save the publication.

...continued on Next Page

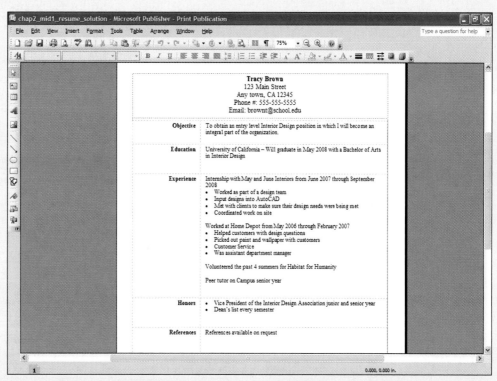

Figure 2.32 Entry Level Résumé

2 The Catalog

CSInc., the computer shop from Chapter 1, produces a simple quarterly catalog to send out to current and potential customers. The catalog features a few new products for sale, new software, and some information about training. The catalog was started by Mike, but he is out sick for the day and your boss needs the catalog ASAP! He has asked you to finish what Mike started. The catalog needs new images to replace several default images, color reverses to match the company's color schemes, new fonts, and a few bulleted items. As you are working, you really start to get into editing the design of this brochure and you decide to layer objects on the page and to emphasize some elements of the publication. The first and last pages of the catalog are finished. Pages two and three are where Mike left off.

a. Start Publisher and open the *chap2_mid2_catalog* publication, and then save the publication as **chap2_mid2_catalog_solution**.

b. On pages 2 and 3, create the color reverses for the 1-800 telephone numbers on each page, as shown in Figure 2.33.

c. If necessary, on the master page, adjust the layout guide on page three to layer appropriately.

d. Change the font size for Featured Product to 16 pt and create the color reverse, as shown in Figure 2.33.

e. Add a 1½ pt border box around the Featured Product objects, as shown in Figure 2.33.

f. On page 3, change the New Software & Training heading to 16 pt font.

g. On page 4, resize the text box to match the one in Figure 2.33.

h. Change the default images on pages 2 and 3 to match those shown in Figure 2.33. If necessary, move or resize the images.

i. Add bullets for the Laptop features section, as shown in Figure 2.33.

...continued on Next Page

j. Add a drop cap style to the Microsoft Office Publisher 2007 information, as shown in Figure 2.33.

k. Save the publication.

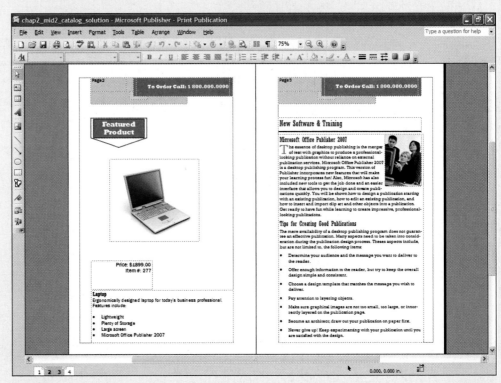

Figure 2.33 The Catalog

3 The Gift Certificate

The running club, Sport's Town, wants you to create a gift certificate that has a design similar to the business card that you created for the first Practice Exercise and the flyer that you created in the hands-on exercises in this chapter. The gift certificate needs to be started from scratch so that you can match images, logos, and color schemes. Irene Brown, the fundraising chairperson, would like to give out gift certificates to join the club. For each person who pays the $15 fee, Sport's Town will donate $5 to a local homeless shelter. Open the *chap2_pe1_business_card_solution* publication and the *chap2_ho2_modified_advertising_solution* publication to use as guides while you are designing this gift certificate.

a. Open a new blank 7 × 3.67 gift certificate found at the very end of the Blank Page Sizes gallery.

b. Save the publication as **chap2_mid3_gift_certificate_solution**.

c. Insert a text box and add the Sport's Town name at the top of the gift certificate. If necessary, center and format the text.

d. Create the color reverse for the name, as shown in Figure 2.34.

e. From the *chap2_pe1_business_card_solution* file, click on the master page, and then, holding down **Ctrl**, point to select the image and the logo. Click **Copy**.

f. Paste the image and the logo onto the gift certificate and move or resize, if necessary, to match that shown in Figure 2.34.

...continued on Next Page

g. Insert a four-row, two-column table, and then add the table information, as shown in Figure 2.34.

h. Format the table to include a deep red border for the entire table, as shown in Figure 2.34.

i. Move and/or reposition the table, as shown in Figure 2.34.

j. Select the first column and change the text to **Comic Sans MS**, **12 pt** font, bold and right-align the text.

k. Switch to the master page and draw out a text box across the entire publication.

l. Select the text box and from the **Fill Color drop-down Fill Effects option**, add a gray fill color with a very light color and a Vertical Shading style.

m. Type the text **Gift Certificate** at the bottom of the text box and change the font to **26 pt Comic Sans MS**, white color.

n. Switch back to the foreground to be sure everything is lined up.

o. Save the publication.

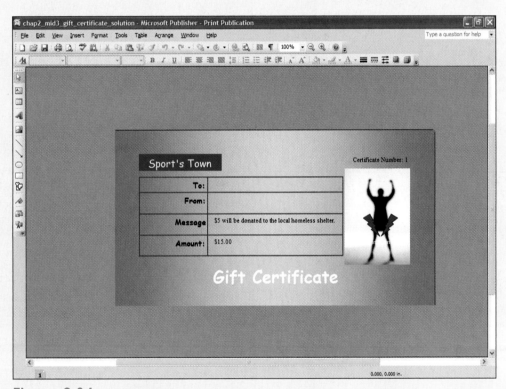

Figure 2.34 The Gift Certificate

Capstone Exercise

You are organizing a guest seminar to help fellow students learn AutoCAD. Your team is creating a flyer, directed to students in Construction Management, providing them with the information needed. You notice that the work that has been done on the flyer so far is of very poor quality. You must fix what has been done, then finish the flyer.

Master Page Clean-Up

a. Open the file *chap2_cap_construction_management*, found in the Exploring Publisher folder. Save the publication as **chap1_cap_ construction_ management_solution.**

b. Go to the master page and remove unnecessary grid lines.

c. There are a lot of unnecessary grid lines, so be careful not to delete something you want to keep. If you accidentally delete something that you did not want to delete, simply hit the **Undo button**.

d. Move the text boxes so they have an orderly format.

e. Move the picture and add another image to the bottom of the flyer.

Change Typography/Formats

a. There are several text boxes. Decide which ones are most important and change the format of them to make them more noticeable.

Do not change the typography of every text box. You do not want to overdo it!

b. If desired, change the style of WordArt used for the title of the flyer.

c. Create a drop cap in the text box at the top of the flyer.

d. Add color reverses to a few text boxes.

e. Save the publication.

Mini Cases

The Band

You and a few of your friends decided to start a band and want to circulate your name through the school. You volunteer to design a flyer using Microsoft Office Publisher 2007. You need to include your band's name, the members of the band and the instruments they play (vocals is considered an instrument), and the genre of music that you play. You have been practicing for a few months and have written a few songs for your first album; include this information on your flyer. Place the logo for your band on the flyer, if you have one, and a picture taken at one of your practices. Open the *chap2_mc1_band* publication and save it as **chap2_mc1_band_solution**.

Performance Elements	Exceeds Expectations	Meets Expectations	Below Expectations
Information on band (Name, genre, members)	Replaced default WordArt name correctly.	Good detail, added band members to text box.	Very little information, not very creative, did not add band members to text box.
Song/album names	Six or more songs typed in table.	Four songs typed in table.	Two songs typed in table.
Graphics	Band picture with correct number of members.	Logo matches band, photo of band.	Clip art logo, nothing to do with band, no band picture.

Favorite Sport

Use the Internet to research your favorite sport; search near your home for a league or club for this sport. Create a flyer displaying the results of your research. This should include the name of the organization, the sport, and the contact information for the local group. Write a short description of the activity that will help persuade other members of the community to join the group. Include some pictures of the activity on the flyer and try to locate some real-life action shots instead of just clip art. Open the *chap2_mc3_favorite_sport* publication and save it as **chap2_mc3_favorite_sport_solution**.

Performance Elements	Exceeds Expectations	Meets Expectations	Below Expectations
Organization Information	Found a specific, local organization and information.	Found a basic regional organization and information.	Found a general or national organization and information.
Attraction paragraph	Sparks a lot of interest.	Sparks some curiosity, will research on own.	Does not spark any further interest.
Images of sport	Purely action photos.	Combination of clip art and photos.	Limited to clip art.

Formatting Hazards

You are shown an example of the hazards of format styles in one of your classes by a guest lecturer from a local graphic design firm. After the presentation, he provides you with a sample exercise demonstrating what he presented during the lecture. Your instructor has asked you to complete the example he provided and submit it for a grade. Open the *chap2_mc2_formatting_disaster* publication and save it as **chap2_mc2_formatting_disaster_solution**. Follow the instructions typed on the publication.

Performance Elements	Exceeds Expectations	Meets Expectations	Below Expectations
Changed WordArt	Applied color and a new shape.	Changed WordArt.	Deleted WordArt.
Fixed color reverses	Applied light text on dark background or dark text on light background.	Changed colors, but still hard to read.	Left color reverses alone.
Removed overformatting	Most formatting changed, some added back.	Not enough formatting changed.	All formatting removed.

Accounting Publications: Working with Business Forms

Objectives

After you read this chapter, you will be able to:

1. Understand business forms **(page 104)**.

2. Know the basic uses for business forms **(page 105)**.

3. Know how to use popular predesigned forms **(page 106)**.

4. Understand popular forms **(page 106)**.

5. Edit business information sets **(page 118)**.

6. Create and edit a personal logo **(page 119)**.

7. Edit, size, and reposition a personal information component **(page 128)**.

Hands-On Exercises

Exercises	Skills Covered
1. WORKING WITH A PREDESIGNED FORM (page 110) **Open:** Predesigned Template **Save as:** chap3_ho1_hope's_invoice_solution	• Open a Predesigned Template • Replace the Template Text • Add the Remaining Text • Add the Final Invoice Items • Delete the Organization Template Logo • Insert, Resize, and Move a Picture • Add the Details • Format Fill Colors • Finish Formatting the Fill Colors
2. CREATING PERSONAL INFORMATION SETS (page 121) **Open:** Predesigned Template **Save as:** chap3_ho2_hope's_po_solution	• Open a Predesigned Business Form • Open the Business Information Dialog Box • Enter the Business Information Data • Edit a Logo • Change the Logo Picture
3. INSERTING AND EDITING PERSONAL INFORMATION SETS (page 130) **Open:** chap3_ho3_fax **Save as:** chap3_ho3_fax_solution	• Open a Partially Completed Publication • Insert the First Business Information Component • Move, Size, and Format the First Component • Insert and Edit the Remaining Components • Continue Formatting the Business Information Components • Finish Formatting the Business Information Components • Edit a Logo • Size the Logo Picture

CASE STUDY
Looking Like a Professional!

Janet Hope has been running a small catering service from her home for about three years. Janet specializes in small parties, luncheons, and special events. Janet hopes to one day own a shop on Main Street in her home town.

Case Study

Since the business's inception, Janet has spread the word about it by passing out business cards, and her business has grown mainly through word of mouth. Janet is the only employee. She does not have a client list nor does she keep track of expenses. She figures out how much she will charge her clients without thinking about how much money she puts into creating her wonderful appetizers, cakes, mini-sandwiches, and flavored teas. In addition, when the party or event is over, Janet typically hands her client a handwritten invoice on a sheet from a restaurant-like order pad. Janet's business has grown, and she realizes that she needs to keep better records; and for the first time in three years, a client asked for a typed, itemized invoice for tax purposes.

Janet remembered that she owns a copy of the Microsoft Publisher program that came with her family computer. She remembers reading something about business forms while looking through the program one day last year. Janet decided that since she needs to organize and update her business records, Publisher offers the best way to begin designing her own forms. She began by designing a new invoice form that she can use with each new client.

Your Assignment

- Read Chapter 3, paying special attention to the information on working with predesigned forms.
- Think about how Janet could design a new invoice for her catering business.
- Be sure to consider how Janet could use Publisher to design her new business forms.
- Design a new invoice using the predesigned forms that includes the name of her business, Hope's Catering, a new logo, her business address, and finally appropriate formatting.
- Print out a copy of your final form design to submit to your instructor.

Business Forms

You have learned the basics of Microsoft Publisher in Chapter 1 and learned how to create publications from scratch in Chapter 2. Learning to create more sophisticated publications, as you do in this chapter, will significantly improve your desktop publishing skills. This chapter provides an introduction to basic business forms, including the process of working with predesigned forms in Publisher. We begin by defining various business forms and describing why you might want to use Microsoft Publisher to create them. We show you how to work with predesigned forms, personal information sets, color schemes, and logos. Figures 3.1 and 3.2 display sample business forms: a basic invoice and a quotation report. Look closely at the two samples. It took us approximately 15 minutes to design the sample invoice form. Then, we saved the sample invoice form under another name and changed the design to one for a quotation form in about two minutes. We used basic predesigned forms in Publisher, and after entering the basic information for the form, we changed some fonts and changed the picture.

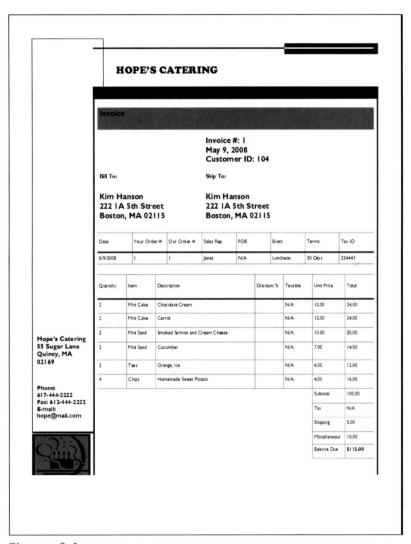

Figure 3.1 Sample Invoice

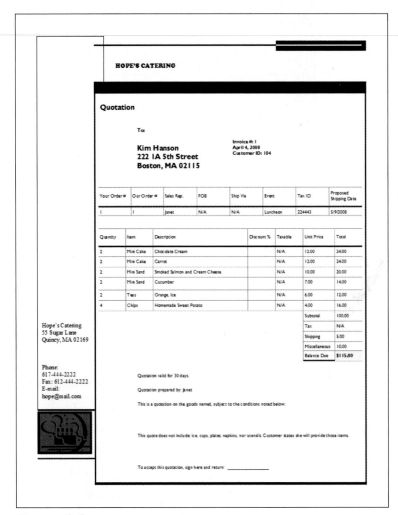

Figure 3.2 Sample Quotation Report

Understanding Business Forms

Business forms are organized documents that help to control everyday operating processes.

Record keeping is a procedure that keeps financial records in order.

Business forms are organized documents that help to control everyday operating processes, such as ordering, billing, faxing, and more. Most businesses (profit or nonprofit) would not survive if there were no control over basic record keeping. **Record keeping** is a procedure that keeps financial records in order. Record keeping may include: inventory control, sales quotes, expense reports, purchase orders, statements, and lots more. Forms help your business appear more professional. Around tax time, completed and organized business forms could make you a happier business owner. Look at Figures 3.1 and 3.2. Would you rather send your client an invoice and quote as shown in the figures, or a handwritten note on an invoice or quotation pad purchased from your local office supply store? Our guess would not be the latter. However, you could spend a lot of money paying someone to design and create these basic record keeping forms.

(Most businesses (profit or nonprofit) would not survive if there were no control over basic record keeping.)

TIP Custom Designs

The start-up costs associated with opening your own small business most often are quite significant. Using Microsoft Publisher to design and create your own business forms can reduce these costs. That way, the lead time for production of new forms may be minimal, because all you may have to do is open up the form on your computer and print more copies.

Why Use Publisher

In today's economy, more and more individuals and families are opening small businesses. More tax-based incentives for owning a small business seem to be introduced each year. However, even with this trend, people do not want to throw money away. Using Microsoft Publisher to create your business forms can save you money and time. Publisher is an excellent choice for designing and printing many of your necessary business forms, because creating forms in Publisher is easy. Not only are you in control of your own record keeping, but because you are also the designer, you can more easily manage how your business is represented.

Knowing the Basic Uses for Business Forms

(Most business forms have similar form elements within each publication.)

Most business forms have similar form elements within each publication. As shown in Figure 3.3, the sample time billing form has text boxes in which to type a date, a table in which information can be categorized, a place for a logo or picture, shaded elements, and different font schemes. Depending on whether you choose to work with a form already designed in Publisher or start a form from scratch, you have the ability to choose different design elements, such as the oval shape and dotted arrow shown in this particular example. Just as with any publication, certain aspects can be changed, such as line thickness and colors. Elements can be moved, copied, pasted, deleted, and much more.

Figure 3.3 Form Basics

Knowing How to Use Popular Predesigned Forms

A ***predesigned form*** is a template.

As shown in Figure 3.4, predesigned forms are selected from the Publication Types task pane. A ***predesigned form*** is basically a template that contains formatting, text, and graphical or financial data placeholders. Publisher provides a large number of predesigned forms from which to choose. In Microsoft Office Publisher 2007, there are ten different business form categories, each including 35 designs, for a total of 350 predesigned form templates.

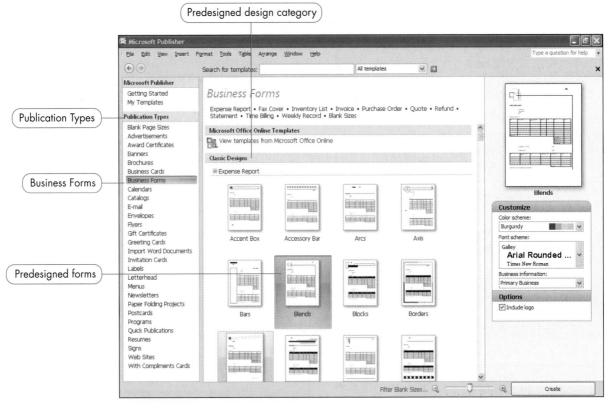

Figure 3.4 Predesigned Forms

TIP Marketing

Not only can Microsoft Publisher help you custom design your business forms, the possibilities for promoting and advertising are endless. Using similar font and color schemes for your forms and advertisements may help to promote a consistent message to your customer.

Understanding Popular Forms

The most common predesigned forms include invoices and statements. However, fax cover sheets, inventory lists, and purchase orders (shown in Figures 3.5, 3.6, and 3.7) are just as common. In addition, there are other categories that are beneficial for any business, including:

An ***Expense Report*** is used to list an employee's expenses.

- ***Expense Report***: Used to list an employee's expenses, such as business trip expenses. You want to be able to list items, such as car, hotel, food, and/or entertainment expenses. When filing income taxes, these records can be very helpful.

A **Fax Cover Sheet** is used to send information along with the organization's fax documents.

An **Inventory List** is used to list in-stock inventory.

An **Invoice** is used to bill customers for services or supplies.

A **Purchase Order** is used to request services or supplies.

A **Quote Form** is used to bid for jobs.

A **Refund Form** is used to keep track of any refunds to clients.

A **Statement** is used to itemize invoices for periodic billing.

Time Billing is used to bill for time-based services.

A **Weekly Record** is used to keep track of employee work hours.

- *Fax Cover Sheet*: Used to send information along with the organizations's fax documents. The fax cover sheet typically precedes the documents to be faxed. The fax cover sheet contains places to list the sender's name, the recipient, the date, and other detailed information.

- *Inventory List*: Used to list in-stock inventory. The form contains places to list each item, the form of payment, description of the item, date the item was purchased, warranty information, and more.

- *Invoice*: Used to bill customers for services or supplies. This form contains the client number and address, and a description of the item or service that was purchased.

- *Purchase Order*: Used to request services or supplies. This form contains places to list each item, a description of the item, the number of units ordered, any applicable taxes, discounts, and more.

- *Quote Form*: Used to bid for jobs or outline how much services or supplies will cost the client.

- *Refund Form*: Used to keep track of any refunds to clients. Contains places to list each item, the date it was purchased, any applicable tax refund, and more.

- *Statement*: Used to itemize invoices for periodic billing.

- *Time Billing*: Used to bill for time-based services.

- *Weekly Record*: Used to keep track of employee work hours, both regular and overtime.

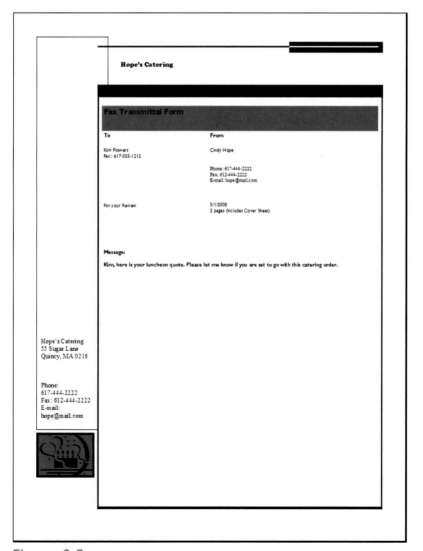

Figure 3.5 Fax

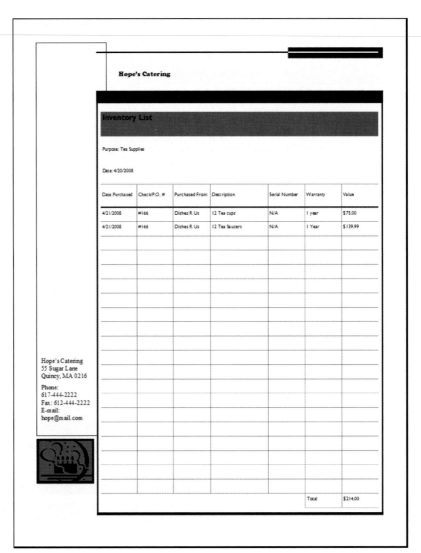

Hope's Catering

Inventory List						

Purpose: Tea Supplies

Date: 4/20/2008

Date Purchased	Check/P.O. #	Purchased From	Description	Serial Number	Warranty	Value
4/21/2008	#166	Dishes R Us	12 Tea cups	N/A	1 year	$75.00
4/21/2008	#166	Dishes R Us	12 Tea Saucers	N/A	1 Year	$139.99
					Total	$214.00

Hope's Catering
55 Sugar Lane
Quincy, MA 0216

Phone:
617-444-2222
Fax: 612-444-2222
E-mail:
hope@mail.com

Figure 3.6   Inventory List

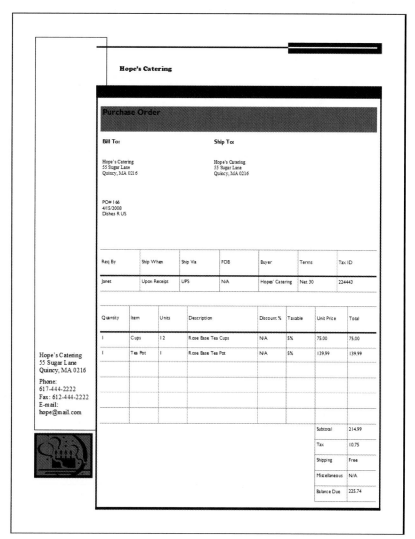

Hope's Catering

Purchase Order

Bill To:	Ship To:
Hope's Catering 55 Sugar Lane Quincy, MA 0216	Hope's Catering 55 Sugar Lane Quincy, MA 0216

PO# 166
4/15/2008
Dishes R US

Req By	Ship When	Ship Via	FOB	Buyer	Terms	Tax ID
Janet	Upon Receipt	UPS	N/A	Hopes' Catering	Net 30	224443

Quantity	Item	Units	Description	Discount %	Taxable	Unit Price	Total
1	Cups	12	Rose Base Tea Cups	N/A	5%	75.00	75.00
1	Tea Pot	1	Rose Base Tea Pot	N/A	5%	139.99	139.99
						Subtotal	214.99
						Tax	10.75
						Shipping	Free
						Miscellaneous	N/A
						Balance Due	225.74

Hope's Catering
55 Sugar Lane
Quincy, MA 0216

Phone:
617-444-2222
Fax: 612-444-2222
E-mail:
hope@mail.com

Figure 3.7   Purchase Order

Hands-On Exercises

1 | Working with a Predesigned Form

Skills covered: 1. Open a Predesigned Template **2.** Replace the Template Text **3.** Add the Remaining Text **4.** Add the Final Invoice Items **5.** Delete the Organization Template Logo **6.** Insert, Resize, and Move a Picture **7.** Add the Details **8.** Format Fill Colors **9.** Finish Formatting the Fill Colors

---

Step 1
Open a Predesigned Template

Refer to Figure 3.8 as you complete Step 1.

a. Start Publisher and click the **Business Forms category** from the Publication Types task pane.

b. Scroll down and click the **Layers Invoice** from the publications gallery, as shown in Figure 3.8.

c. Click the **Create button**.

d. Save the publication as **chap3_ho1_hope's_invoice_solution**.

> **TROUBLESHOOTING:** If this is the first time you have worked with forms in Publisher, a box may appear after you select the Layers Invoice asking you to add personal information such as your name and address so that you do not have to do this for every publication you create. Once you click OK, the Personal Information dialog box opens, where you supply this information. Click Update or click Cancel to close the dialog box and begin choosing options for your flyer. Later in the chapter, we will work with Personal Information.

The publication gallery is now replaced with a publication window displaying a template for the Business Form Layers Invoice you selected, and the Publication Types task pane is replaced by the Format Publication task pane.

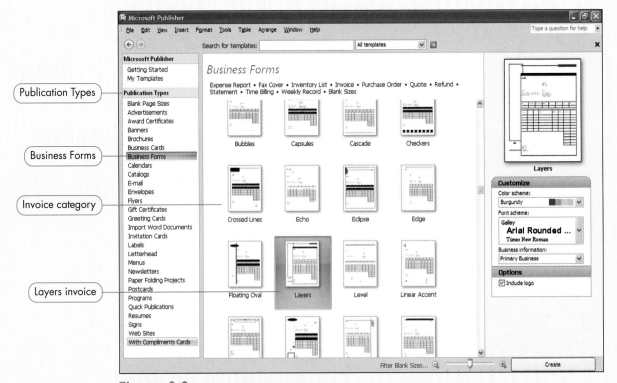

Figure 3.8 Layers Invoice

Refer to Figure 3.9 as you complete Step 2.

a. If necessary, click to Zoom the screen to 100% to increase your working area.

b. Scroll up to select the **Business Name text box** at the top of the form, and then type **Hope's Catering**.

c. Format the font to **Cooper Black**, **16 pt** font size.

d. Replace the Bill To: and Ship To: address with the addresses shown in Figure 3.9.

e. Format the font for both the Bill To: and Ship To: addresses to **12 pt** font size and bold, as shown.

f. Change the line spacing to **0** for both the Bill To: and the Ship To: addresses from the **Paragraph command** on the **Format menu**.

g. Replace shown in the address and telephone information on the bottom left of the form, as shown in Figure 3.9.

h. Change the address the line spacing to **0** from the **Paragraph command** on the **Format menu** for both the address and telephone information on the bottom left.

TROUBLESHOOTING: You may have to select several lines at a time to change the line spacing and then continue this process until all text can be seen in these text boxes.

i. Format the font for both to **Gill Sans MT**, **9 pt** font size.

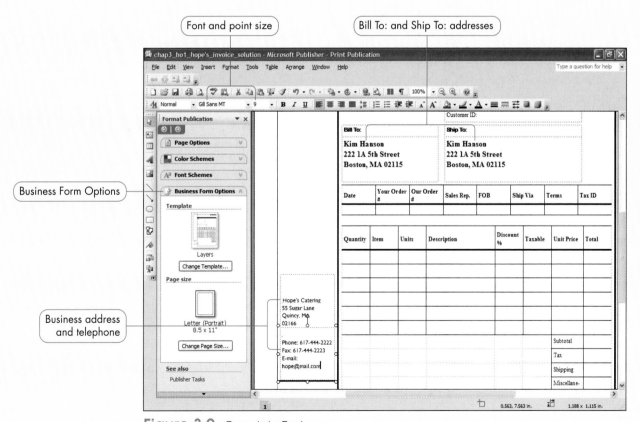

Figure 3.9 Template Text

Refer to Figure 3.10 as you complete Step 3.

a. If necessary, scroll up or down and/or left or right to move back to the top of your invoice.

b. Click to select the Invoice #, invoice date, and Customer ID text, and then hit **Delete** on your keyboard.

c. In the same text box, type in the information as shown in Figure 3.10.

d. Format the font to **12 pt** and **bold**.

e. Change the line spacing to **0** from the **Paragraph command** on the **Format menu**.

f. Type in the date, order number, sales rep, and the remaining information on the invoice information row, as shown in Figure 3.10.

g. Select Ship Via and replace the text with **Event** to match Figure 3.10.

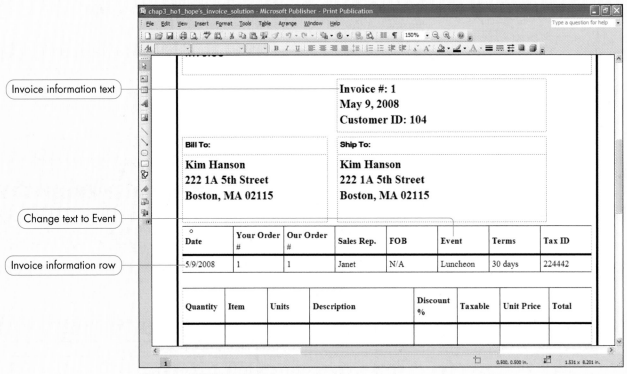

Figure 3.10 Remaining Text

TIP   Compatibility

Microsoft Office Publisher 2007 has a number of useful characteristics, one of the most important being its compatibility with earlier versions of Microsoft Publisher. Publisher 2003 files can be opened with Publisher 2007 and earlier versions of the software as well, making sharing files between users easier.

Step 4

Add the Final Invoice Items

Refer to Figure 3.11 as you complete Step 4.

a. Type each of the invoice items into the form table as shown in Figure 3.11.

To move from one cell to the next in the table, hit the Tab key on your keyboard.

b. Type in each of the totals for each individual item.

c. Type in the subtotal, tax, shipping, miscellaneous, and balance due amounts.

d. Format the balance due amount to **bold**.

e. Click outside the balance due text box to deselect the area.

f. Select all text in the individual invoice area, including the table labels, and change the font to **Gills Sans MT**, **7 pt** font.

g. Save the publication.

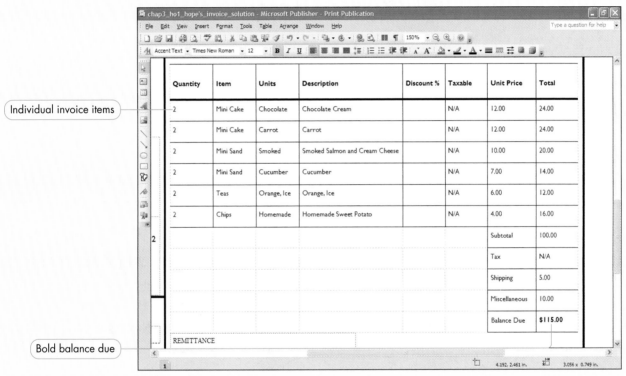

Individual invoice items

Quantity	Item	Units	Description	Discount %	Taxable	Unit Price	Total
2	Mini Cake	Chocolate	Chocolate Cream		N/A	12.00	24.00
2	Mini Cake	Carrot	Carrot		N/A	12.00	24.00
2	Mini Sand	Smoked	Smoked Salmon and Cream Cheese		N/A	10.00	20.00
2	Mini Sand	Cucumber	Cucumber		N/A	7.00	14.00
2	Teas	Orange, Ice	Orange, Ice		N/A	6.00	12.00
2	Chips	Homemade	Homemade Sweet Potato		N/A	4.00	16.00
					Subtotal		100.00
					Tax		N/A
					Shipping		5.00
					Miscellaneous		10.00
					Balance Due		**$115.00**

REMITTANCE

Bold balance due

Figure 3.11 Invoice Items

Step 5

Delete the Organization Template Logo

Refer to Figure 3.12 as you complete Step 5.

a. Scroll down and left so that you can see the template logo at the bottom left of the invoice form.

b. Click to select the logo, and then hit **Delete** on your keyboard.

A dialog box may appear asking if you want to change to a design that does not include a logo. If this happens, click Yes to delete the logo from the invoice business form.

c. Save the publication.

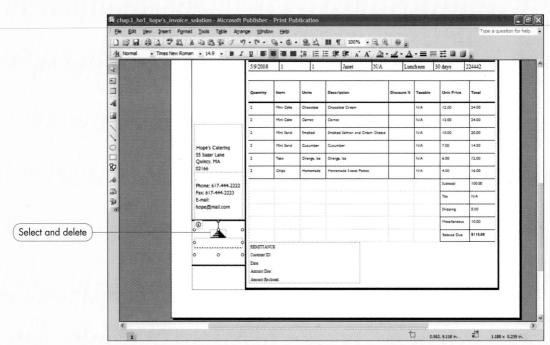

Figure 3.12 Delete Logo

Step 6
Insert, Resize, and Move a Picture

Refer to Figure 3.13 as you complete Step 6.

a. Pull down the **Insert menu**, point to **Picture**, and click **Clip Art**.

The Insert Clip Art task pane opens.

b. Type **Birthday cakes** in the Search for text box.

c. Choose the same clip art we chose or a similar birthday cake as shown in Figure 3.13.

d. Save the publication.

Figure 3.13 Insert Picture

TIP   Your Own Pictures

When custom designing your business forms using Microsoft Publisher, you are not limited to static templates. You can include all sorts of pictures in your designs. Many businesses use photographs that illustrate their business. These photos may be of clients or employees, or maybe a particular tool they use in day-to-day business. Be sure to obtain legal permission to use any employee photograph in your publications.

Step 7
Add the Details

Refer to Figure 3.14 as you complete Step 7.

a. Point to the upper right sizing handle on the picture and click to drag inward to resize the picture.

b. Click the mouse in the middle of the picture and drag down to move it back to the logo area, as shown in Figure 3.14.

c. If necessary, resize or continue moving to place the picture exactly where you want it on the form.

d. Save the publication.

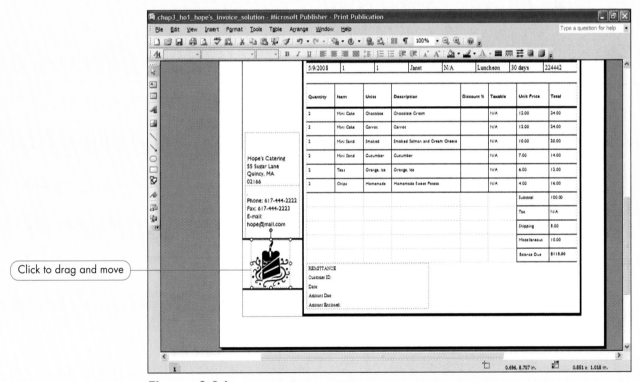

Figure 3.14 Resize and Move Picture

TIP Nudge Option

Sometimes when placing graphics in your publication, you will find that you need to move the graphic only slightly from its position. Each time you press ALT and the arrow keys (up, down, left, and right), your selected graphic moves one pixel. Using the Options dialog box from the Tools menu and Edit tab, you can change the nudge distance. By clicking the check box next to the Arrow keys nudge options, you can change the distance of the nudge options when using the keyboard command to nudge an object.

Step 8
Format Fill Colors

Refer to Figure 3.15 as you complete Step 8.

a. Scroll up to the top of the invoice, and then select the text box for the business name.

b. Click the drop-down arrow for the **Fill Color button**, and then choose **More Fill Colors**.

c. In the **Colors dialog box**, select the light cream fill color, as shown in Figure 3.15, and then click **OK**.

The business name text box fill color is now the cream color you chose in the Colors dialog box.

d. Save the publication.

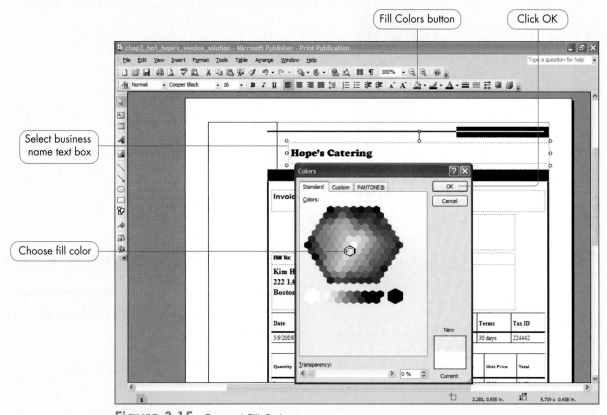

Figure 3.15 Format Fill Color

Step 9
Finish Formatting the Fill Colors

Refer to Figure 3.16 as you complete Step 9.

a. Change each of the address text boxes to the same cream fill color as shown in Figure 3.16.

b. Change the Invoice text box background to the red fill color as shown in Figure 3.16.

c. Change the picture background to the red fill color as shown in Figure 3.16.

d. Change the Balance Due table cell to the bright yellow fill color as shown in Figure 3.16.

e. Save the publication.

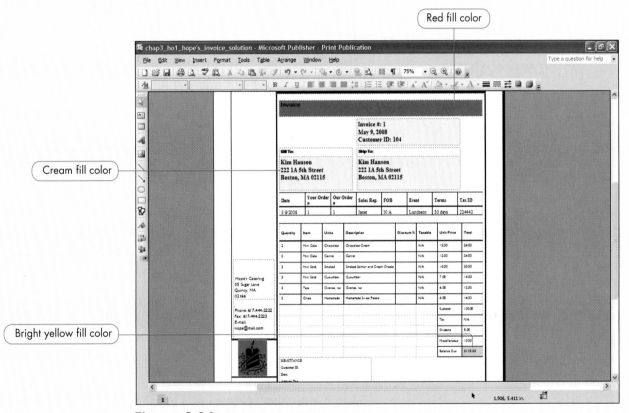

Figure 3.16   Finish Formatting

 TIP   Font Size

You can avoid using the mouse to change font size when you are working on a publication. To increase or decrease the font to the next size, select the text you wish to change, and then press Ctrl+SHIFT+> to increase the size and Ctrl+SHIFT+< to decrease the size. There is also a shortcut that will increase or decrease the font by 1 pt. Press Ctrl+) to increase the font or Ctrl+(to decrease the font.

Business Information Sets

These information sets can be used with any publication, but for the purpose of this chapter, we will concentrate on a primary business set. The business information set includes the following core categories:

- Individual name: Your name or the name of the person you want associated with the business information set.
- Job position or title: Your job position or title or the job positon or title of the person you want associated with the business information set.
- Organization name: Your company name.
- Address: Your company address.
- Phone, fax, and e-mail: Your company phone, fax, and e-mail.
- Tag line or motto: A slogan or a business phrase that you would like to include on your publications.
- Logo: A logo for your company. You can design your own logo or choose from several provided by Microsoft Publisher.

Each of the seven core components are inserted into a publication separately; none of the components can be combined. You can insert as many of the components as you want into a publication. For instance, if you are working with a business form quote, you may want to insert the address into more than one location. If you are working with a time sheet, you may want to insert your name multiple times. In addition, the information for each core category can be edited or removed entirely.

Editing Business Information Sets

One of the nice things about using Publisher to design your business forms is that you can set up what Microsoft calls *business information sets*. Business information sets contain information about you or your business. You create business information sets once, but use them over and over. The *Edit Business Information Set dialog box* allows you to create as many business information set names as you wish. The default name that appears in the dialog box is *Primary Business*. You can change the name by typing in a new name at the Business Information Set name text box. This is where you name the business information set so that you can use it over again.

> You create business information sets once, but use them over and over.

Business information sets contain information about you or your business.

The **Edit Business Information Set dialog box** allows you to create as many Business Information Set names as you wish.

Personal Information Data

Microsoft Publisher has many, many tools to help make your job easier. When you install Microsoft Publisher, the personal information set contains default information. When you begin to work with publications, the Business Information dialog box, as shown in Figure 3.17, may appear at any time so that you can replace the default information. If it does not appear, you can display the Business Information dialog box from the Edit menu. Once you have opened the Business Information dialog box, then all you have to do is click Edit or New to edit an existing business information set or to create a new one, as shown in Figure 3.18. Then, you simply select which components you want to change by replacing any default text with your own text for the seven core components. After you edit or create a new business information set, you can then update the publication to include the components.

> Microsoft Publisher has many, many tools to help make your job easier.

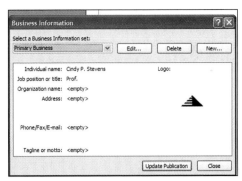

Figure 3.17 Business Information Set

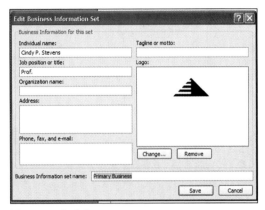

Figure 3.18 Edit or Create Business Information Set

Troubleshooting the Personal Information Set

Synchronization means that any formatting changes made in a publication will be automatically changed in similar elements.

If your business information does not change after you edit the information in the Business Information dialog box, *synchronization* may be turned off in your Publisher options. In Publisher, synchronization means that any formatting changes made in a publication will be automatically changed in similar elements on the same publication. If synchronization is turned off, then the changes you have made in the Business Information dialog box will not be updated in your current publication. To correct this problem, simply click on the Tools menu and Options command. Click on the User Assistance tab and click the Automatically Synchronize Formatting button to fix the problem.

Creating and Editing a Personal Logo

Publisher contains many different types of logo images to use in your publications. However, you may want to create your own logo, and then add it to your business information set to use each time you create a new pubication. To edit the default logo in Publisher you must first open a predesigned publication that contains a default logo, or you can even use a blank publication and insert a logo placeholder to work with. To change the text of the logo, simply select it to replace the default text. To replace the picture, right-click the picture to select a new one, as shown in Figure 3.19, from the shortcut menu.

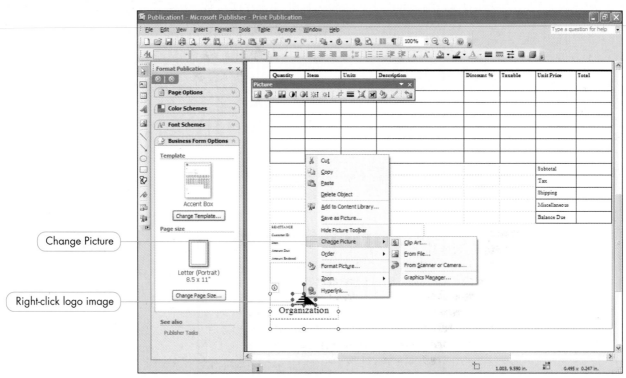

Change Picture

Right-click logo image

Figure 3.19 Edit a Logo Image

TIP Logos

Logos surround us every day. They provide a quick way for people to recognize your business. Be sure when designing your logo to keep it simple. Too many lines, shapes, colors, or words detract from the meaning. Consider using just the initials of the business in the logo or perhaps using a simple abstraction of the first letter of your business name. You do not have to be an expert to design your own business logo. However, you do want to pay attention to detail. A logo represents your business, and a highly effective logo shows your attention to detail. If you choose to use one of the existing logos provided in the Publisher program, you certainly can make changes to it. For instance, you may want to change either the fill color or the logo, the picture, the text, or even the border color or thickness. If you are not sure how you want your logo to look, search the Internet for logo samples to get some ideas. However, be careful not to steal somebody else's idea.

2 | Creating Personal Information Sets

Skills covered: 1. Open a Predesigned Business Form **2.** Open the Business Information Dialog Box **3.** Enter the Business Information Data **4.** Edit a Logo **5.** Change the Logo Picture

---

Step 1
Open a Predesigned Business Form

Refer to Figure 3.20 as you complete Step 1.

a. Start Publisher.

The application window opens with the Publication Types task pane on the left and the publication preview gallery in the middle of the screen.

b. From the Publications Types task pane, click **Business Forms**.

c. Scroll down until the Purchase Order category appears in the preview gallery.

d. Select (click once) the **Layers Purchase Order**, as shown in Figure 3.20. Click the **Create button**.

The publication gallery is now replaced with a publication window displaying a template for the Business Form Layers Purchase Order you selected, and the Publication Types task pane is replaced by the Format Publication task pane.

e. Save the publication as **chap3_ho2_hope's_po_solution**.

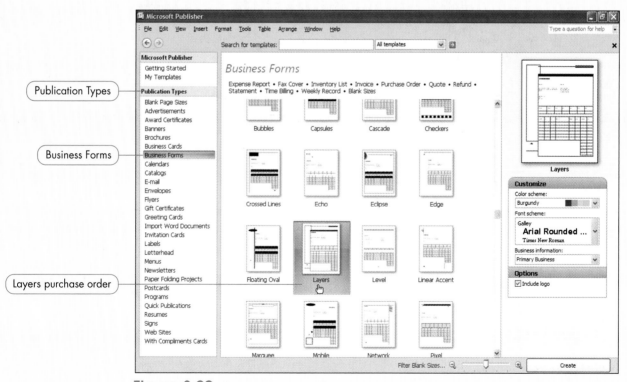

Figure 3.20 Layers Purchase Order

Refer to Figure 3.21 as you complete Step 2.

a. If necessary, click to Zoom the screen to 75% or 100% to increase your working area.

b. Click on the **Edit Menu**, and then click **Business Information command** at the bottom of the drop-down menu.

c. If necessary, click the **New button** to open the Create New Business Information Set dialog box, as shown in Figure 3.21.

TROUBLESHOOTING: Do not worry if your screen does not look exactly the same as ours. Your Publisher program may already include your name and other information due to working with previous exercises.

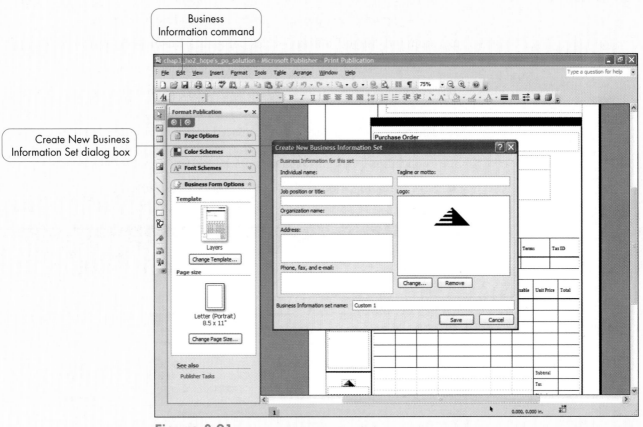

Figure 3.21 Business Information Set

TIP Do Not Forget WordArt

Microsoft WordArt is another way to create decorative text to add interest to your publication. Choose WordArt from the Drawing toolbar. Enter the desired text, then click OK to create the WordArt object. You can click and drag the sizing handles to change the size or proportion of the text. Use any tool on the WordArt toolbar to further change the appearance of the object.

Step 3

Enter the Business Information Data

Refer to Figure 3.22 as you complete Step 3.

a. If there is default text already entered into your Business Information dialog box, select the text to delete.

In each of the core categories (excluding logo category), enter the text as shown in Figure 3.22 or enter your own information. (Your information does not have to match our screen.)

b. Click in the **Individual Name text box** and enter the name, **Janet Hope**, as shown in Figure 3.22.

c. Click in the **Job position or title text box** and enter the job position or title, **Owner**, as shown in Figure 3.22.

d. Click in the **Organization name text box** and enter the business name, **Hope's Catering**, as shown in Figure 3.22.

e. Click in the **Address text box** and enter the company address, **55 Sugar Lane**, **Quincy**, **MA 02169**, as shown in Figure 3.22.

f. Click in the **Phone, Fax, and e-mail text box** and enter the company phone **617-444-2222**, fax **617-444-2221**, and e-mail **hope@email.com**, as shown in Figure 3.22.

g. Click in the **Tag line or motto text box** and enter the slogan, **Yummies Delivered!**, as shown in Figure 3.22.

h. Click in the **Business Information set name text box** and enter **Hope's Catering**, as shown in Figure 3.22.

i. Press the **Print Screen button** on your keyboard, and then open Word to paste this screen and print a copy to submit to your instructor.

j. Click **Save** in the Business Information Dialog Box to save the changes, and then click the **Update Publication button**.

The form may not look quite the way you want it to look at this time. Do not worry, in the third hands-on exercise we will show you how to insert individual Business Information set components into your publication for better formatting.

k. Save the publication.

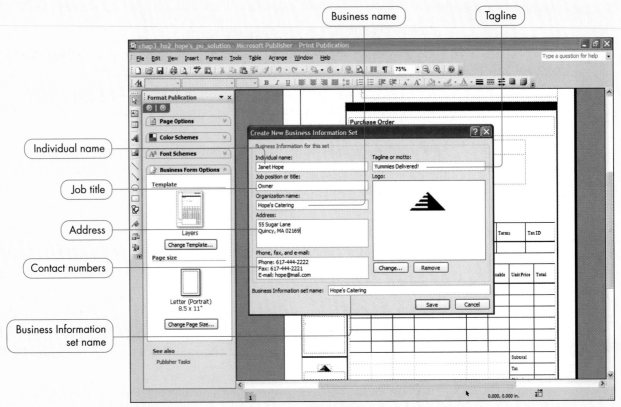

Figure 3.22 Business Information Set Data

The Drawing Toolbar

The Drawing toolbar is common to all applications in Microsoft Office. Click the down arrow next to the AutoShapes button to display the various shapes, and then click Block Arrows to display the arrows that are available. Select an arrow. The mouse pointer changes to a tiny crosshair that you click and drag to create the arrow within the publication. Right-click the arrow, and then click the Add Text command to enter text within the arrow. Use the other buttons to change the color or other properties.

Step 4
Edit a Logo

Refer to Figure 3.23 as you complete Step 4.

a. If necessary, click to Zoom the screen to 75% or 100% to increase your working area.

b. Scroll down so that you can work with the Logo image at the bottom left corner of the form, as shown in Figure 3.23.

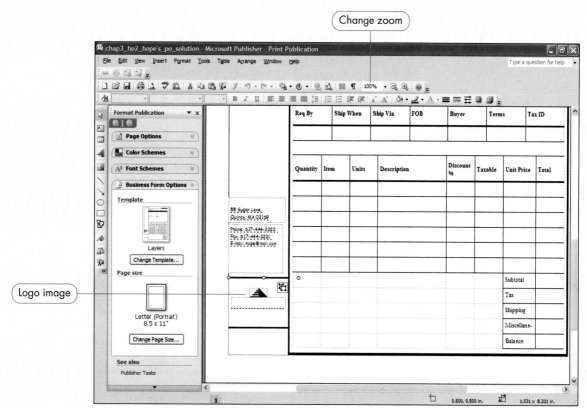

Change zoom

Logo image

Figure 3.23 Edit Logo

TIP   Resizing an Object

There are times in Publisher when the center of your object is in the right place, but you just need to make the object bigger. To do this, click the object, and then hold down Ctrl while you resize the object. When you are done resizing, release the mouse button before you release Ctrl.

Step 5
Change the Logo Picture

Refer to Figure 3.24 as you complete Step 5.

a. Click once on the logo to activate the sizing handles, and then click again to activate just the picture on the logo.

b. With the logo picture activated, right-click to bring up the shortcut menu, and then point to the **Change Picture command**.

c. Choose the **Clip art category**, and then search for **Birthday cakes** to insert a new picture similar to the one shown in Figure 3.24.

d. Click once on your picture choice to change the default logo image to your new clip art image.

Do not worry that your picture is very small. In Hands-On Exercise 3, you will learn how to edit personal information sets, including logos. You can zoom out in your publication as shown in the figure.

e. Save the publication.

f. Close Microsoft Publisher, unless you plan to work on Hands-On Exercise 3.

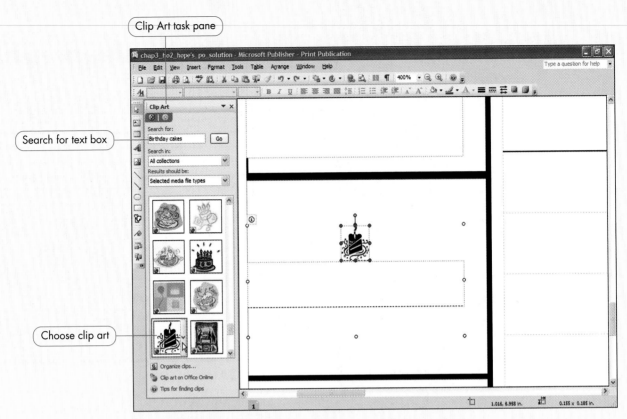

Figure 3.24 Change Logo Picture

Including Personal Information Components

Once you set up the information in your Business Information Set dialog box, the business information, such as name, address, phone, fax, and e-mail, automatically appears on each new predesigned form. However, at times, you may want to create a business form, or other publication, from scratch. Inserting personal information sets anywhere in a publication is possible. You can also insert any of the seven core categories into a blank publication, as shown in Figure 3.25. To insert a business information component into your publication, first select Business Information from the Insert menu, and then choose a component from Insert Business Information on the task pane. When you choose to insert one of the components individually, a text box including the component is inserted into the publication.

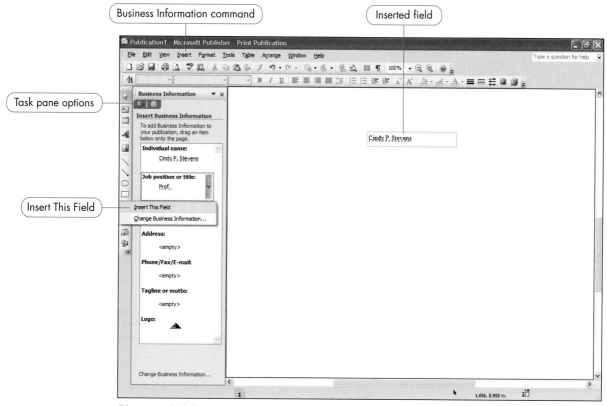

Figure 3.25 Including Business Information Components

TIP   Using a Professional Printer

Sometimes when you have a professional printer print your business forms, you will notice a slight color difference between what you designed and what is actually printed. This is due to the fact that your monitor may be set to a different brightness or contrast level. Be sure to proof the final design as it will be printed before you end up with a stack of business forms that are the wrong color.

Editing, Sizing, and Repositioning a Personal Information Component

After inserting a business information component, you can edit, resize, and/or move the component anywhere on the publication page.

After inserting a business information component, you can edit, resize, and/or move the component anywhere on the publication page. To edit a component, select the text. Then you can change it, add to it, and/or change the font or font size, and even add fill color to the component's text box. Text can also be aligned differently and/or bulleted. To resize the component, you would click any of the sizing handles to drag the text box in to decrease its size or out to increase. Remember, however, that changing the size of the text box does not change the size of the text. Finally, to move the component, click and hold your mouse and drag to reposition the component anywhere on the Publisher page. If necessary, you can also delete an individual component added to a publication by clicking it once and pressing Delete on your keyboard or by clicking the Cut button on the Standard toolbar. (Alternatively, you can choose Cut from the Edit menu.) Figure 3.26 shows individual components added to a blank publication with each component edited, resized, and moved.

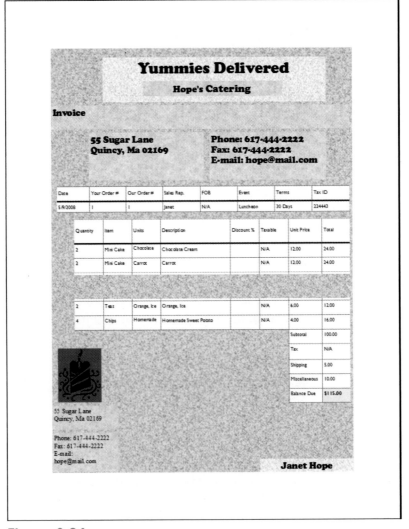

Figure 3.26 Editing, Sizing, and Repositioning

TIP Edit Your Work

After staring at your design for a while, you may start missing even the most obvious mistakes in your work. Make sure to run the spelling checker on your publication. Finally, print a rough draft of the publication and have someone else check your work. Microsoft Publisher enables you to edit your work in Word as well. Right-click any text box that you want to check for errors. Click the Change Text command that will appear in the shortcut menu, and then click Edit Story in Microsoft Word. Keep in mind that the Publisher text boxes will not appear when you choose to edit text in Word.

Hands-On Exercises

3 | Inserting and Editing Personal Information Sets

Skills covered: 1. Open a Partially Completed Publication **2.** Insert the First Business Information Component **3.** Move, Size, and Format the First Component **4.** Insert and Edit the Remaining Components **5.** Continue Formatting the Business Information Components **6.** Finish Formatting the Business Information Components **7.** Edit a Logo **8.** Size the Logo Picture

---

Step 1
Open a Partially Completed Publication

Refer to Figure 3.27 as you complete Step 1.

a. Start Publisher, if necessary, and open the *chap3_ho3_fax* file.

Alternately, you can click the open button on the Standard toolbar to browse for the file.

b. Save the publication as **chap3_ho3_fax_solution**.

c. Click the Zoom out to 75% or 100% to see the fax form better.

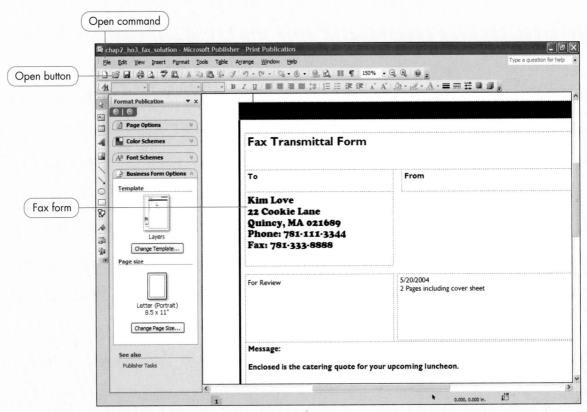

Figure 3.27 Open Publication

Step 2
Insert the First Business Information Component

Refer to Figure 3.28 as you complete Step 2.

a. Scroll to the top of the fax cover sheet.

b. Click the **Business Information command** on the **Insert Menu**.

c. Click the down arrow next to the **Organization name component** from the task pane on the left, as shown in Figure 3.28, and then click **Insert This Field**.

Do not worry if your organization name is different from ours if you have set up your Business Information dialog box differently.

d. The Organization name component will now appear on the publication.

e. Save the publication.

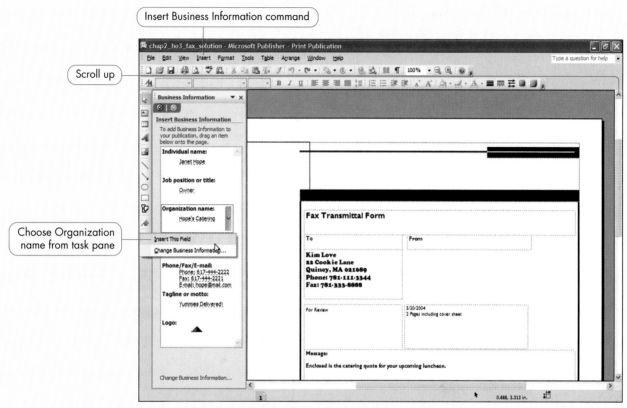

Figure 3.28 Insert the Organization Name

TIP   Switching Views

Hit F9 on the keyboard to go up to the next zoom size. This will change the current view of your publication to a larger view. Hit F9 again to go back down. You can also click on the Boundaries and Guides command on the View menu to see what your publication will look like without the imaginary placeholder lines. You can also click Ctrl+Shift+L to display your entire publication on your screen. However, it is just as simple to click Print Preview from the File menu.

Refer to Figure 3.29 as you complete Step 3.

a. Click on the **Organization name text box** and hold your mouse to drag the component to the top of the flyer, as shown in Figure 3.29.

b. Click to resize the text box as shown in the figure.

c. Select the Organization name text and change the font to **16 pt**, **Copper black** (or you may choose any other typeface and font size for your publication).

d. If necessary, resize the Organization name text box and/or reposition it on your publication to match that shown in Figure 3.29.

e. Save the publication.

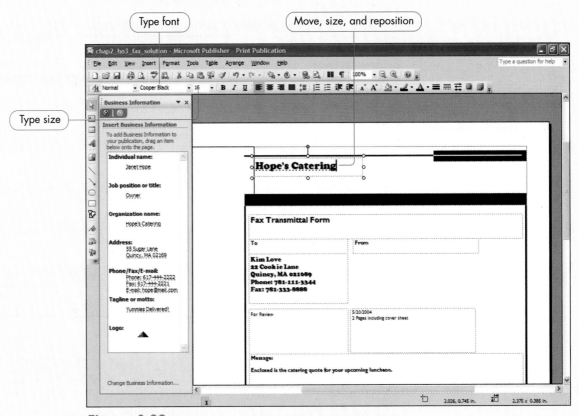

Figure 3.29 Move, Size, and Reposition Component

Refer to Figure 3.30 as you complete Step 4.

a. Insert, move, resize, and format each of the remaining core categories (excluding the logo category), as shown in Figure 3.30. These other components include the following:

Individual name—Insert the name twice, as shown in Figure 3.30. Change the font to **10 pt**, **Copper black**. Resize the text boxes and also reposition them on the publication to match Figure 3.30.

Job position or title—Insert the Job title, as shown in Figure 3.30. Change the font to **10 pt**, **Copper black**. Resize the text boxes and also reposition them on the publication to match Figure 3.30.

Address—Insert the company address, as shown in Figure 3.30. Change the font to **10 pt**, **Copper black**. Resize the text boxes and also reposition them on the publication to match Figure 3.30.

Phone, fax, and e-mail—Insert this information twice, as shown in Figure 3.30. Change the font to **10 pt**, **Copper black**. Resize the text boxes and also reposition them on the publication to match Figure 3.30.

Tag line or motto—Insert the tag line, as shown in Figure 3.30. Change the font to **14 pt**, **Copper black**. Resize the text boxes and also reposition them on the publication to match Figure 3.30.

b. Save the publication.

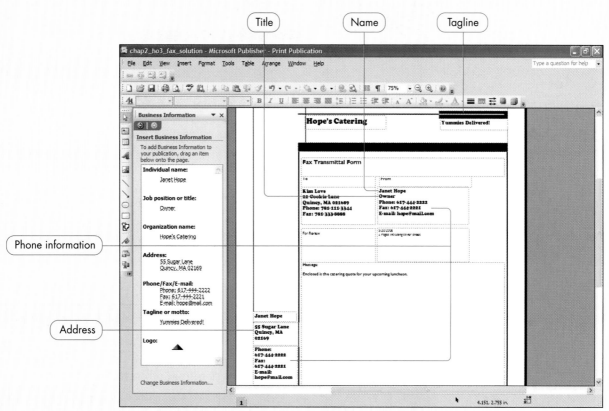

Figure 3.30 Insert and Edit Remaining Components

Refer to Figure 3.31 as you complete Step 5.

a. If necessary, scroll up to the top of the fax cover sheet, and then select the **Organization name text box**, as shown in Figure 3.31.

b. Click on the **Fill Color button arrow**, and then select **More Fill Colors**.

c. Choose the **light cream** color or choose any other color you wish.

d. Click on the **Fill Color button arrow** again, and then choose **Fill Effects**.

e. On the **Gradient tab**, change the **Transparency** for both From: and To: to **30%** and click **OK** to apply the new changes.

f. Save the publication.

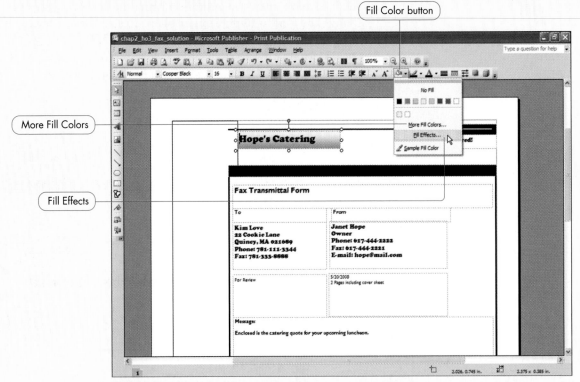

Figure 3.31 Continue Formatting

   **Windows Command**

If you are working on multiple publications at once, the contents of the Windows menu let you switch between publications easily. The Windows menu will display all of the publications that are open, and the one that is currently displayed will be highlighted with a check mark. Selecting Arrange All in the Windows menu will display all of the open publications in one window, allowing you to compare publications side by side.

Step 6

Finish Formatting the Business Information Components

Refer to Figure 3.32 as you complete Step 6.

a. Add fill colors and fill effects to each of the remaining personal information components (excluding the logo category), as shown in Figure 3.32 (your fill colors and fill effects do not have to match this figure exactly), including:

- Individual name—Format the owner's name fill color to a **light gray** with **30%** transparency fill effects.

- Job position or title—Do not add any fill color.

- Address—Format the address to a **light cream** color with **30%** transparency fill effects.

- Phone, fax, and e-mail—Format the phone information to a **light cream** color with **30%** transparency fill effects.

- Tag line or motto—Format the fill color to a **light gray** with **30%** transparency fill effects.

- Fax text box—Format the fax text box to a **light cream** color with **30%** transparency fill effects.

b. Save the publication.

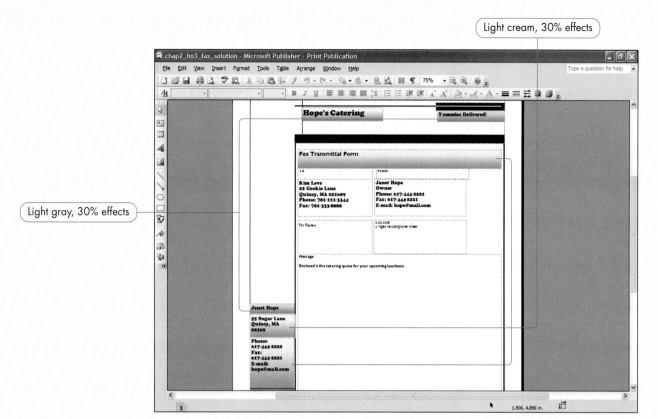

Light cream, 30% effects

Light gray, 30% effects

Figure 3.32 Finish Formatting

Step 7
Edit a Logo

Refer to Figure 3.33 as you complete Step 7.

a. Scroll down to the bottom of the fax form, if necessary, and then select the small logo picture to activate it.

Click on the logo once, and then click on the small picture once to work with the picture.

b. From the **Arrange menu**, click the **Ungroup command**, as shown in Figure 3.33.

If a warning box appears asking you if you really want to ungroup these objects, click **Yes** to ungroup these objects. We will regroup the objects at a later time.

c. Save the publication.

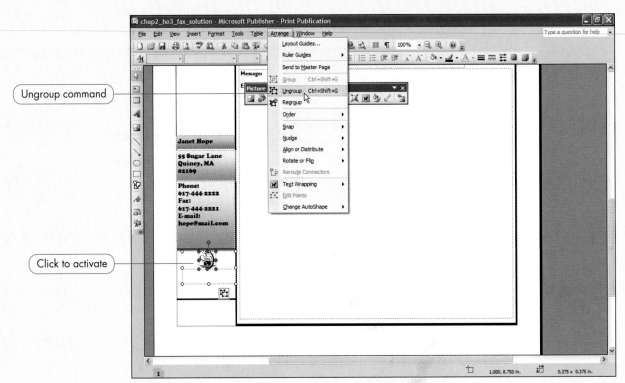

Figure 3.33 Edit a Logo

Step 8
Size the Logo Picture

Refer to Figure 3.34 as you complete Step 8.

Once you have ungrouped the logo objects, you can now resize the picture.

a. Click on one of the corner sizing handles on the picture and drag out to make the picture larger.

b. Click and move either of the logo text boxes to reposition them on the screen and continue resizing the picture to match Figure 3.34.

c. Click inside the logo text box below the logo picture and type the word **Yummy!**, as shown in Figure 3.34.

d. If necessary, change the typeface to **14 pt**, **Copper Black**.

e. Holding down **Ctrl** on your keyboard, select the picture and the text box containing the word *Yummy*. Then, click the **Group command** on the **Arrange menu**.

f. Save the publication.

g. Close Microsoft Publisher unless you plan to continue with the Practice Exercises.

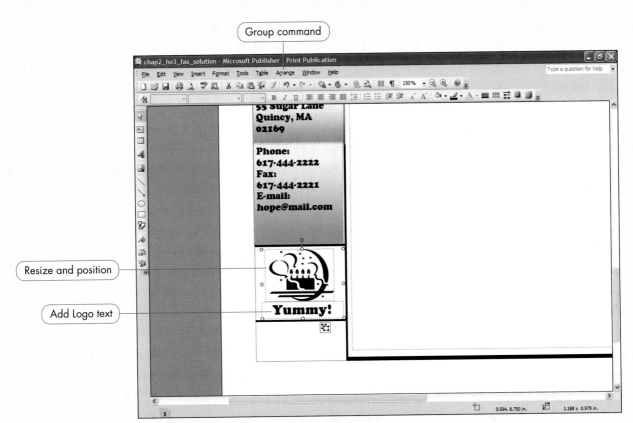

Figure 3.34 Size the Logo Picture

Summary

1. **Understand business forms.** Creating business forms with Microsoft Publisher may help to save time and money. Business forms are organized documents that are used to help control everyday operating processes, such as ordering, invoicing, faxing, and more.

2. **Know the basic uses for business forms.** Both profit and nonprofit companies use business forms to help manage basic record keeping. Record keeping may include: inventory control, sales quotes, expense reports, purchase orders, statements, and lots more.

3. **Know how to use popular predesigned forms.** Predesigned forms can be formatted and changed to adjust to your needs. Text boxes can have fill color added, text within text boxes can be formatted for different typefaces or font sizes, and borders or shading can be added to any element within your business forms.

4. **Understand popular forms.** Publisher is an excellent choice for designing and printing many of your necessary business forms, because creating forms in Publisher is easy. Not only are you in control of your own record keeping, but because you are also the designer, you can more easily manage how your business is represented. Forms help make your business appear more professional and will help keep your finances in order to prepare your taxes. Publisher is easy to use to design business forms and there are 350 different predesigned business forms to choose from within 10 different categories.

5. **Edit business information sets.** Editing your business information set components also helps to save time when working with business forms and other types of publications. There are seven business information component items that can be edited to quickly add commonly used information over and over within a publication. Business information component items can also be inserted individually into a predesigned publication or a blank publication.

6. **Create and edit a personal logo.** Your business forms can contain a predesigned template logo provided by Publisher, or a custom-designed logo can be formatted for different text and/or a different picture.

7. **Edit, size, and reposition a personal information component.** Most business forms have similar form elements within each publication, such as text boxes in which to type a date, a table in which information can be categorized, a place for a logo or picture, shaded elements, and different font schemes. All of the items can be edited, sized, or removed from the form.

Key Terms

Multiple Choice

1. An invoice form is used to:

   (a) Request services or supplies

   (b) Bid for jobs or outline how much services will cost the client

   (c) Bill others for services and supplies

   (d) Bill for time-based services

2. Record keeping in a business can include:

   (a) Inventory control

   (b) Sales quotes

   (c) Purchase orders

   (d) All of the above

3. Which menu contains the command to change your business information?

   (a) Insert menu

   (b) Edit menu

   (c) Tools menu

   (d) Arrange Window

4. What happens when you delete a logo from a publication?

   (a) A dialog box appears asking if you really want to delete the logo.

   (b) A dialog box appears prompting you to switch to a design that does not include a logo.

   (c) The logo just gets deleted.

   (d) None of the above.

5. Which command will increase the font size of your selected text to the next font size?

   (a) Ctrl+Shift+>

   (b) Ctrl+Shift+<

   (c) Ctrl+]

   (d) Ctrl+[

6. Which command, in the Format Publication task pane, will allow you to quickly change the design of your publication?

   (a) Page Options

   (b) Template

   (c) Color Schemes

   (d) Font Schemes

7. What are the main business information sets?

   (a) Primary Business, Secondary Business

   (b) Other Organization, Home/Family

   (c) All of the above

   (d) None of the above

8. The Print Screen button on your keyboard allows you to:

   (a) Capture a screen shot for use in another publication

   (b) Automatically print the publication you are working on

   (c) Automatically print a picture of the view on your monitor

   (d) None of the above

9. Which category is not included in business information sets?

   (a) Name

   (b) Address

   (c) Tag Line or Motto

   (d) Font Scheme

10. What can you do to a business information component once it is placed in the publication?

    (a) Nothing, it has to stay the way it is

    (b) Edit or resize the component

    (c) Move the component someplace else in the publication

    (d) Both (b) and (c)

11. What happens when you select a color scheme in your personal information?

    (a) The color scheme is applied only to that publication.

    (b) The color scheme will be applied to all future publications.

    (c) The color scheme will only be applied if you tell Publisher to apply the color scheme.

    (d) None of the above.

12. What is the first step to synchronize the data in your business information?

    (a) Click on the User Tab.

    (b) Select the Tools menu.

    (c) Click Automatically synchronize formatting.

    (d) Select the Options command.

13. In order to activate the logo picture you must:

    (a) Click on the logo once.

    (b) Click on the small picture within the logo.

    (c) Both (a) and (b).

    (d) Neither (a) nor (b).

14. A form does not include which of the following?

    (a) Text boxes to type in

    (b) A place for a logo or picture

    (c) Page numbers

    (d) Shaded elements

15. Why is using Publisher an excellent choice for designing and printing your business forms?

    (a) It is easy to use.

    (b) You are in control of your own record keeping.

    (c) You are your own designer.

    (d) All of the above.

16. When working in a table, what will happen when you press the Tab key?

    (a) Your typing will be indented.

    (b) The cursor will move between cells within the table.

    (c) Nothing.

    (d) The information in the cell will be deleted.

17. How is each of the core components of your business information inserted into the publication?

    (a) Separately.

    (b) You can insert each component only once.

    (c) You can combine components.

    (d) Two at a time.

18. Which shortcut will display the entire page of the publication you are designing?

    (a) Ctrl+Shift+L

    (b) Ctrl+L

    (c) Ctrl+Shift

    (d) Ctrl+Z

Practice Exercises

1 Inventory Form

All business owners, and individuals, for that matter, should keep track of their inventory items. It is too easy to misplace paperwork and warranty information years after a purchase. Getting into the habit of recording this information so that you can have it readily available will save time and money if the equipment breaks. In this exercise, you will practice with an already existing inventory list form. You will add text, replace default text, replace the logo image, and change the formatting of the publication using Figure 3.35 as a guide.

a. Start Publisher. Open the *chap3_pe1_inventory* publication and save it as **chap3_pe1_inventory_solution**.

b. Select the default text **Check/P.O. #** and change it to **Check #**.

c. Select the **Value** default text and change it to **Amount**.

d. Enter the following purchases on the inventory form:

Date Purchased	Check #	Purchased From	Description	Serial Number	Warranty	Amount
April 9, 2009	Ck#445	Best Computer	Notebook Computer	11122233344	5 Years	1999.00
April 9, 2009	Ck#445	Best Computer	Notebook Computer	11122233346	5 Years	1999.00
April 9, 2009	Ck#445	Best Computer	Notebook Computer	11122233347	5 Years	1999.00
April 9, 2009	Ck#446	Circuit Buy	Printer	0000000001	3 years	399.00
April 9, 2009	Ck#446	Circuit Buy	Printer	0000000002	3 years	399.99

e. Select the following row and click Bold on the Formatting toolbar:

Date Purchased	Check #	Purchased From	Description	Serial Number	Warranty	Amount

f. Enter the total **6795.00**, as shown in Figure 3.35.

g. Click your mouse in front of the total 6795.00 and from the **Insert menu** and **Symbol command**, insert a **$ sign**.

h. Add a $ sign to each of the individual amounts on the inventory form as well.

i. You can also just type the $ sign. We just wanted to show you how to use the Symbols dialog box for this practice exercise.

j. Click in the text box that reads *Inventory List* and click the **Center button** on the Formatting toolbar.

k. Click in the **name and address text box** and change the fill color to **light gray** with **30%** transparency, as shown in Figure 3.35.

l. Apply the same fill color and transparency format to the Inventory List text box.

m. Highlight the **Total text boxes** and change the fill color to **yellow** with **30%** transparency.

n. Change the logo icon image to match Figure 3.35.

o. Save the publication.

...continued on Next Page

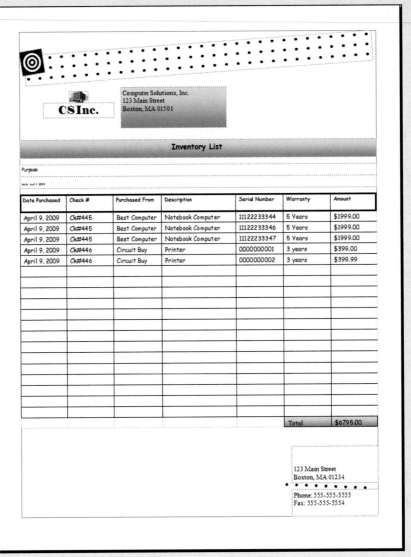

Figure 3.35 Inventory Form

2 Changing Publication Design

Your supervisor has decided to change the look of all the business forms. You decide to help him with this task and begin by changing the design of the statement publication first, making sure that the old elements fit in with the new design. Use Figure 3.36 as a guide.

a. Start Publisher. Open the *chap3_pe2_statement* publication from the student disk and save it as **chap3_pe2_statement_solution**.

b. From the Format Publication task pane, click to change the template design to the **Axis Statement gallery type**.

Be sure to apply the new template to the current publication.

c. Click to select the **Business name text** and change the font to **Franklin Gothic Book, 20 pt**.

d. Enter the following statement items:

...continued on Next Page

Date	Type	Invoice #	Description	Amount	Payment	Balance
4/15/09	Consumer	123444	Repair to Server	$150.00	$0.00	$150.00
4/17/09	Consumer	123445	Repair to PC	$30.00	$0.00	$30.00
4/30/09	Consumer	123446	Software Upgrade—Labor	$80.00	$0.00	$80.00
4/30/09	Consumer	123447	Software Upgrade—Software	$135.00	$0.00	$135.00

   e. Enter the total **$395.00** in the **Total text box**.

   f. Click to select and enlarge the text **Please include the Statement # on your check** to a **9 pt font**, **bold**. If necessary, resize the text box.

   g. From the Objects toolbar, click to draw out and add text boxes next to the Statement #, Date, and Customer #, and then add the information.

   h. Format the font for the Statement #, Date, and Customer ID to **7 pt**, **Franklin Gothic Book** to match the rest of the statement form items, as shown in Figure 3.36. If necessary, resize the text box.

   i. Change the color of the Business Name box to a **light blue** with **30%** transparency, as shown in Figure 3.36.

   j. Change the address and phone information font to **9 pt**, **Franklin Gothic Book**.

   k. Change the text on the lower text box on the form to read: **Please contact us at the numbers to the left if you have any questions!**

   l. Click the **Background command** from the **Format menu** and change the background color of the publication to a **light gray gradient fill (horizontal)**, as shown in Figure 3.36.

TROUBLESHOOTING: When you do this, some of the text boxes may also then have the gray background now. If this did happen, change each of the text boxes to a white fill color to match that shown in Figure 3.36.

   m. Resize the address and phone information text boxes to eliminate excess white space in the publication.

   n. Format the total text box to **yellow** with **30%** transparency, as shown in Figure 3.36.

   o. Change the logo image and choose **no fill color** to match that shown in Figure 3.36.

   p. Ungroup the logo image from the logo text and enlarge the logo image.

   q. Regroup the logo image and the logo text.

   r. Save the publication.

...continued on Next Page

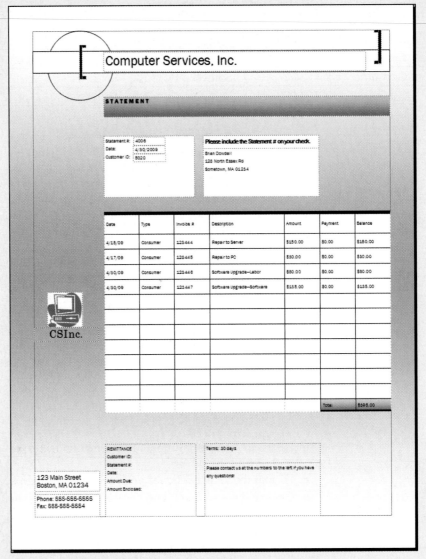

Figure 3.36 Statement Form

3 Weekly Records

The exercises in this chapter have dealt with a number of businesses and several different types of forms. You have already designed a billing statement and inventory list for CSInc., and in this exercise, you will create a weekly record for CSInc.'s employees to use. Your goal is to have similarity between the publications. This consistency promotes a good image. You will start with a predesigned weekly record form and then add text and a logo, and format the publication using Figure 3.37 as a guide.

    a. If necessary, open Publisher.

    b. Under the Business Forms task pane, click to select the **Axis design** from Weekly Record gallery.

    c. Save the publication as **chap3_pe3_weekly_record_solution**.

    d. Click in the **Business Name text box** and type the full name of the business, **Computer Services, Inc.**, at the top of the form and format the font to **Franklin Gothic Book, 20 pt**.

    e. Select the text **Weekly Time Record** and change the font to **Franklin Gothic book, 11 pt**.

    f. From the Objects toolbar, click to draw out and add text boxes for the employee, manager, phone, e-mail, and Tax ID, and then fill in the information as shown in Figure 3.37.

    g. Change the font for these items to **Franklin Gothic Book, 9 pt**.

    h. Enter the following weekly times and hours, which includes 8 hours of Saturday overtime:

...continued on Next Page

Day	In	Out	In	Out	Regular Hours	Overtime Hours	Sick	Vacation
Monday – Friday	8:30am	12:30pm	1:30pm	5:30pm	40	0	0	0
Saturday	8:30am	12:30pm	1:30pm	5:30pm	0	8	0	0

i. Enter the regular rate at **$18.00** per hour and **$27.00** per hour overtime.

j. Enter all the totals as shown in Figure 3.37.

k. Change the font for the entire form to **Franklin Gothic Book** and increase the point size to the next point size up. If necessary, resize the table columns.

l. Change the background color of the publication to **light gray gradient fill (horizontal)**, as shown in Figure 3.37.

When you do this, some of the text boxes will also then have the gray background. Change these text boxes to a white background to match Figure 3.37.

m. Format the color of the Weekly Time Record text box to a **light blue** with a **30%** transparency.

n. Format the color of the Total to **yellow** with **30%** transparency.

o. Add the address and phone information to the two left text boxes, as shown in Figure 3.37. If necessary, change the Line Spacing to **0 pt** from the **Paragraph command** on the **Format menu**.

p. Change the logo image to match that shown in Figure 3.37 and resize the image.

q. Add the logo text to match that shown in Figure 3.37.

r. Save the publication.

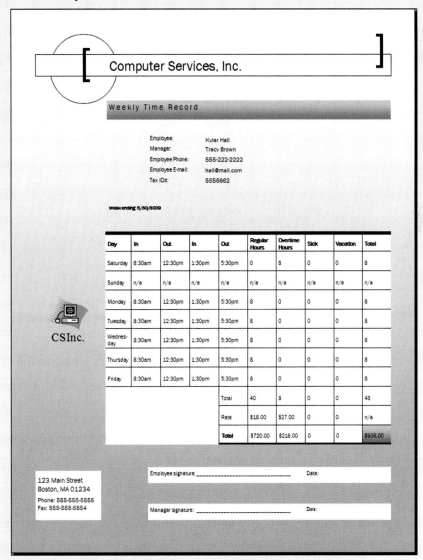

Figure 3.37 Weekly Form

...continued on Next Page

CSInc. needs a new fax form to add to their collection of forms. In this exercise, you will design a new fax form for CSInc. to match the previously created forms. You will work with a predesigned fax form gallery template to begin, using Figure 3.38 as a guide.

a. If necessary, open Publisher.

b. From the Publication Types task pane, choose the **Axis Fax Cover design gallery template**. If default Business Information fills in, do not worry. We will edit the text next.

c. Save the Publication as **chap3_pe4_fax_solution**.

d. Click in the business name text box at the top of the form and add the business full name, **Computer Services, Inc.**

e. Change the business name font to **20 pt** size.

We will leave the font style Times New Roman since this is a common fax transmittal font style.

f. Add the address and phone information to the two left text boxes, as shown in Figure 3.38. If necessary, change the Line Spacing to **0 pt** from the **Paragraph command** on the **Format menu** and adjust the height of the text boxes to get rid of white space.

g. Change the logo image to match that shown in Figure 3.38 and resize the image.

h. Add the logo text to match that shown in Figure 3.38.

i. Click on the picture and from the Picture toolbar, change the color to black and white. Colors are not necessary for electronic fax transmission.

j. Change the background color of the publication to **light gray gradient fill (horizontal)**, as shown in Figure 3.38.

When you do this, some of the text boxes will also then have the gray background. Change these text boxes to a white background to match Figure 3.38.

k. Format the color of the Fax Transmittal Form text box to a **light gray** with a **30%** transparency.

l. Save the publication.

...continued on Next Page

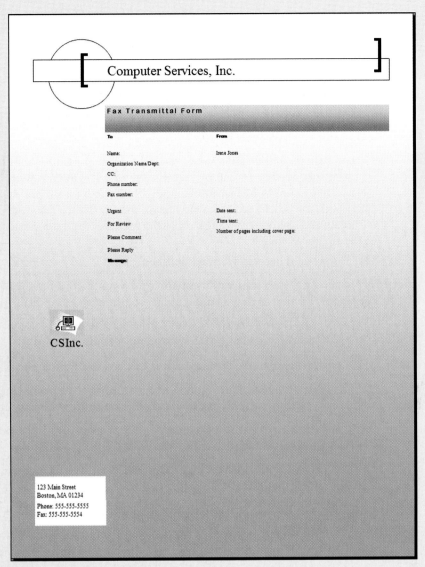

Figure 3.38 Fax Form

...continued on Next Page

It is springtime and you just opened up your own landscaping business. You have just enough financing to buy the needed yard equipment, such as lawn mowers and all the needed gardening tools. You also have just enough start-up money to purchase supplies for six clients, such as sod, flowers, bushes, and mulch. Your first potential customer has requested a quote for a spring cleanup, which would include some planting. If she is happy with your quote and the work, she will have you back for weekly lawn service over the summer months. Your tax man suggested that you keep very organized and accurate records. He said it will help with filing taxes each year. You have decided to use Publisher to maintain all business forms. You have a new computer and a color printer, so you can add some nice detail. Your task is to create a quote form to give to your first customer and also one that can be used over and over for future customers using Figure 3.39 as a guide.

a. If necessary, open Publisher.

b. Open the Cascade quote form from the Business Forms gallery and save the publication as **chap3_mid1_quote_solution**.

c. Type the business name, **Brian's Landscaping**, at the top of the quote and change the font to **Albertus Extra Bold** (or other font), **20 pt**.

d. Format the Business Name text box to a **light green** fill color with a **30%** transparency.

e. Type the address and phone information as shown in Figure 3.39 and change the font to **Albertus Extra Bold** (or other font), **10 pt**. Change the line spacing to **0 pt**.

f. Ungroup the logo image and change, resize, and reposition the image logo to match that shown in Figure 3.39.

g. Add the logo text, **The Green Keeper**, and change the font to **Albertus Extra Bold** (or other font).

The font size will change to fit into the logo text box as you type.

h. Change the font of the text *Quotation* to **Albertus Extra Bold** (or other font), **14 pt** and format the text box to a **light green** color with **30%** transparency.

i. Add the customer name and address and change the font to **Albertus Extra Bold** (or other font), **9 pt** to match with the above.

j. Add the three text boxes for quote #, date, and customer ID and fill in that information. Change the font to **Albertus Extra Bold** (or other font), **9 pt**.

k. Type the quote form information as shown and change the font to **Albertus Extra Bold** (or other font), **8 pt**:

Your Order #	Our Order #	Sales Rep.	FOB	Ship Via	Terms	Tax ID	Proposed Shipping Date
1	1	Brian	n/a	n/a	30 days	2223336	4/30/09

l. Type the individual quote items as shown and change the font to **Albertus Extra Bold** (or other font), **8 pt**:

...continued on Next Page

Quantity	Item	Units	Description	Discount %	Taxable	Unit Price	Total
1 Case	Pansies	10	Plant	10%	Included	$25.00	$25.00
1 Case	Violas	10	Plant	10%	Included	$30.00	$30.00
2 Cases	Perennials	20	Plant	10%	Included	$25.00	$50.00
1 Case	Azalea Bush	4	Plant	10%	Included	$40.00	$40.00
1	Yard Cleanup	n/a	Labor	10%	n/a	$100.00	$100.00
1	Mow Grass	n/a	Labor	10%	n/a	$75.00	$75.00

m. If necessary, adjust any column sizes.

n. Type the subtotal, discount, and final total numbers as shown in Figure 3.39.

o. Add a **yellow** fill color with **30%** transparency to the final total, as shown in Figure 3.39.

p. Type the quote details as shown at the bottom of the form.

q. Save the publication.

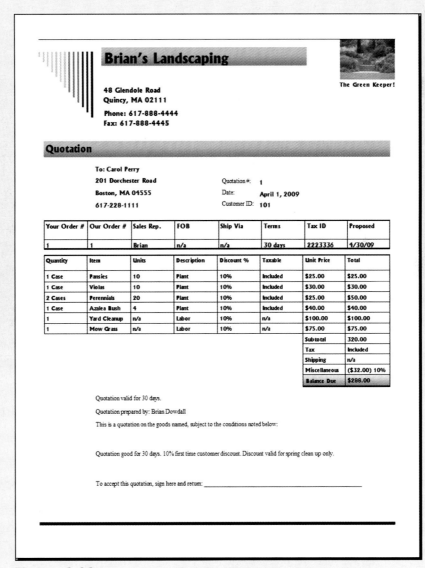

Figure 3.39 Brian's Landscaping Quote

...continued on Next Page

You did such a great job on Carol's spring cleanup that she hired you for the summer. You have been mowing her grass for a month now and it is time to request payment. Your task is to create a billing statement to send to her and to other future customers. You want the billing statement to match the quote form that you sent her. Using Figure 3.40 as a guide, you will add text, change the logo, and apply the same formatting used for the Quotation form in Mid-Level Exercise 1.

a. If necessary, open Publisher, and then choose the Cascade Statement form from the Business Forms gallery.

b. Save the publication as **chap3_mid2_statement_solution**.

c. Type the business name at the top of the statement form, as shown in Figure 3.40.

d. Change the logo to match that shown in Figure 3.40.

e. Type the business address and phone information.

f. Type the customer name, address, and phone information.

g. Change the text *Invoice* # on the weekly services to **Quote #**.

h. Type the weekly services as shown:

Date	Type	Quote #	Description	Amount	Payment	Balance
4/6/2009	Labor	1	Mow Lawn	$75.00	$0.00	$75.00
4/13/2009	Labor	1	Mow Lawn	$75.00	$0.00	$75.00
4/20/2009	Labor	1	Mow Lawn	$75.00	$0.00	$75.00
4/27/2009	Labor	1	Mow Lawn	$75.00	$0.00	$75.00

i. Type the total at the bottom of the services, as shown in Figure 3.40.

j. Add the statement details at the bottom of the form.

k. Change all fonts to **Albertus Extra Bold** (or other font) and the font size to **8.8 pt** to match Figure 3.40.

l. Change the fill color and transparency on all text boxes to match Figure 3.40.

m. Save the publication.

...continued on Next Page

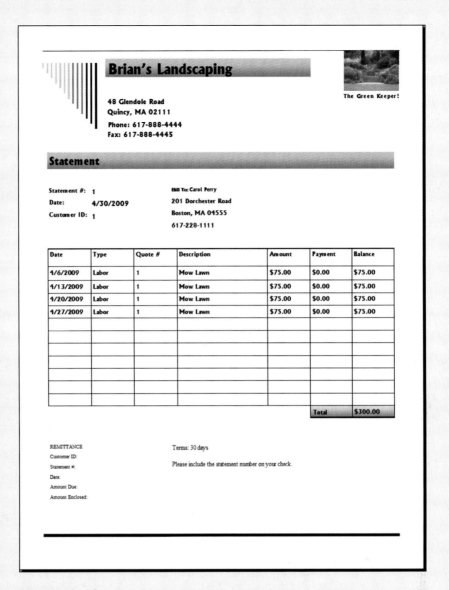

Figure 3.40 Brian's Landscaping Statement

3 Conference Expenses

Tri-County Real Estate has been in business for a little over a year now. The broker, Terry Brown, worked for another real estate agent for 15 years and then decided to open his own business. He has six real estate agents working for him at this time. He has decided to send his top real estate agent, Irene Jones, to the National Real Estate Conference in June 2009. This is a pretty big conference and the agents return with great new sales ideas, marketing strategies, financial forecasting, and much more. This is the first conference since Terry opened his broker's agency; thus, he does not have a method for his agents to report expenses. Your task is to create an expense report that Terry can use over and over for future reporting and to include all of Irene's business expenses from this first conference held in New York City. Use Figure 3.41 as a guide while creating this form.

  a. If necessary, open Publisher.

  b. Select the Borders Expense form from the Business Forms on the Publications Types task pane.

  c. Save the form as **chap3_mid3_expense_solution**.

  d. Add the business name and address as shown in Figure 3.41.

...continued on Next Page

e. Change the font size for the business name to **20 pt** font. Adjust the text box if necessary.

f. Add the Employee, Department, To:, and From: information text boxes as shown in Figure 3.41.

g. Change the logo image and text to match that shown in Figure 3.41.

h. Add the following expenses:

Date	Description	Transportation/Mileage	Lodging	Meals
6/1/2009	Delta Airlines	$199.00	n/a	$75.00
6/1/2009	Hilton New York	n/a	$375.00	$147.00
6/2/2009	Hilton New York	n/a	$375.00	$138.00
6/3/2009	Hilton New York	n/a	$375.00	$80.00
6/4/2009	Delta Airlines	$199.00	n/a	$45.00

i. Be sure to include the following entertainment expenses:

Date	Person(s) Entertained	Title	Business Purpose	Name of Place	Total
6/1/2009	Kevin Hall	Regional Broker	Sales Meeting	Hilton Restaurant	$147.00
6/2/2009	Chad Barfoot	Sales Broker	Sales Meeting	Hilton Restaurant	$138.00

j. Enter n/a for all appropriate areas, as shown in Figure 3.41.

k. Enter all totals where appropriate, as shown in Figure 3.41.

l. Add a **light yellow** fill color to the two totals.

m. Change the color scheme from the task pane to **Civic**.

n. Save the publication.

...continued on Next Page

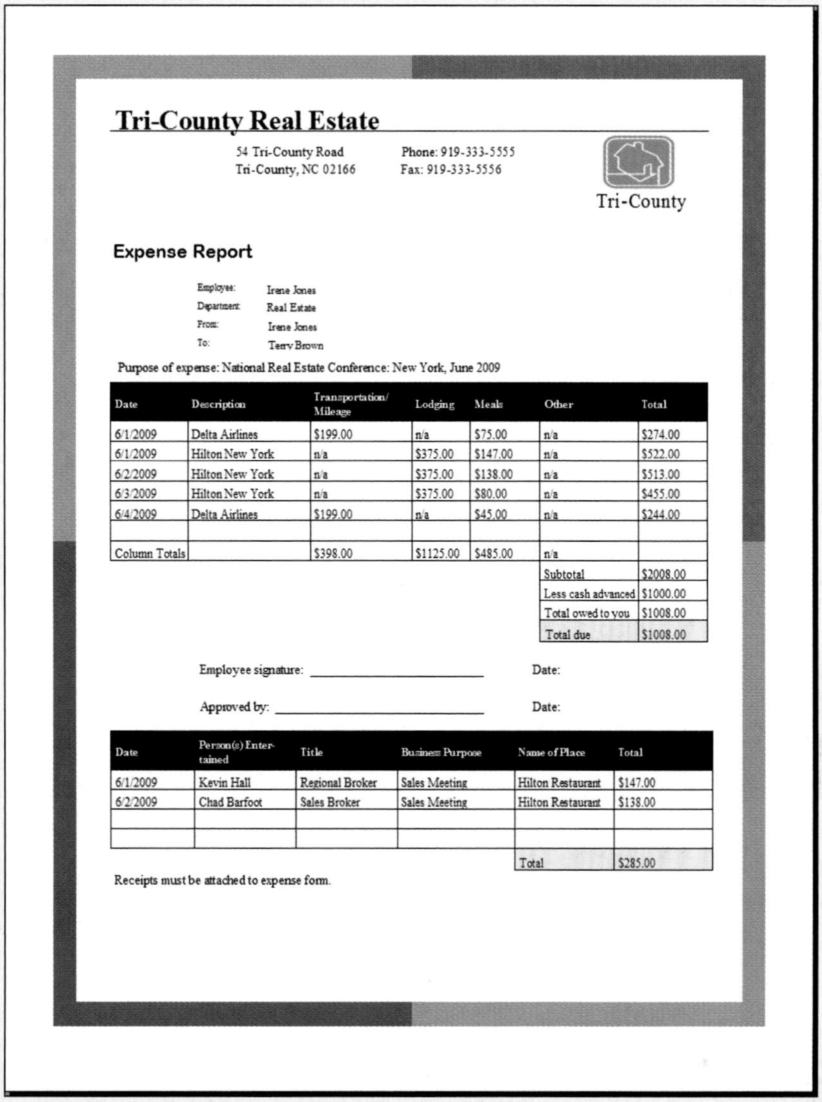

Tri-County Real Estate

54 Tri-County Road
Tri-County, NC 02166

Phone: 919-333-5555
Fax: 919-333-5556

Tri-County

Expense Report

Employee: Irene Jones
Department: Real Estate
From: Irene Jones
To: Terry Brown

Purpose of expense: National Real Estate Conference: New York, June 2009

Date	Description	Transportation/ Mileage	Lodging	Meals	Other	Total
6/1/2009	Delta Airlines	$199.00	n/a	$75.00	n/a	$274.00
6/1/2009	Hilton New York	n/a	$375.00	$147.00	n/a	$522.00
6/2/2009	Hilton New York	n/a	$375.00	$138.00	n/a	$513.00
6/3/2009	Hilton New York	n/a	$375.00	$80.00	n/a	$455.00
6/4/2009	Delta Airlines	$199.00	n/a	$45.00	n/a	$244.00
Column Totals		$398.00	$1125.00	$485.00	n/a	

Subtotal	$2008.00
Less cash advanced	$1000.00
Total owed to you	$1008.00
Total due	$1008.00

Employee signature: _____   Date: _____

Approved by: _____   Date: _____

Date	Person(s) Entertained	Title	Business Purpose	Name of Place	Total
6/1/2009	Kevin Hall	Regional Broker	Sales Meeting	Hilton Restaurant	$147.00
6/2/2009	Chad Barfoot	Sales Broker	Sales Meeting	Hilton Restaurant	$138.00
				Total	$285.00

Receipts must be attached to expense form.

Figure 3.41 Tri-County Expense Form

Capstone Exercise

You are taking a summer job at a small convenience store down the street called Johnson's. Both Mr. and Mrs. Johnson do not have computer skills and keep their books by hand. You offer to set up a few templates for them to input their information quickly. They use inventory lists, invoices, and purchase orders most frequently. Your task is to set up a business information set that can be used to quickly create these forms. You plan to teach the Johnsons how to do this so that when you leave after the summer they can continue using Publisher to create additional business forms.

You will need the following information to set up a new business information set:

Johnsons, Owners
1 Main Street
Melrose, MA 02176
Phone: 781-555-1234
Fax: 781-555-6789
E-mail: johnsons@food.com

Inventory List

a. If necessary, open Publisher.

b. From the Business Form Publication Types task pane, open the Accent Box Inventory form.

c. From the **Edit menu**, open the **Business Information Set dialog box**.

d. Select New to create a new business information set for Johnson's.

e. Add the business name, title, and organization name where appropriate.

f. Enter the organization's address and other contact information.

g. Click to save the business information set.

h. Click to update the current publication.

i. Edit the organization logo by adding the business name to the Logo text box and also changing the image to something more appropriate.

j. Include a few examples of something that would be found on their Inventory List, such as milk and bread.

k. Change any of the font point sizes and change the color scheme to black.

l. Save the publication as **chap3_cap_inventory_ solution**.

Invoice

a. From the Business Forms Invoice gallery, open the **Accent Box invoice**.

b. From the **Edit menu**, update the business information set.

c. From the **Insert menu, Business Information command**, insert the information into the Invoice, Bill To: and Ship To: boxes.

d. Include example(s) of something that would be found on the invoice.

e. Change any font point sizes and change the color scheme to **black**.

f. Edit the organization logo by adding the business name to the Logo text box and also changing the image to something more appropriate to match the inventory list.

g. Type any of the additional information where appropriate such as dates, customer ID#s, and Invoice number.

h. Save the publication as **chap3_cap_invoice_ solution**.

Purchase Order

a. From the Business Forms Purchase Order gallery, open the Accent Box Purchase Order form.

b. From the **Edit menu**, update the business information set.

c. From the **Insert menu**, insert the information into the Bill To: and Ship To: boxes.

d. Change any font point sizes and change the color scheme to **black**.

e. Edit the organization logo by adding the business name to the Logo text box and also changing the image to something more appropriate to match the inventory list.

f. Type any sample additional information where appropriate.

g. Save the publication as **chap3_cap_po_solution**.

Mini Cases

Use the rubric following the case as a guide to evaluate your work, but keep in mind that your instructor may impose additional grading criteria or use a different standard to judge your work.

Consulting Firm

GENERAL CASE

You're an employee at a consulting firm. Before you can get your paycheck, you must fill out your timecard. Using the template file *chap3_mc1_weekly*, you will fill in the weekly hours that you worked. You have worked over 40 hours this week at a rate of $10.00 per hour, which included 3 hours each of overtime on Saturday, Sunday, Tuesday, and Thursday, so you qualify for overtime pay. You also took a vacation day on Monday, so include that in your timecard. Save the publication as **chap3_mc1_weekly_solution**.

Performance Elements	Exceeds Expectations	Meets Expectations	Below Expectations
Hours	Set up hours as directed.	Set up most of the hours.	Did not set up any hours.
Format	No errors in format.	A few errors.	Many errors in format.
Information	All information included.	Most company information included.	Forgot company information.

Accounts Financial Statements

RESEARCH CASE

Using the Internet, research commonly used accounts, such as: Accounts Receivable, Supplies, Accounts Payable, Sales Revenue, Advertising Expense, and Supplies Expense. Using the Publisher template *chap3_mc2_accounts*, enter the account names that you found on the Internet, and then check off the appropriate box where the "normal balance" of the account is located. The normal balance is the debit or credit amount that increases or decreases the balance in the account. Cash has already been done for you as an example. Save the Publisher file as **chap3_mc2_accounts_solution**.

Performance Elements	Exceeds Expectations	Meets Expectations	Below Expectations
Chart of accounts	Multiple accounts for each portion of the statement.	At least one debit and credit account in both the Balance Sheet and the Income Statement.	Some portions of the statements do not have any accounts.
Variety of accounts	Large variety, specific accounts.	Several, commonly used accounts.	Little variety, very few accounts.

Burke's Antiques

DISASTER RECOVERY

You are working for a store that sells antiques; the collection ranges from cameras to furniture to cars. The owner of Burke's Antiques, Mr. Burke, has designed a simple flyer to place around town advertising the store. He is concerned, however, that when he prints the flyer the blue lines under the address and telephone numbers will be printed also. You explain to him that the blue lines will not print and you also explain to him that he can use the Print Preview command to see exactly what the flyer will look like after he prints it out on his color printer. He still does not like the little blue lines under the text and asks you to show him how to remove them. Using the file *chap3_mc3_antiques*, show Mr Burke how to remove the blue lines using the Command button drop down, Convert to Plain Text command, after he types the address and phone information. Also, using WordArt change the company name to the name of his store. Save the file as **chap3_mc3_antiques_solution**. Send this file electronically to your instructor so she/he can see that the blue lines have been removed.

Performance Elements	Exceeds Expectations	Meets Expectations	Below Expectations
Information	Creative title, all required information.	Required information, title.	Missing information.
Blue lines	No longer appear.	No longer appear on either the address or the phone but not both.	Still appear.

Online Publishing: Creating a Web Site

Objectives

After you read this chapter, you will be able to:

1. Understand Web site basics **(page 159)**.

2. Understand copyright issues **(page 159)**.

3. Use the Easy Web Site Builder **(page 160)**.

4. Send a publication by e-mail **(page 174)**.

5. Create an electronic form **(page 182)**.

6. Understand Web form control properties **(page 182)**.

Hands-On Exercises

Exercises	Skills Covered
1. OUR FIRST WEB SITE (page 162) **Open:** Predesigned Template **Save as:** chap4_ho1_pilates_and_yoga_solution	• Choose an Easy Web Site Builder • Choose Your Web Site Goals • Change Your Business Information Set • Add Content to Your Home Page • Change the Picture and Delete the Logo • Change the Background Color • Format Fill Colors • Design Page Two • Design the Remaining Pages • Preview Your Web Site in Internet Explorer
2. E-MAIL A WEB PUBLICATION (page 175) **Open:** chap4_ho2_e-mail **Save as:** chap4_ho2_e-mail_solution	• Open a Publication • Change the Background • Choose a Different Color Scheme • Format Fill Color and Fill Effects • Preview the E-Mail Publication • Send the Publication as an E-Mail • View the E-Mail
3. CUSTOMIZING A WEB SITE (page 184) **Open:** chap4_ho1_pilates_and_yoga_solution **Save as:** chap4_ho3_form_solution	• Open an Existing Web Publication • Add Background Sound to the Home Page • Preview the Background Sound • Add a Hyperlink • Add a New Blank Web Page • Create an Electronic Web Form • Set the List Box Form Controls • Finish Customizing Your E-Form

CASE STUDY

Time to Get Online!

Case Study

Tracy Darpen opened a new Pilates and Yoga fitness studio six months ago, and she has been building membership through word of mouth and by handing out flyers since then. Tracy has decided that she would also like to build and maintain a Web site, posting her Web site with her local Internet Service Provider. After asking around about the costs of having someone design her Web site, Tracy realized that she does not have the funds to pay someone to design and create her Web site.

However, Tracy remembered that she owns the Microsoft Publisher program that came with her new computer. She already knows how to use Microsoft Word, the Internet, and e-mail, so Tracy decides to check out the Publisher program. Her Internet Service Provider assured her that they will help her get her Web site up and running after she produces the Web pages. They also told Tracy they would give her a quick tutor session on how to FTP updated pages as she needs to make changes, instead of relying on them to do so. After a few days of investigating Publisher, Tracy decides to design and create her own Web site.

Your Assignment

- Read Chapter 4, paying special attention to the information on the Easy Web Site Builder.
- Think about how Tracy could design a new Web site for her Pilates and Yoga Studio.
- Be sure to consider how Tracy could use Publisher to build her Web site either using a template or building from scratch.
- Design a new Web site using the predesigned easy builder templates that include:
  - The name and description of her business
  - A description of her classes
  - A schedule
  - An e-mail contact
  - A new logo
  - Her business address

Online Publishing

In today's economy, and with the prevalence of technology, many businesses can now use the Internet to provide information, to advertise, and to present their business in a professional-looking manner. Because the Internet is so popular, it is an ideal tool to support and market services and products. After a company's Web site has been created, people will find out about it in various ways. Some will read the URL address on a business card or flyer. Others will see your Web site when scanning the yellow pages. Some may find it just by searching the Internet or through word of mouth. In this high-tech world, it would be uncommon to find a business without a Web site.

> (Because the Internet is so popular, it is an ideal tool to support and market services and products.)

Understanding Web Site Basics

The **Internet** is a network of networks that connects computers anywhere in the world.

The **World Wide Web** (**WWW**, or simply, the Web) is a very large subset of the Internet.

Hyperlinks provide a link to other Web pages, documents, images, and more on the Internet.

HyperText Markup Language (HTML) is a markup language that describes how text, graphics, and/or other items will look when viewed as a Web page.

Markup codes (tags) placed before and/or after the text or graphics describe how the page should appear when viewed in a browser.

The Internet and World Wide Web have changed society. Perhaps you are already familiar with the basic concepts that underlie the Internet, but a brief review is in order. The *Internet* is a network of networks that connects computers anywhere in the world. The *World Wide Web* (*WWW*, or simply, the Web) is a very large subset of the Internet, consisting of those computers that store a special type of document known as a Web page.

The interesting thing about a Web page is that it contains references called *hyperlinks* to other Web pages, which may in turn be stored on different computers, located anywhere in the world. Therein lies the power of the Web: it provides users with the ability to click on link after link and move effortlessly from one document to the next.

Web pages are currently developed in a special language called *HyperText Markup Language (HTML)*. HTML is a markup language that describes how text, graphics, and/or other items will look when viewed as a Web page. A set of *markup codes* (tags) placed before and/or after the text or graphics describes how the page should appear when viewed in a browser. HTML tells the browser, such as Internet Explorer, how to display the page(s). For instance, the set of tags <b></b> typed around the word happy (i.e., <b>Happy</b>) would tell the browser to show the word in bold text. Placing <i></i> around the word would display italicized text. What do you think the browser would display if you placed a <u></u> around the word? If you guessed underline, then you are already starting to comprehend basic HTML.

Initially, the only way to create a Web page was to learn HTML. However, Microsoft Publisher and a number of other programs simplified the process because you can create Web pages by using several methods. Publisher enables you to use the Easy Web Site Builder with the predesigned templates or do it from scratch. Microsoft Publisher generates the HTML statements for you so that you can continue to enter text and/or change the formatting just like any other type of publication.

Understanding Copyright Issues

A **copyright** provides legal protection for a written or artistic work.

Because you will be working with the Internet and possibly placing your files on a Web server, a review of copyright information is necessary. Also, if you plan to download anything from the Internet to use on your pages, a review will be helpful. A *copyright* provides legal protection for a written or artistic work, including literary, dramatic, musical, and artistic works such as poetry, novels, movies, songs, computer software, and architecture. It gives the author of a work the exclusive right to the use and duplication of that work. A copyright does not, however, protect facts, ideas, systems, or methods of operation, although it may protect the way these things are expressed.

(Does copyright protection prevent you from quoting a document found on the Web in a research paper?)

Infringement (of a copyright) occurs any time a right reserved by the copyright owner is violated without permission of the owner.

The **public domain** gives everyone the right to freely reproduce and distribute the material.

A **fair use** policy gives permission to use a portion of a work for educational, nonprofit purposes, or for the purpose of critical review or commentary.

Software piracy is the unauthorized duplication or use of software products such as Microsoft Office.

The **Easy Web Site Builder** helps you to organize your Web site.

The following copyright concepts affect what a person can use on a Web site. The owner of the copyright may sell or give up a portion of his or her rights. For example, an author may give distribution rights to a publisher and/or grant movie rights to a studio. *Infringemen (of a copyright)* occurs any time a right reserved by the copyright owner is violated without permission of the owner. Anything on the Internet should be considered copyrighted unless the document specifically says it is in the *public domain*, in which case the author is giving everyone the right to freely reproduce and distribute the material. Does copyright protection prevent you from quoting a document found on the Web in a research paper? Does copyright protection imply that you cannot download an image for inclusion in a term paper? The answer to what you can use from the Web depends on the amount of the information you reference, as well as the intended use of that information. Facts themselves are not covered by copyright, so you can use statistical data without fear of infringement. It is considered *fair use*, and thus not an infringement of copyright, to use a portion of a work for educational, nonprofit purposes, or for the purpose of critical review or commentary. In other words, you can use a quote, downloaded image, or other information from the Web, provided you cite the original work in your footnotes and/or bibliography.

Software piracy (the unauthorized duplication or use of software products such as Microsoft Office) presents a unique problem with respect to copyright protection because of the ease with which it can be done. A program that takes years of development and costs millions of dollars can be copied in a few seconds and results in economic harm to the developer. Software piracy harms everyone in the long run, including you, the end user. It results in higher prices for legitimate licenses, reduced levels of support, and delays in the development of new software. The law imposes stiff penalties for copyright infringement. You may think that this is unduly harsh, but the intent behind the copyright law is to provide economic incentive to an artist or software developer in order that they invest the necessary resources to create the work. You should honor and respect the copyright process.

Using the Easy Web Site Builder

Microsoft Publisher provides an *Easy Web Site Builder* for creating Web pages and Web sites in a quick, efficient, and easy way. The Web Sites category from the Publication Types task pane contains the following categories: Newer Designs, Classic Designs, and Blank Sizes. Within each category there are multiple predesigned templates to choose.

Figure 4.1 displays a Web page created using the Easy Web Site Builder. The Easy Web Site Builder helps you to organize your Web site. When building it, the Studio design near the bottom of the Classic Designs category list was chosen. The process to build the site took approximately 15 minutes. Publisher predesigned templates contain placeholders for text, clip art, hyperlinks, and content-based information, as well as different formatting options, such as font and color schemes, background color, borders and shading, fill color, design elements, and more. Using the Easy Web Site Builder, the background color from the extisting template, some fonts, the clip art, and some fill colors were changed.

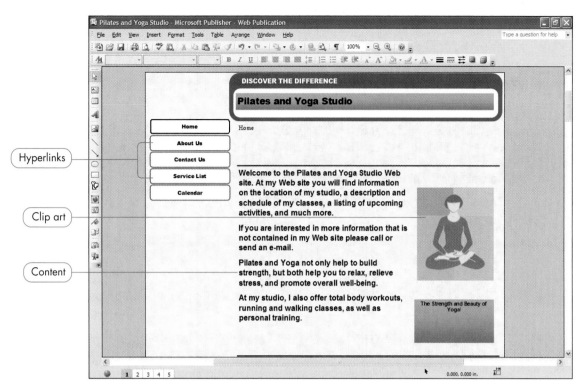

Figure 4.1 Easy Web Site Builder

Hands-On Exercises

1 | Our First Web Site

Skills covered: 1. Choose an Easy Web Site Builder **2.** Choose Your Web Site Goals **3.** Change Your Business Information Set **4.** Add Content to Your Home Page **5.** Change the Picture and Delete the Logo **6.** Change the Background Color **7.** Format Fill Colors **8.** Design Page Two **9.** Design the Remaining Pages **10.** Preview Your Web Site in Internet Explorer

---

Step 1
Choose an Easy Web Site Builder

Refer to Figure 4.2 as you complete Step 1.

a. If necessary, start Publisher.

b. Click **Web Sites** in the Publication Types task pane.

The category expands to show the types of subcategories available.

c. Scroll down in the publication preview gallery to select the **Studio Web site design** under the Classic Designs category, as shown in Figure 4.2.

d. Leave the default colors and fonts for now and click the **Create button**.

Figure 4.2 Choose an Easy Web Site Builder

Step 2
Choose Your Web Site Goals

Refer to Figure 4.3 as you complete Step 2.

After selecting the Studio Web site design and hitting the Create button, a dialog box will appear asking you to select the goals for your Web site.

a. Click in each of the following check boxes, as shown in Figure 4.3, to select the following goals for your Web site:

- Tell customers about my business
- Tell customers how to contact us

- Describe services
- Display a calendar or schedule

b. After checking each box, click **OK**.

c. Save the publication as **chap4_ho1_pilates_and_yoga_solution**.

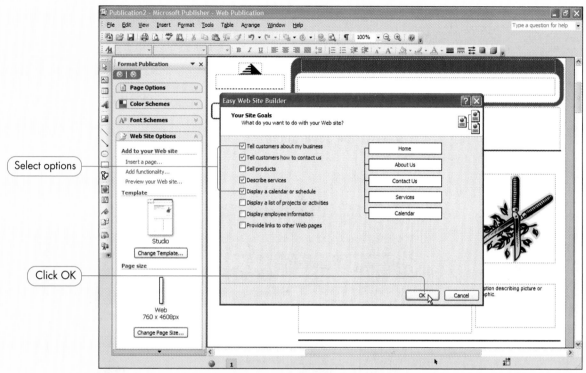

Figure 4.3 Choose Your Web Site Goals

TIP Keep It Simple

When starting to design your Web site, remember that less is sometimes more. Adding too many graphics or too much text on a site can make it difficult to read. Add only necessary information and keep the language simple. Likewise, trying to keep the content organized by using adequate white space on the page will help visitors find information. Another good rule of thumb is to avoid too much scrolling on your site. A good balance of links and scrolling will help visitors to better navigate the site.

Step 3
Change Your Business Information Set

Refer to Figure 4.4 as you complete Step 3.

a. Open the **Business Information Set dialog box** from the **Edit menu** and click the **New button**.

If there is text already entered into your Business Information Set dialog box, you will need to select the text to delete each time you replace the text.

b. In each of the categories (excluding the logo category), enter the text as shown in Figure 4.4 or enter your own information (your information does not have to match the screen in Figure 4.4), including the following:

- Individual name—Your name or the name of the person you want associated with the business information set.

- Job position or title—Your job position or title or the job positon or title of the person you want associated with the business information set.
- Organization name—Your company name.
- Address—Your company address.
- Phone, fax, and e-mail—Your company phone, fax, and e-mail.
- Tagline or motto—This would be a slogan or a business phrase that you would like to include on your publications.
- Business Information set name—Name the Business Information set to use over and over.

c. Click **Save** to save the Business Information set.

d. Click **Update** to quickly update the personal information on the pages of your Web site.

e. Save the publication.

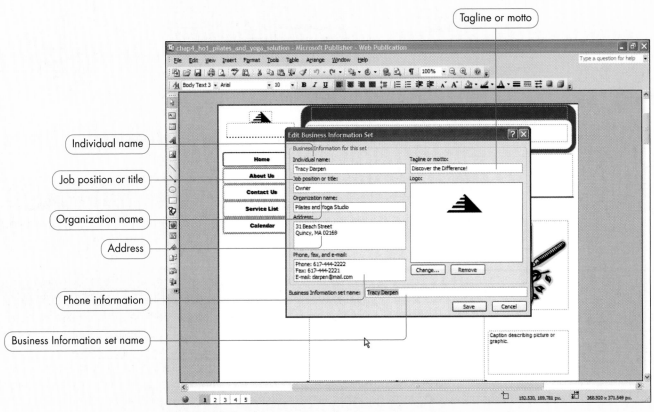

Figure 4.4 Change Your Business Information Set

Step 4

Add Content to Your Home Page

Refer to Figure 4.5 as you complete Step 4.

a. Replace the default paragraphs on the home page with the text shown in Figure 4.5. (Your text does not have to match our publication exactly.)

b. Replace the default tagline text under the picture with the different text also shown in Figure 4.5.

c. Be sure to check your publication for spelling errors by using spelling checker.

d. Select the newly typed text and format the font to **12 pt**, **Bold**.

e. Select the newly typed picture tagline text and format the font to **Bold**, **Center**.

f. Save the publication.

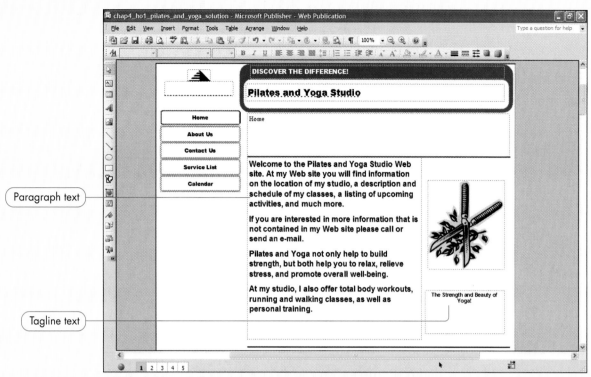

Figure 4.5 Add Content to Your Home Page

TIP   Inserting a Word Document

Microsoft Publisher and Word were designed to be used together. Everything you do to your document in Word, such as adding headers and footers or bullets and tables and applying other formatting, will convert to Publisher. To insert a Word document into your publication, click on Import Word Document in the File menu. Locate the document that you want to import, select the file name, and click OK. Using the Word Import Options in the task pane, you can make any changes you want to the document.

Step 5
Change the Picture and Delete the Logo

Refer to Figure 4.6 as you complete Step 5.

a. Right-click on the default picture, and then choose the **Change Picture**, **Clip Art command**.

The task pane will change to allow you to search for an appropriate picture.

b. Type **Yoga** in the Search for text box, and then click the **Go button**.

c. Scroll through the clip art selections to find the same clip art as in Figure 4.6 (or you may choose a different picture).

d. Click on the picture in the task pane to replace the default picture, as shown in Figure 4.6.

e. Scroll up, if necessary, so that you can see the template logo at the top of your home page. Do not worry if your logo looks different than the one in Figure 4.6.

f. Click to select the logo, and then hit **Delete** on your keyboard.

g. Save the publication.

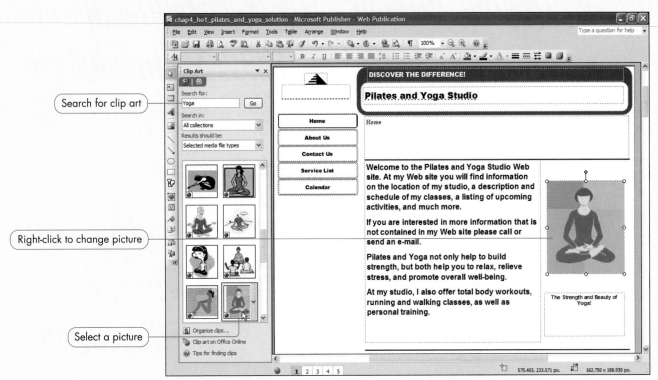

Search for clip art

Right-click to change picture

Select a picture

Figure 4.6 Change the Picture and Delete the Logo

Step 6
Change the Background Color

Refer to Figure 4.7 as you complete Step 6.

a. Choose the **Background command** from the **Format menu** to format the background.

The task pane will display different background colors and designs to choose from. Alternatively, you can choose the More Backgrounds command from the bottom of the task pane to see additional colors and designs.

b. Choose the same or similar background as that shown in Figure 4.7. (Your background does not have to match that shown in the figure exactly.)

c. Save the publication.

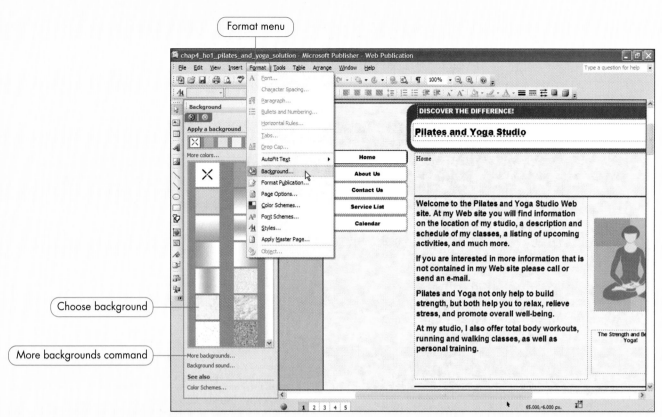

Format menu

Choose background

More backgrounds command

Figure 4.7 Change the Background Color

TIP Background Color

The colors you use on your Web site must be easy to view on the screen. If your text and background colors are too similar, they may be difficult to view. Black text on a white background is the easiest on the eye, but other color combinations can be used as well. A light pink text on a medium pink background will probably not be easy for a viewer to read.

Step 7
Format Fill Colors

Refer to Figure 4.8 as you complete Step 7.

a. If necessary, open the task pane from the **View menu**, and then choose **Orchid** from the Color Scheme options.

b. Scroll up, if necessary, to the top of your home page, and then select the text box for the business name.

c. Click on the **Fill Color button arrow**, and then select **More Fill Colors**.

d. Choose a **light purple** color, as shown in Figure 4.8, or choose any other color you wish. (Your publication does not have to match the figure exactly.)

e. Click on the **Fill Color button arrow** again, and then choose **Fill Effects**.

f. Change the transparency to **30%** and click **OK** to apply the new changes. (Your publication does not have to match Figure 4.8 exactly.)

g. Scroll to the middle of your home page, and then click on the **Picture tagline text box**.

h. Change the fill color and fill effects to match the above.

i. Scroll to the bottom of your home page, and then change the fill color and fill effects of the address and phone information to match the above.

j. Save the publication.

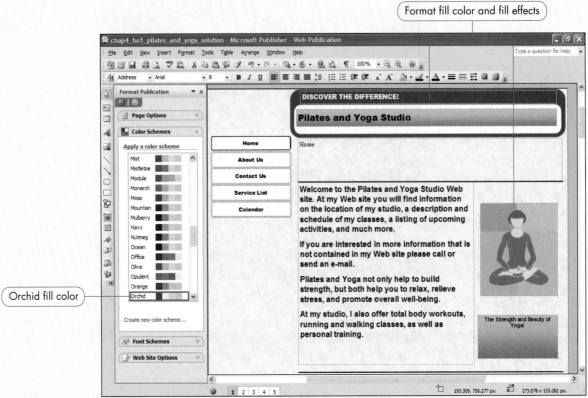

Figure 4.8 Format Fill Colors

Step 8
Design Page Two

Refer to Figure 4.9 as you complete Step 8.

a. Click on **page 2** at the bottom of your Publisher screen.

b. Replace the default paragraphs on page 2 with the text shown in Figure 4.9. (Your text does not have to match this publication exactly.)

c. Select the newly typed text and format the font to **11 pt**, **Bold**.

d. Replace the default tagline text under the picture with different text, also shown in Figure 4.9.

e. Select the newly typed picture tagline text and format the font to **Bold**, **Center**.

f. Right-click on the default picture, and then choose the **Change Picture**, **Clip Art command** to choose a more appropriate picture to match that in Figure 4.9.

g. Delete the logo picture at the top left corner of page 2.

h. Change the background using the **Format menu**, **background command** to closely match that shown in Figure 4.9.

i. Select the **Business name text box**, the **Picture tagline text box**, and the **Contact information text box** to change the fill color and fill effects to closely match that shown in Figure 4.9.

j. Save the publication.

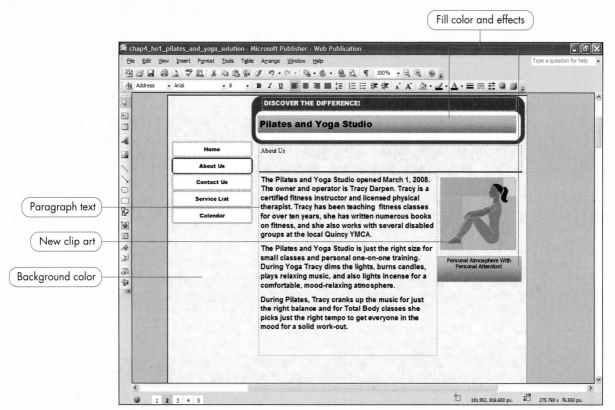

Fill color and effects

Paragraph text

New clip art

Background color

Figure 4.9 Design Page Two

Refer to Figures 4.10, 4.11, and 4.12 as you complete Step 9.

a. Click on each of the remaining three pages to make the following changes:

- Replace the default text on the pages shown in the figures. (Your text does not have to match these publications exactly.)
- Delete any text boxes not needed and move any text boxes to layer appropriately, as shown in the figures.
- Where necessary, use the **Insert Business Information command** to quickly insert a component.
- Select the newly typed text and format the font to increase the font size and to **bold** and **center** the text where appropriate.

b. On page 4, replace the default tagline text under the pictures with different text also shown in the figures.

c. On page 4, select the newly typed picture tagline texts and format the font to **bold** and **center**, if necessary.

d. On page 4, right-click on the default pictures, and then choose the **Change Picture, Clip Art command** to choose more appropriate pictures for each of the remaining pages to match those shown in the figures.

e. Delete the logo pictures at the top left corner of each of the remaining pages.

f. Change the background of each remaining page using the **Format menu**, **background command** to closely match those shown in the figures.

g. Apply fill color and fill effects where appropriate, as shown in the figures.

h. Save the publication.

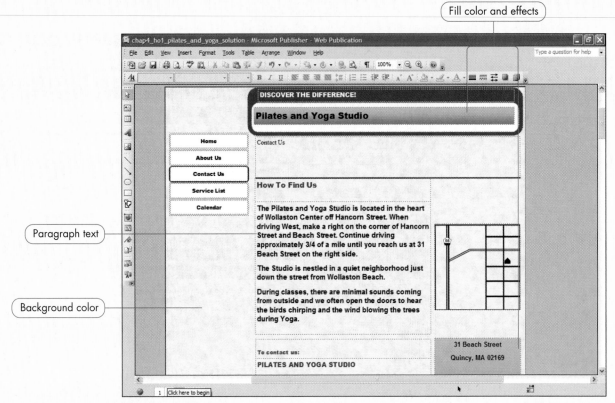

Figure 4.10 Page Three

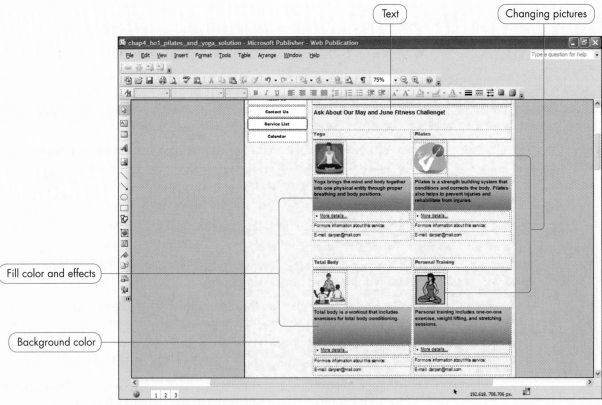

Figure 4.11 Page Four

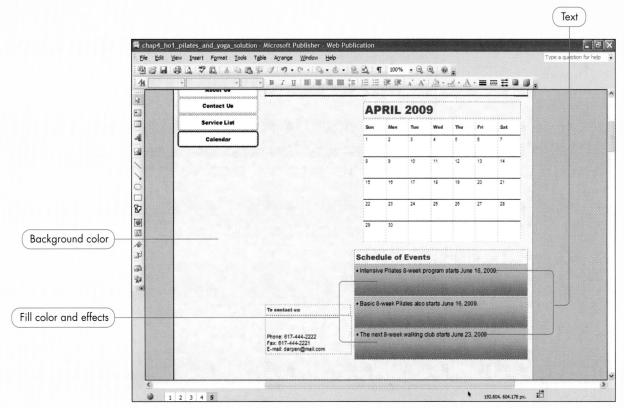

Text

Background color

Fill color and effects

Figure 4.12 Page Five

Refer to Figure 4.13 as you complete Step 10.

a. Click on **page 1** so that your home page is displayed.

b. If necessary, click the drop-down arrow to select **Format Publication** on the task pane.

c. Under Web Options, in the middle of the task pane, click the link to **Preview your Web site**.

d. Your default browser will open to display your Web site, as shown in Figure 4.13.

If you notice anything that needs to be adjusted, close your browser, go back to Publisher to make any adjustments, and then simply click the link again to view your Web site locally in your browser.

e. Save the publication.

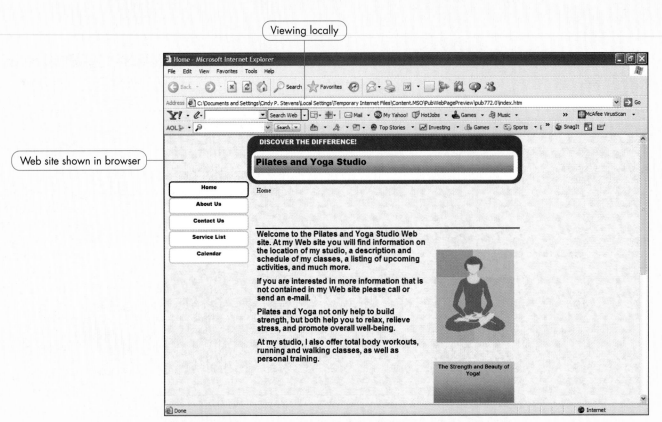

Figure 4.13 Preview Your Web Site in Internet Explorer

TIP Publish Your Site

When you are ready to publish your Web site, contact your Internet Service Provider to find out how they want you to publish your site to their server. More than likely, they will direct you to use an FTP program. FTP is a file transfer protocol language used to send files from one computer to another computer over the Internet. You can use an FTP program to transfer your files. However, you can also use the Publish to the Web command available from the File menu.

E-Mail Web Sites

E-mail Web pages and sites are used to market your products and services.

Microsoft Publisher provides predesigned templates for creating e-mail-based Web pages and sites. ***E-mail Web pages and sites*** are used to market your products and services. E-mail advertising is a low-cost way to keep in contact with your customers. E-mail also provides your customers with information on new products and/or services. The E-mail link from the Publication Types task pane contains the following categories under Newer Designs and Classic Designs: Event/Activity, Featured Product, Letter, Product List, Newsletter, Event/Speaker, and finally Blank Sizes.

(E-mail advertising is a low-cost way to keep in contact with your customers.)

Figure 4.14 displays an Event/Speaker Web page created using a predesigned template about to be sent via Outlook Express. The Eclipse Event/Speaker design template near the middle of the category list was chosen. It took approximately 10 minutes to create the Web page. The templates vary; however, most include placeholders for text, clip art, hyperlinks, and content-based information, as well as different formatting options, such as font and color schemes, background color, borders and shading, fill color, design elements, and more. We changed the color scheme from the existing template and we also changed some fonts, the clip art, and some fill color.

Figure 4.14 E-Mail Web Site

TIP Configuring Outlook

The first time you open Outlook or Outlook Express a command box will appear configuring Outlook to work with Publisher. If you plan to send e-mail Web pages or sites via Outlook, you will need to let this configuration take place. You will be prompted to restart your computer upon configuration completion. Outlook or Outlook Express must be set up as your default e-mail program to send Publisher publications.

Sending a Publication by E-Mail

Microsoft Publisher gives you the ability to send most publications via e-mail. The e-mail recipient does not need to have Microsoft Publisher installed on his/her computer to view the e-mail page. The publication shown in Figure 4.14 is a Web template designed specifically for the purpose of sending the publication via e-mail. In order to send your publications via e-mail, you must have Microsoft Office Oulook 2007 or Microsoft Outlook Express (version 5.0 or later) set as your default e-mail program. To send a publication via e-mail, simply choose the *Publisher Tasks* link from the Format Publication task pane to send as a message within the e-mail or attachment. The Publisher Tasks link provides commands for previewing your e-mail publication, checking for errors, and posting to a Web site. You can also set up a mailing list, address an individual e-mail publication, and use links that Microsoft provides to find and/or purchase a mailing list. Alternatively, you can also send the publication as an attachment using the *Send Publication as Attachment* command, from the Send E-mail command on the file menu, allows you to send an e-mail message that includes an attached Publisher file. It is also a good idea to preview your e-mail page and also to check for any errors using the Publisher Tasks link from the Format Publication task pane. After you click to send as a message, a Design Checker command will prompt you to fix any errors as shown in Figure 4.14 above.

The ***Publisher Tasks*** link provides commands for previewing your e-mail publication, checking for errors, posting to a Web site, and more.

The ***Send Publication as Attachment command***, from the Send E-mail command on the file menu, allows you to send an e-mail message that includes an attached Publisher file..

Troubleshooting Sending E-Mail

When sending an e-mail publication, you could run into a few problems. Here is a list of the most common problems along with a possible solution for each:

- I can send the publication via e-mail but some fonts are exported as an image: Certain fonts that are called non-Web fonts may turn into an image that looks like symbols, instead.

- There is no command to send my publication as an e-mail from the File menu: You probably do not have Microsoft Office Outlook 2007 or Microsoft Outlook Express (version 5.0 or later) installed and/or configured as your default e-mail program.

- I can send the publication via e-mail but the text is coming out blurry: The background color and the text color on your e-mail Web page may be too close in color. Try using light fonts on a dark background or dark text with a light background.

Hands-On Exercises

2 | E-Mail a Web Publication

Skills covered: 1. Open a Publication **2.** Change the Background **3.** Choose a Different Color Scheme **4.** Format Fill Color and Fill Effects **5.** Preview the E-Mail Publication **6.** Send the Publication as an E-Mail **7.** View the E-Mail

---

Step 1
Open a Publication

Refer to Figure 4.15 as you complete Step 1.

a. If necessary, start Publisher, then open the *chap4_ho2_e-mail* publication in the Exploring Publisher folder.

b. Save the publication as **chap4_ho2_e-mail_solution**.

This publication was completed using the E-mail Web publication templates. It is based on the Eclipse Event/Speaker template. The content has been provided for you, as shown in Figure 4.15.

c. If necessary, change the Zoom to 75% or 100%, whichever you prefer to work with the publication.

Figure 4.15 Eclipse E-Mail Publication

TIP E-Mail Fonts

You may wish to personalize your e-mail messages, but keep in mind that specialized fonts may not show up on another person's computer. If a font is not installed on a computer, the message will be displayed using the default font. Using a common font such as Arial or Times New Roman is more likely to ensure that the receiver of your message will see the same message that you sent.

Refer to Figure 4.16 as you complete Step 2.

a. Choose the **Background command** on the **Format menu** to format the background.

The task pane will display different background colors and designs to choose from.

Alternatively, you can use the **More Backgrounds command** from the bottom of the task pane to see additional colors and designs.

b. Choose the same or a similar background, as shown in Figure 4.16. (Your background does not have to match that shown in the figure exactly.)

c. Save the publication.

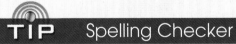

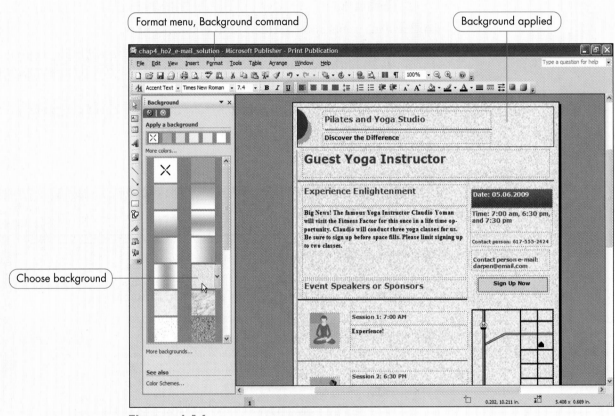

Figure 4.16 Change the Background

TIP   Spelling Checker

It is nice to see those red wavy lines appear under misspelled words in your publications letting you know when you have made a spelling error. However, what if you type a proper name and the red wavy line continues to appear? New words can be added to the spelling dictionary in Microsoft Publisher. These words may include proper nouns or industry-specific words. To add a new word to the dictionary on the Tools menu, point to Spelling and then click Spelling. Click Add for each word that you want to add to the dictionary when it is found as a misspelling by the spelling checker.

Step 3
Choose a Different Color Scheme

Refer to Figure 4.17 as you complete Step 3.

a. If necessary, change to Format Publication and click **Color Schemes** from the drop-down menu on the task pane, as shown in Figure 4.17.

b. Experiment with different color schemes until you are satisfied.

We chose the **Lagoon color scheme**. (You do not have to choose the same color scheme. Your publication can be different from Figure 4.17.)

c. Save your publication.

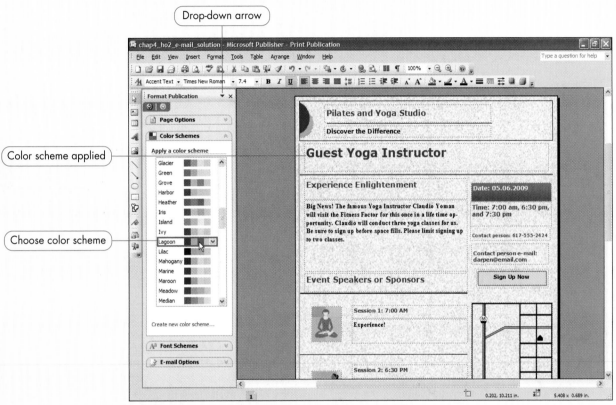

Figure 4.17 Color Scheme

Step 4
Format Fill Color and Fill Effects

Refer to Figure 4.18 as you complete Step 4.

a. If necessary, scroll up to the top of your e-mail publication, and then select the text box for the business name.

b. Click on the **Fill Color button**, and then select **More Fill Colors**.

c. Choose a **light green** color, as shown in Figure 4.18, or choose any other color you wish. (Your publication does not have to match the figure exactly.)

d. Click on the **Fill Color button** again, and then choose **Fill Effects**.

e. Change the transparency to **30%** or more and click **OK** to apply the new changes. (Your publication does not have to match Figure 4.18 exactly.)

f. Scroll to the middle of your publication, and then click on the **Sign Up Now text box**.

g. Change the fill color and fill effects to match the colors you chose above.

h. Scroll to the bottom of your publication, and then change the fill color and fill effects of the address to match the colors you chose above.

i. Save the publication.

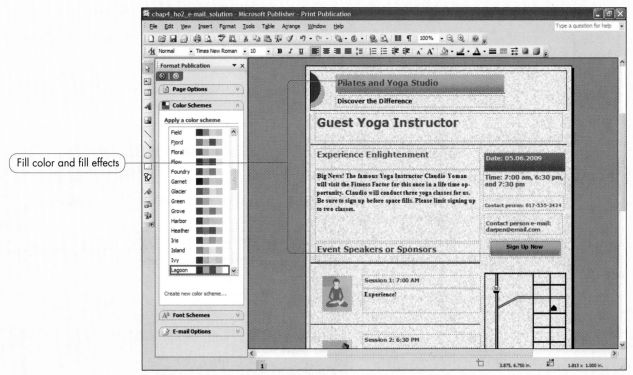

Fill color and fill effects

Figure 4.18 Fill Color and Fill Effects

Refer to Figure 4.19 as you complete Step 5.

a. Choose **Publisher Tasks** from the Format Publication task pane.

b. Click the **Send in e-mail command** under Distributing your publication.

c. Then click the **Send as a message command**.

d. Then click the **Preview command**.

Your browser will open to display your e-mail publication. If you spot something that needs to be edited, simply close your browser and return to Publisher to fix the publication.

e. Close your browser.

f. Save the publication.

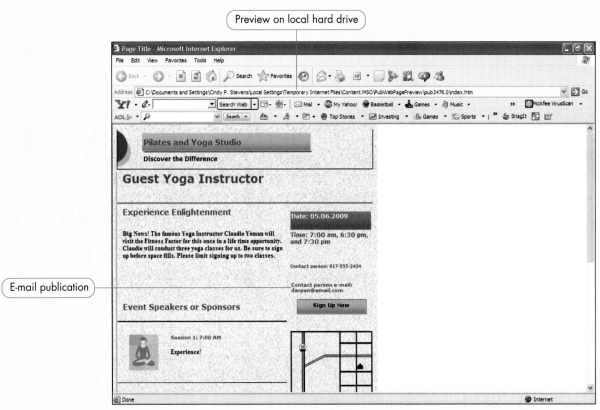

Preview on local hard drive

E-mail publication

Figure 4.19 Preview

TIP Free E-Mail

There are many sites that offer free e-mail. Subscribers are able to access their e-mail from any computer. Sometimes, having multiple e-mail addresses is useful. When running your own business, having an e-mail address that is separate from your personal account may be a necessity.

Step 6
Send the Publication as an E-Mail

Refer to Figure 4.20 as you complete Step 6.

a. From the task pane, click to choose the **Address and send command**.

b. Then click to choose the **Type individual addresses command**. (Alternatively, you can choose the **Send this page as an e-mail button** on the Standard toolbar.)

The e-mail header will appear on the publication screen, as shown in Figure 4.20.

c. Fill in the header information as follows:

• To: Send the e-mail to yourself for practice.

• Subject: Type Web E-mail.

d. Click the **Send button** to send the e-mail.

e. Save the publication.

Figure 4.20 Send the E-mail

TIP E-Mail

When sending e-mails, you may not want all of your recipients to know everyone to whom you sent the e-mail. To hide e-mail addresses and names, type them into the Bcc: line in your e-mail header. This should be the third line, after the To: line and the Cc: line. Do not forget to include a subject line so that recipients know what they are receiving in the e-mail.

Step 7
View the E-Mail

Refer to Figure 4.21 as you complete Step 7.

a. Open Outlook Express or Microsoft Office Outlook and click the **Send/Receive button** to retrieve your e-mail.

Your publication will appear in the e-mail message area, as shown in Figure 4.21.

b. Print the e-mail message from your e-mail program. Close your e-mail program.

c. Print the e-mail publication from Microsoft Publisher and submit both printouts to your instructor.

d. Save the publication.

e. Close Microsoft Publisher unless you plan to continue to Hands-On Exercise 3.

Figure 4.21   View the E-Mail

Customizing Web Pages

(Whether you create a Web site from the design templates, the e-mail templates, or from a blank publication, you can customize your pages with certain Web elements.)

Whether you create a Web site from the design templates, the e-mail templates, or from a blank publication, you can customize your pages with certain Web elements. For instance, the pages can be formatted to add a different background (as discussed previously). Customize using different color schemes (as discussed previously), background sound, additional hyperlinks, and more graphics (as discussed previously). In addition, you can add an electronic Web form to your pages and then customize the Web form properties.

TIP   Placing an Order

By using the Web Form controls, you can add an order form to your Web site. Using online ordering is a great way to expand your business. However, be careful when taking orders over the Internet. Be sure that you offer a secure way for credit card numbers to be used as a form of payment.

Creating an Electronic Form

(Web forms let your Web sites work for you.)

Web forms enable your visitors to place orders, submit information, join a mailing list, or provide feedback.

Form controls enable a visitor to your Web site to submit information and/or feedback.

Web forms let your Web sites work for you. Available **Web forms** enable your visitors to place orders, submit information, join a mailing list, or provide feedback. Microsoft Publisher offers six types of **Form controls** that enable a visitor to your Web site to submit information and/or feedback, including the following:

- Check boxes: Check boxes allow a visitor to choose one or more choices.
- Option buttons: Option buttons allow a visitor to choose only one from a set of choices.
- List box: A List box allows a visitor a choice of certain listed items. The List box also contains a scroll bar if there are items within the box.
- Textbox: A Textbox provides one line in which a visitor can type information.
- Text area: A Text area provides multiple lines in which a visitor can type information.
- Submit button: A Submit button is what the visitor can click in submit the information found on the form.

TIP   Links

You may find many sites useful or interesting and want to share them with visitors to your Web site. Hyperlinks can take the viewer to these sites. Be sure to check with the site host before adding a link to your site.

Understanding Web Form Control Properties

Control properties enable you to set specific functionality to the type of form control, such as text properties, style of button, and more.

You can set **Control properties** for all six Web form controls listed in the previous section. Control properties enable you to set properties specific to the type of form control such as text properties and style of button. When you double-click any of the form controls, a dialog box appears so that you can set properties specific to the type of form control. For example, the Textbox and Text area form control properties control the appearance of the text and the way you want the data sent back to you. The Button form controls enable you to choose a picture instead of a button and to specify how you want the form information sent back to you. You will experiment with several Form controls in our next hands-on exercise.

Adding Background Sound

Background sound files can be added to your Web publication. When the Web page is opened on the Internet, if the user has speakers, the sound will play in the background.

The **Web Options command** allows you to add a title to your Web publication, add sound to your publication, and add Web page descriptors to your Web site.

The **Web Options dialog box** allows you to add a title to your Web site, add keywords for search engines, and add a sound file and control the amount of time the sound file plays.

The **Insert Hyperlink dialog box** gives you several options, such as linking to an existing Web site or file, linking to the current site's documents, linking to a new document, or even linking to an e-mail address.

Web publications can be customized to include *background sound* when the site opens in a viewer's browser. By using the *Web Options command* on the Tools menu, you can add sound to the background of your publications. The *Web Options dialog box* allows you to add a title to your Web site, add keywords for search engines, and add a sound file and control the amount of time the sound file plays. The background sound can be inserted from a specific sound file that you create or download from the Internet. In addition, Microsoft Publisher comes with many sound file choices. Or, you can download sound files from the Microsoft Online site, the same site used earlier. You can customize the background sound to play continously on the Web page or set the sound to play for a specified amount of time.

Adding Hyperlinks

As discussed at the beginning of this chapter, a hyperlink contains references to other Web pages either within the same site or an external Web site. Hyperlinks can be added to text or pictures in Microsoft Publisher. Hyperlinks can be created by selecting the text or picture and clicking the Hyperlink button on the Standard toolbar or the Hyperlink command on the Insert menu. The *Insert Hyperlink dialog box*, shown in Figure 4.22, gives you several options, such as linking to an existing Web site or file, linking to the current site's documents, linking to a new document, or even linking to an e-mail address. The Hyperlink dialog box also enables you to display text instead of the URL address and to remove or edit a hyperlink.

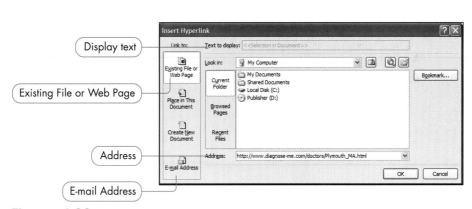

Figure 4.22 Creating a Hyperlink

Hands-On Exercises

3 | Customizing a Web Site

Skills covered: 1. Open an Existing Web Publication **2.** Add Background Sound to the Home Page **3.** Preview the Background Sound **4.** Add a Hyperlink **5.** Add a New Blank Web Page **6.** Create an Electronic Web Form **7.** Set the List Box Form Controls **8.** Finish Customizing Your E-Form

---

Step 1
Open an Existing Web Publication

Refer to Figure 4.23 as you complete Step 1.

a. If necessary, start Publisher.

b. Click the **File menu** and open the publication created in the first hands-on exercise in this chapter, *chap4_ho1_pilates_and_yoga_solution*.

c. Save the publication as **chap4_ho3_form_solution**, as shown in Figure 4.23.

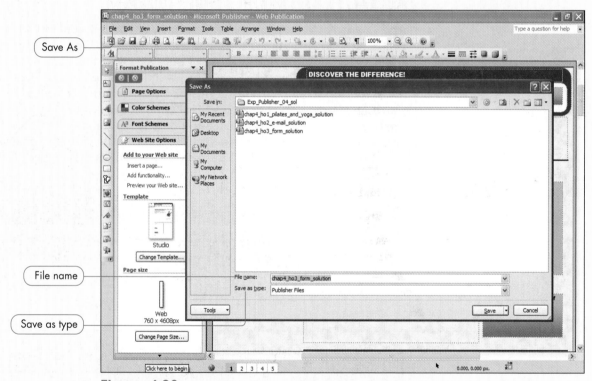

Figure 4.23 Save Web Site

Step 2
Add Background Sound to the Home Page

Refer to Figure 4.24 as you complete Step 2.

a. Choose the **Web Page Options command** from the **Tools menu** to open the Web Page Options dialog box, as shown in Figure 4.24.

b. Click the **Browse button** to find a default sound. (Alternately, you can browse for a sound file that you recorded or a different sound that you downloaded from the Internet.)

c. Choose the default sound file entitled *Fall_01* that came with the Publisher program.

TROUBLESHOOTING: Do not worry if you cannot find this sound file. You can just pick a different sound file suited for this Web site.

d. Once you find the sound file you want, simply double-click the file and the file name will be entered into the File name box.

e. Set the Loop for **2** times (or however many times you would like the sound to play over again).

f. Click **OK** and save your publication.

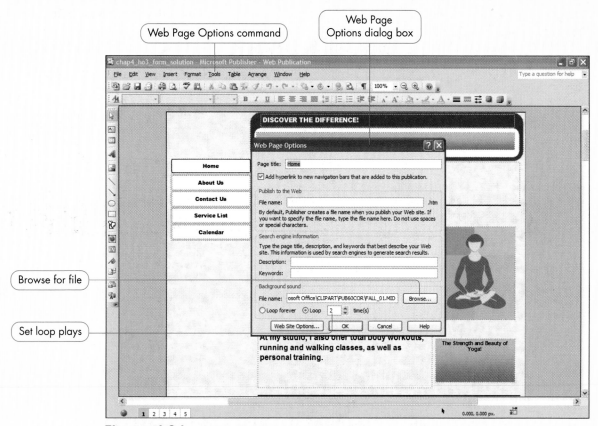

Figure 4.24 Add Background Sound

TIP Sounds

Be careful when adding background sounds to your Web pages. Some people find added sounds to be unprofessional. In addition, if you choose to use background sound, be sure that it is either your own original music or music you have obtained legally to use.

Step 3
Preview the Background Sound

Refer to Figure 4.25 as you complete Step 3.

a. If necessary, open the task pane and click **Format Publication** from the drop-down menu.

b. On the task pane under Web Page Options, click the **Preview your Web site link**, as shown in Figure 4.25.

Internet Explorer (or your default browser) will open, and the Web site will appear locally from your hard drive.

When your Web site opens in your browser, if you have speakers on your computer and if you have the sound turned on or volume turned up, you will hear the background sound that was added to your home page.

If you click on the other pages, you will notice the sound does not play because we only added sound to the home page.

c. Close your browser.

d. Save the publication.

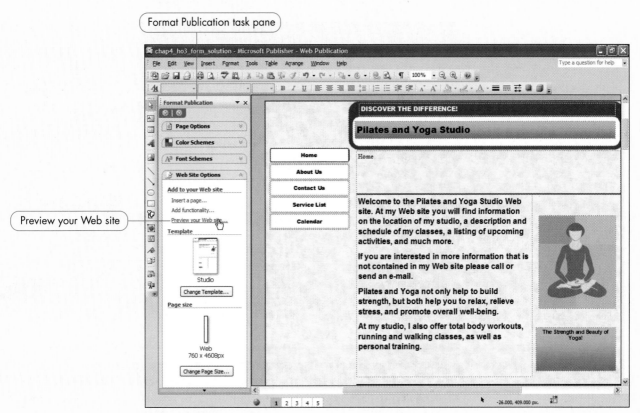

Format Publication task pane

Preview your Web site

Figure 4.25 Preview the Background Sound

Refer to Figure 4.26 as you complete Step 4.

a. If necessary, scroll down to the bottom of your home page.

b. Select the text for the e-mail address, **darpen@mail.com**, and then click the **Insert Hyperlink button** on the Standard toolbar.

c. In the **Link to side pane**, click **E-mail Address** to type the address in the text box, as shown in Figure 4.26.

When you start to type the address, Publisher will add **mailto:** at the beginning of the address for you.

d. Click **OK** to add the e-mail hyperlink.

Once you click OK, the e-mail address will be underlined and will also be formatted as colored text.

e. Save the publication.

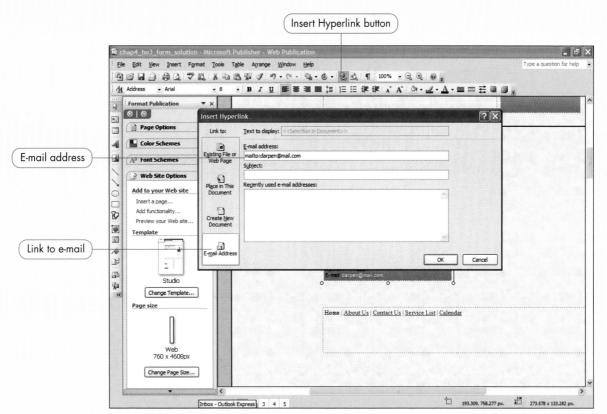

Insert Hyperlink button

E-mail address

Link to e-mail

Figure 4.26 Add a Hyperlink

TIP   Shortcut

To insert a hyperlink to a selected object, use the Ctrl+K shortcut. This command links the picture or graphic to another page on the Web site or to another Web site altogether. Remember, if you are adding a hyperlink to an outside Web site (a site other than your own), make sure that you check often to be sure the site is still active or has not moved. Also, if you are adding a link to one of your own pages, please note that, if you move that page to another directory, you must also update the hyperlink.

Step 5
Add a New Blank Web Page

Refer to Figure 4.27 as you complete Step 5.

a. Click on the **Calender page** (page 5) of your Web site.

b. To insert a new blank page after the calender page, open the task pane to Format Publication options, and then click **Insert a page**, as shown in Figure 4.27.

The Insert Web Page Dialog box will appear, as shown in Figure 4.27.

c. Click the **Blank Page option**, and then click **OK**.

Publisher will add a new blank page after the calendar page that will include the Web site template items, such as business name and page links.

d. Save the publication.

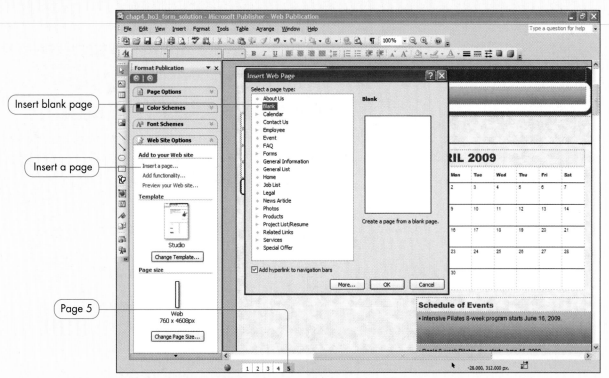

Figure 4.27 Add a New Blank Page

Refer to Figure 4.28 as you complete Step 6.

a. Create the List box form control:

- At the top of the blank page, insert a text box from the drawing toolbar and type the following, as shown in Figure 4.28: **Which of the following classes would you like to receive more information about?**

- Choose **List box** from the **Insert Form Control** on the **Insert menu** and draw out a list box underneath the text box you just created, as shown in Figure 4.28.

- Drag to move both and resize each similar to that shown in Figure 4.28.

b. Create the Textbox form control:

- From the Toolbox, click **Textbox** to draw out a text box and type the following: **What is your e-mail address or telephone number?**

- Choose **Textbox** from the **Insert Form Control** on the **Insert menu** to insert a text box underneath the text box you just created, as shown in Figure 4.28.

- Drag to move both and resize each similar to that shown in Figure 4.28.

c. Create the Text area form control:

- From the drawing toolbar, click **Textbox** to insert a text box and type the following: **Please type any detailed qustions you might have in this area below**.

- Choose **Text area** from the **Insert Form Control** on the **Insert menu** and insert a text area underneath the text box you just created, as shown in Figure 4.28.

- Drag to move both and resize each similar to that shown in Figure 4.28.

d. Choose **Submit** from the **Insert Form Control** on the **Insert menu**.

- Drag to move the button to a place similar to the one shown in Figure 4.28.

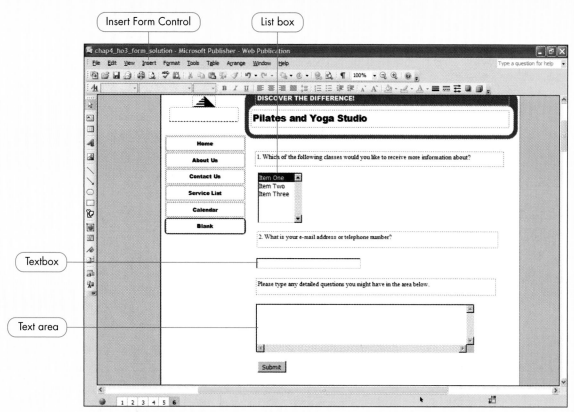

Figure 4.28 Create an Electronic Web Form

Refer to Figure 4.29 as you complete Step 7.

a. Double-click the **List box form control**.

b. In the List Box Properties dialog box, choose **Item One** in the Appearance box, and then click the **Modify command**, as shown in Figure 4.29.

c. Type the first item, **Pilates**.

d. Select each of the remaining two items, and then the **Modify command** to change the remaining two items to **Yoga** and **Personal Training**.

e. After labeling the items, click the **Form Properties button** to choose the data retrieval method and click **Send data to me in e-mail**.

f. Type the e-mail address, as shown in Figure 4.29.

g. Click **OK** within each dialog box, and then save the publication.

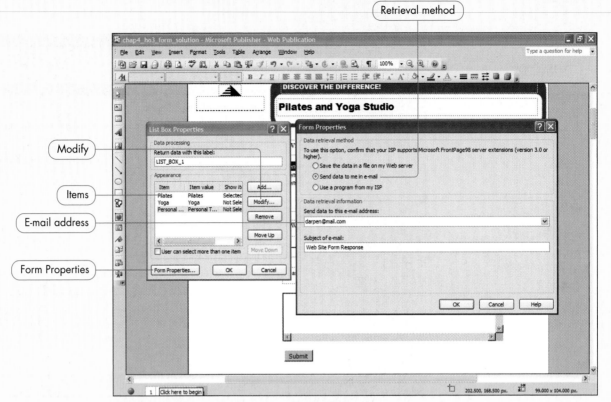

Figure 4.29 Set the List Box Form Controls

Step 8
Finish Customizing Your E-Form

Refer to Figure 4.30 as you complete Step 8.

a. Customize your Electronic Form to look similar to that shown in Figure 4.30 as follows:

- Delete the logo at the top left of the page.

- Add a background to your electronic form using the **Background command** on the **Format menu** to match the rest of your Web site.

- Format the text boxes for a **light purple** fill color to match the rest of your Web site.

- Format the text boxes with a **30%** transparency fill effect to match the rest of your Web site.

- Click on the **Blank button**, and then click the **Edit Options wand**, as shown in Figure 4.30, on the Blank page button to change the text to read **Feedback** instead of *Blank*.

b. Preview your Web site.

Keep in mind that you will not be able to actually submit the Web form until you have placed your Web site on a Web server.

c. Save the publication.

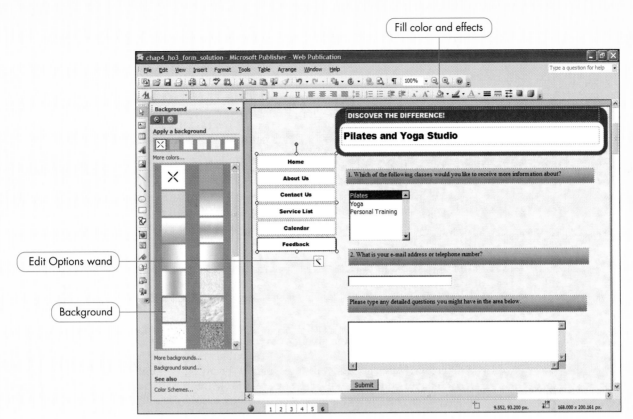

Figure 4.30 Finish Customizing Your E-Form

Summary

1. **Understand Web site basics.** Creating Web sites with Microsoft Publisher is simple and fun to do. Web pages are developed in a special language called HTML (HyperText Markup Language). Microsoft Publisher generates the HTML statements for you—you can continue to enter text and/or change the formatting just like any other type of publication.

2. **Understand copyright issues.** A copyright provides legal protection to the written or artistic work, including literary, dramatic, musical, and artistic works such as poetry, novels, movies, songs, computer software, and architecture. If you plan to download anything from the Internet to use on your pages, you must do so legally.

3. **Use the Easy Web Site Builder.** The Easy Web Site Builder allows you to choose which components you want to include in your Web site on different pages.

4. **Send a publication by e-mail.** Microsoft Publisher gives you the ability to send any publication via e-mail. The e-mail recipient does not need to have Microsoft Publisher installed on their computer to view the e-mail page. Any publication can be converted to a Web page, and Microsoft Publisher also provides many Web and/or e-mail template designs to work with. Web pages and/or e-mail Web sites can be customized to add different background colors, background sound, graphics, color schemes, and hyperlinks.

5. **Create an electronic form.** Microsoft Publisher also has the tools to create electronic Web forms. Web forms enable your Web sites to work for you. With Web forms, your visitors may be able to place orders, submit information, join a mailing list, or provide feedback.

6. **Understand Web form control properties.** Form controls include items, such as check boxes, option controls, text boxes, and more. Form control properties are attributes that you can change about a form control. Form control properties give your customers many choices to quickly choose from or allow them to enter information quickly in an attempt to provide feedback.

Key Terms

Multiple Choice

1. What does the acronym HTML stand for?

   (a) HyperType Makeup Language

   (b) HyperText Markup Language

   (c) HyperText Microsoft Language

   (d) HelpfulTest Markup Language

2. The World Wide Web or Web is:

   (a) The only way to convey information

   (b) A large subset of the Internet

   (c) Complicated

   (d) Only used by large corporations

3. Which of the following does a copyright protect?

   (a) Written or artistic work

   (b) Gives the author the exclusive right to the use and duplication of the work

   (c) Facts and ideas

   (d) Both (a) and (b)

4. When does an infringement of copyright occur?

   (a) When you quote from a text or Web site

   (b) When you use copyrighted material without the permission of the owner

   (c) When the work is public domain

   (d) When using statistical data

5. Why does software piracy harm everyone?

   (a) It results in higher prices for legitimate licenses

   (b) Reduced levels of support

   (c) Delays in development of new software

   (d) All of the above

6. Web templates contain which of the following?

   (a) Placeholders for text, clip art, hyperlinks, and content-based information

   (b) Different formatting options

   (c) Both (a) and (b)

   (d) Neither (a) nor (b)

7. When you open the Easy Web Site Builder, what is the default number of pages?

   (a) 1

   (b) 4

   (c) 3

   (d) 10

8. After replacing any of the business information, which button do you have to press to change the information throughout the Web site?

   (a) Change

   (b) Enter

   (c) Update

   (d) Edit

9. What color line will appear under your text if a word is spelled incorrectly?

   (a) Purple

   (b) Green

   (c) Blue

   (d) Red

10. How do you change a default picture in your publication?

    (a) Right-click on the default picture, and then choose the Change Picture, Clip Art Command.

    (b) Search for the appropriate picture.

    (c) Click on the picture in the task pane to replace the default picture.

    (d) All of the above.

11. Which of the following can you do with the default background?

    (a) Change it to another solid color.

    (b) Choose a gradient color.

    (c) You cannot change the background color.

    (d) Both (a) and (b).

12. Which e-mail program must you have installed in your computer to send a publication via e-mail?

    (a) Microsoft Office Outlook 2007

    (b) Microsoft Outlook Express (version 5.0 or later)

    (c) MSN Mail

    (d) Either (a) and (b)

13. Why would the text be blurry when sending a publication by e-mail?

    (a) The monitor may be defective.

    (b) The background color and text color may be too close in color.

    (c) The recipient does not have Microsoft Publisher installed on their computer.

    (d) None of the above.

Multiple Choice Continued...

14. Which step would you take to preview your e-mail publication?

    (a) Click the E-mail preview command from the Save e-mail command.

    (b) Save the publication, and then open it using your Internet browser.

    (c) Print the Publication.

    (d) You cannot preview the publication.

15. What can you do with a background sound?

    (a) Have it play continuously.

    (b) Set it to play for a certain amount of time.

    (c) Set it to play only when the viewer requests the sound.

    (d) Both (a) and (b).

16. When you click on Insert Hyperlink, what are the options for each hyperlink?

    (a) Link to an existing file or Web site

    (b) Link within the current site's documents or a new document

    (c) Link to an e-mail address

    (d) All of the above

17. Item, Item Value, and Show Item as are all found in which command box?

    (a) List Box Properties

    (b) Text Box Properties

    (c) Command Button Properties

    (d) Multi-line Text Box Properties

18. How do Web forms enable your Web site to work for you?

    (a) Your visitors can place orders

    (b) Submit information

    (c) Join a mailing list

    (d) All of the above

Practice Exercises

1 E-Mail Event

As an active member of your Student Government Association you have been asked to design the advertisements for an upcoming speaker session on copyright issues that your association is sponsoring. You have decided to use the e-mail Web site tool that you just learned about in Microsoft Publisher. Complete the publication as directed using Figure 4.31 as a guide. Open the *chap4_pe1_event* publication and proceed as follows:

a. Open the *chap4_pe1_event* publication based on the Arrows E-mail Event/Speaker pre-designed template and save it as **chap4_pe1_event_solution**.

b. Change the Color Scheme to **Technic** to match Figure 4.31.

c. Change the Background to **Picture Fill (Swirls)** to match that shown in Figure 4.31.

d. Design a logo for the Student Government Association to match Figure 4.31.

e. Click in the description paragraph on the publication, point to the **Language command** on the **Tools menu**, and click **Hyphenation** to turn off hyphenation.

f. Preview the e-mail publication in your browser.

g. Save the finalized e-mail publication.

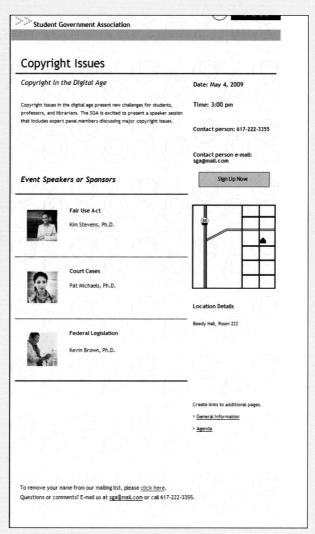

Figure 4.31   E-Mail Event

...continued on Next Page

To make her Web site more user friendly, the owner of the Pilates Studio has decided to provide several hyperlinks to pages within her Web site. Complete the publication as directed using Figure 4.32 as a guide. Open the *chap4_ho1_pilates_yoga_solution* publication finished in the first hands-on exercise and proceed as follows:

a. Open the *chap4_ho1_pilates_yoga_solution* publication and save it as **chap4_pe2_ hyperlink_solution**.

b. On Page 1, select to highlight the word **Pilates** in the third paragraph of text and click to add a hyperlink from the **Place in This Document command** to the Service page, as shown in Figure 4.32.

c. On Page 1, select to highlight the word **Yoga** in the same paragraph and click to add a hyperlink from within the document to the Service page.

d. On Page 2, select to highlight the word **Pilates** in the last paragraph and click to add a hyperlink from within the document to the Service page.

e. On Page 2, select to highlight the word **Yoga** in the third paragraph and click to add a hyperlink from within the document to the Service List page.

f. On Page 4, select to highlight the words **Fitness Challenge** and click to add a hyperlink from within the document to the Calendar page.

g. On Page 5, select to highlight the word **Pilates** in the first event listed under the events schedule and hyperlink to the Service List page.

h. Save the publication.

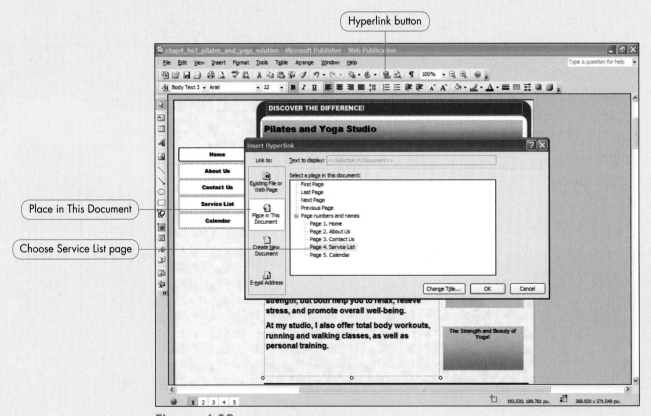

Figure 4.32 Adding Hyperlinks

...continued on Next Page

You own the largest used bookstore on the East Coast. You never have had a Web site, but your son has learned how to use Microsoft Publisher and wants to start building one for you. You plan to start out very simple with a basic home page, products page, and an online order form. The main home page has been created for you. Your job is to add the products page and the order form page using Figure 4.33 as a guide for inserting new pages.

a. Open the *chap4_pe3_books* publication and save it as **chap4_pe3_books_solution**.

b. Using the **Insert menu page command** insert a Product List page and add the following book information for each product area:

Book Title	Description	Item Number	Price
Dusty Road	Fiction	222-33-456-211	$5.99
Long Way Home	Fiction	235-44-567-888	$5.99
Brian's Story	Fiction	567-43-555-194	$5.99
Helping Yourself	Self-help	333-56-777-546	$4.99
Blue Sky's	Non-fiction	999-45-333-777	$2.99
Down South	Travel	765-45-222-657	$2.99

c. Delete the logo on the Products page.

d. Change each of the default images to something more appropriate on the Products page.

e. Using the **Insert menu page command**, insert an Order Form page.

f. Change the default text on the Form page at the top to read: **Enter your order information below**.

g. Delete the logo on the Form page.

h. Change the default image on the Form page to something more appropriate.

i. Save the publication.

...continued on Next Page

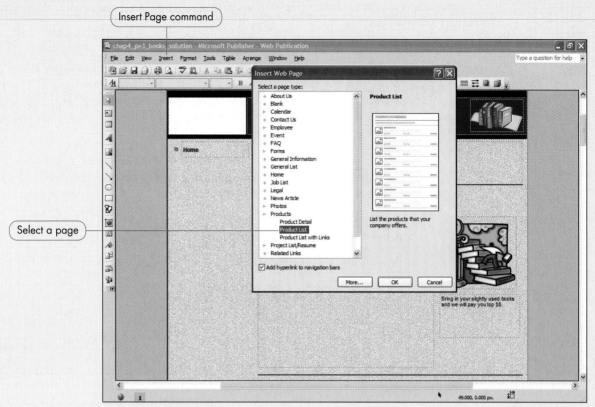

Insert Page command

Select a page

Figure 4.33 Books

4 E-Mail Résumé

While learning to use Publisher, you discover that you can send any publication as an e-mail attachment or within the e-mail message. Now that you know how to send publications over e-mail, you have a great idea for job hunting and plan to send your résumé out to several human resources departments to seek employment. To be cautious, however, you decide to send your résumé in an e-mail to yourself first to experiment with this tool. Use Figure 4.34 as a guide to send this e-mail.

a. Open the file *chap2_mid1_resume_solution* that you saved from Chapter 2 and save it as **chap4_pe4_resume_solution**.

b. From the Format Publication task pane, click the **Publisher Tasks link** at the bottom of the task pane.

c. Click the **Send in an e-mail command**, as shown in Figure 4.34.

d. Click the **Send as a Message command**.

e. Click **Preview** to see what your e-mail will look like in your browser.

f. Close the browser.

g. Click the **Address and Send command**.

h. Click the **Type Individual Addresses command**.

i. Enter your e-mail address, and then click **Send** to send the e-mail to yourself.

j. Open either Outlook Express or Outlook to obtain your e-mail.

k. Print the e-mail to submit to your teacher as proof you completed this exercise.

...continued on Next Page

Publisher Tasks task pane

Send in an e-mail

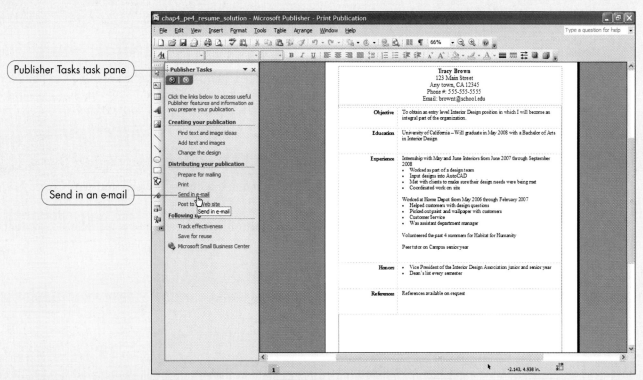

Figure 4.34 E-Mail Résumé

The owner of the Secondhand Bookstore wants to set up an address list of frequent customers so that he can send out monthly advertisements and flyers through e-mail. His son has agreed to begin an address list using the Mailings and Catalogs dialog box in Publisher. Set up an initial address list using the following instructions as a guideline. Use Figure 4.35 as a guide.

a. If necessary, open Publisher and open a blank publication of any size.

b. From the **Mailings and Catalogs command** on the **Tools menu**, click **Create Address List**.

c. Click the **Customize Columns button**, and then remove the following categories using Figure 4.35 as a guide:

- Title
- Company Name
- Address Line 2
- Country or Region
- Work Phone

d. Enter the following customer data in the Address List dialog box (do not hit enter before you go to the next step):

First Name	Last Name	Address Line 1	City	State	Zip Code	Home Phone	E-Mail Address
Cindy	Stevens	55 Glensmart Road	Goldsberry	NC	02115	919-444-4343	stevens@email.com (use your e-mail address to test the list in the next exercise)
Brian	Dowdall	21 Porter Street	Goldsberry	NC	02115	919-333-6767	dowdall@email.com
Alyssa	Picou	55 Stevens Lane	Goldsberry	NC	02115	919-567-2345	picou@email.com

e. Hold down **Ctrl** on your keyboard and hit **Print Scrn** on your keyboard.

f. Click **OK** and save the data list as **chap4_mid1_list_solution**.

g. On the blank publication page, click the **Paste button** to paste the screen shot into the publication to submit to your teacher as proof you completed this exercise.

h. Save the publication with the screen shot as **chap4_mid1_list_solution**.

...continued on Next Page

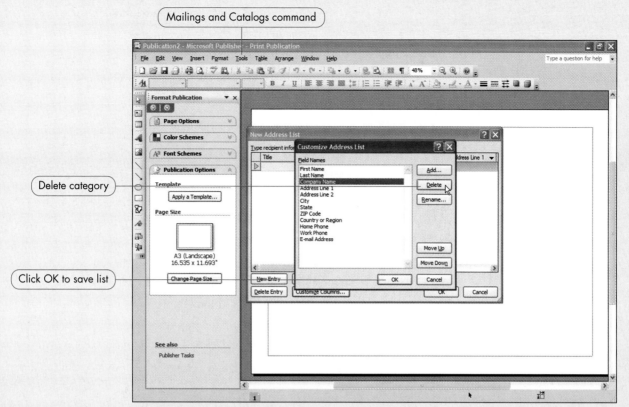

Figure 4.35 E-Mail List

2 Send an E-Mail Publication Using an Address List

Now that you have set up an e-mail address list for the Secondhand Bookstore, it is time to try out this form of advertising. The owner of the Secondhand Bookstore wants to send out his basic Web site as an e-mail advertisement monthly to his regular customers. Using the e-mail address list created in the first mid-level exercise and the Web site created in the third practice exercise, you will practice sending a Web site from e-mail using an e-mail address list. You will work with the **chap4_pe3_books_solution** publication to complete this exercise. Refer to Figure 4.36 as a guide.

a. If necessary, start Publisher and open the file *chap4_pe3_books_solution*.

b. Save the publication as **chap4_mid2_books_email_solution**.

c. From the Format Publication task pane, click the **Publisher Tasks command**.

   TROUBLESHOOTING: You may have to click the down arrow at the bottom of the task pane to see the Publisher Tasks command.

d. Click the **Send in an e-mail command** from the Distributing your Publication list.

e. Click the **Send as a message command** from the Send in an e-mail list, and then choose **Current page only** in the dialog box that appears.

   If you choose to send a Web site with more than one page, most of the formatting will be lost.

f. Click the **Preview command** to see what your publication will look like in a browser.

g. Click the **Address and Send command** from the Send as a message list.

...continued on Next Page

h. Click the **Use a list command** from the Address and Send list.

i. Make sure the Use an existing lists toggle box is marked, as shown in Figure 4.36, and click the **Next command** at the bottom of the task pane.

j. Browse to find the *chap4_mid1_list_solution* file saved in the first mid-level exercise.

k. Double-click the *chap4_mid1_list_solution* file.

l. Click **OK** in the Mail Merge Recipients dialog box.

m. Click the **Next command** at the bottom of the task pane to go to Step 3.

n. Click the **Send e-mail command**.

> **TROUBLESHOOTING:** Publisher may indicate potential design issues with the format of this publication. If you previewed your publication and everything looked fine, then you can proceed.

o. Type **Secondhand Bookstore** in the subject line of the Merge to e-mail dialog box, and then click the **Send button**.

p. Click **OK** to send it, and then open Outlook Express or Outlook to be sure your e-mail was sent.

Because the customer data are not real, e-mails will bounce back to you as undelivered.

q. Open the Sent folder of your e-mail and print a copy of one e-mail to submit to your instructor.

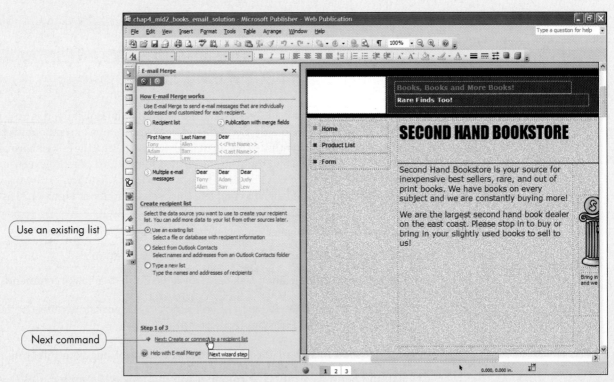

Figure 4.36 Address List

Capstone Exercise

You have a project in your computer class to make an electronic portfolio (EP). This EP will be your very own Web site, where you can showcase all of your achievements. You need to have at a minimum a "Home page," an "About Me" page, a "Courses" page, and a "Related Experiences" page. You can add more pages later if you so desire.

Home Page

a. Open the *chap4_cap_ep* publication and save it as **chap4_cap_ep_solution**.

b. Change the text in the title; you will then use this on every page you make.

c. Change the title of the home page from just *Home* to something else.

d. Change the body text of your home page.

e. Put in your picture (or any other picture) and add a caption if you like.

f. Put in your e-mail address so you can be contacted.

About Me Page

a. Insert the header.

b. Change the body text to information about yourself, such as your education, hobbies, etc.

c. Add another picture of yourself, different from the one on the home page (optional).

d. Place your e-mail address here also.

Courses Page

a. Insert the header.

b. Insert a description for the page.

c. Add in the course name and write a course description.

d. Repeat step c for as many courses as you like.

Experiences Page

a. Insert the header.

b. Insert a description for the page.

c. Add in the type of experience and write a description.

d. Repeat step c for as many experiences as you like.

Mini Cases

Use the rubric following the case as a guide to evaluate your work, but keep in mind that your instructor may impose additional grading criteria or use a different standard to judge your work.

Web Design Team

GENERAL CASE

You have joined your major's Web design team at school. Your first task is to design a template for the site; after the template is made, create the main pages from it. The main pages should include, but are not limited to, the following: main home page for the site, program page, co-op and/or internship profiles page, who's who page featuring faculty, and a resources page providing links to the school's library, writing center, and more. Links to other pages can be made off of the main pages, but it is up to you (or your teacher) if they need to be completed. Try to incorporate the school's colors into the design of the site. If you need some ideas for the design of your site, search for other sites like this online; there are plenty to be found. Open the *chap4_mc1_school* publication or start with any predesigned template and save the file as **chap4_mc1_school_solution**.

Performance Elements	Exceeds Expectations	Meets Expectations	Below Expectations
Site layout/design	Planned out, very easy to navigate.	Simple and straightforward.	Poor design, every page is different.
School colors	Actual school colors.	Few different colors, coordinates well.	Poor color choice, different shades of same color.
Number of pages	5+ pages total.	2–4 pages total.	Just home page.

Programming Codes

RESEARCH CASE

You are learning about making Web sites in your computer class. Your assignment is to make a handout for the class describing a few topics covered in class. The most important topics to research are different types of programming code used for Web site development, different programs used for Web design, and different ways to publish sites. Additional topics can also be covered. Using the *chap4_mc2_coding* flyer publication, add text boxes and type your research in the areas listed above. Save the file as **chap4_mc2_coding_solution**.

Performance Elements	Exceeds Expectations	Meets Expectations	Below Expectations
Types of code	4+ examples.	2–3 examples.	only 1 (HTML).
Web design programs	4+ examples.	2–3 examples.	only 1 (FrontPage).
Publishing software	4+ examples.	2–3 examples.	only 1 (FTP).

American Bikes

DISASTER RECOVERY

You have been put in charge of making your company's American Bikes Web site. You decide to create it in Publisher. However, there was an error when creating the publication and the links to several pages have disappeared. The pages should contain navigation bar links to: Home, About Us, Product List, and Service List. However, the remaining three links have been lost on the navigation bar to About Us, Product List, and Service List on all four pages. You need to repair the links to navigation bars on each page. Open the *chap4_mc3_bikes* publication to repair the links, and then save the file as **chap4_mc3_bikes_solution**.

Performance Elements	Exceeds Expectations	Meets Expectations	Below Expectations
Home page	Added all three navigation bar menu items.	Added two navigation bar menu items.	Added one navigation bar menu item.
About us page	Added all three navigation bar menu items.	Added two navigation bar menu items.	Added one navigation bar menu item.
Products list page	Added all three navigation bar menu items.	Added two navigation bar menu items.	Added one navigation bar menu item.
Service list page	Added all three navigation bar menu items.	Added two navigation bar menu items.	Added one navigation bar menu item.

Glossary

All key terms appearing in this book (in bold italic) are listed alphabetically in this Glossary for easy reference. If you want to learn more about a feature or concept, use the Index to find the term's other significant occurrences.

Background sound   Files can be added to your Web publication. When the Web page is opened on the Internet, if the user has speakers, the sound will play in the background.

Baseline guides   Help to align text.

Blank Page Sizes   A gallery of different page size options. This gallery contains common page sizes, such as landscape or portrait.

Blank Page Sizes Task Pane   Includes page size information, color and font scheme options, and business information options.

Bulleted list   Emphasizes and separates items.

Business forms   Organized documents that help to control everyday operating processes, such as ordering, billing, faxing, and more.

Business information sets   Contain information about you or your business; you create Business information sets once, but use them over and over.

Canvas   A container that can be selected, deleted, moved, rotated, and sized.

Clip art on Office Online   A site provided by Microsoft that contains extra clip art, photos, sounds, and more.

Close command   Closes the current publication.

Color Schemes   A drop-down menu that allows you to choose a blend of predefined color choices.

Control properties   Enable you to set properties specific to the type of form control, such as text properties and style of button.

Copyright   Provides legal protection for a written or artistic work, including literary, dramatic, and musical, as well as artistic works such as poetry, novels, movies, songs, computer software, and architecture.

Default layout   A predefined tempate that contains grid guides, picture placeholders, color and font schemes, and more.

Design sets   Collection of publications with a similar color scheme, font scheme, and more. In this window, you can also click to view templates from Microsoft Office Online where there are even more design choices.

Dropped-capital letter   Also known as a drop cap; a large capital letter at the beginning of a paragraph. It catches the reader's eye and calls attention to the associated text.

Easy Web Site Builder   Used for creating Web pages and Web sites in a quick, efficient, and easy way.

Edit Business Information Set dialog box   A tool that allows you to create as many business information set names as you wish.

E-mail Web pages and sites   Used to market your products and services; E-mail advertising is a low-cost way to keep in contact with your customers.

Exit command   Quits Publisher altogether.

Expense Report   Used to list an employee's expenses, such as business trip expenses. You want to be able to list items, such as car, hotel, food, and/or entertainment expenses. When filing income taxes, these records can be very helful.

Fair use   A policy that gives permission to use a portion of a work for educational, nonprofit purposes or for the purpose of critical review or commentary.

Fax Cover Sheet   Used to send information along with the organization's fax documents. The fax cover sheet typically precedes the documents to be faxed and contains places to list the sender's name, the recipient, the date, and other detailed informaiton.

File menu   Contains commands for opening a new file, saving a file, printing, changing your page setup, and much more. It is a critically important menu in every Windows application.

Fill color   Adds a choice of different colors to text boxes, objects, and more.

Flipping objects   Enables you to flip the object horizontally or vertically.

Font Schemes   A drop-down menu that allows you to choose a major and a minor typeface for the title, headings, and paragraph text of the newsletter.

Foreground   Contains all objects and text that will appear on that page only, as opposed to the background master page.

Form controls   Enable a visitor to your Web site to submit information and/or feedback, including check boxes, option buttons, list box, textbox, text area, and submit button.

Formatting toolbar   Appears below the menu bar and provides access to common formatting operations such as boldface, italics, or underlining. Formatting buttons become active (i.e., able to be used) when you select an object on which they can operate.

Grid guides   Help to align columns and rows.

Grouping objects When separate objects become one grouped set of objects.

Hyperlinks Provide a link to other Web pages, documents, images, and more on the Internet.

HyperText Markup Language (HTML) A markup language that describes how text, graphics, and/or other items will look when viewed as a Web page.

Infringement (of a copyright) Occurs any time a right reserved by the copyright owner is violated without permission of the owner.

Insert Hyperlink dialog box Gives you several options, such as linking to an existing Web site or file, linking to the current site's documents, linking to a new document, or even linking to an e-mail address. Also enables you to display text instead of the URL address and to remove or edit a hyperlink.

Internet A network of networks that connects computers anywhere in the world.

Inventory List Used to list in-stock inventory. The form contains places to list each item, the form of payment, description of the item, date the item was purchased, warranty information, and more.

Invoice Used to bill customers for services or supplies. This form contains the client number and address, and a description of the item or service that was purchased.

Layering Positioning each object on the publication in such a way as to achieve an uncluttered look, among other objects.

Layout guides Underlying, but nonprinting, set of blue and green horizontal and vertical lines that determine the placement of the major elements. These guides repeat on each page of a publication, establishing its overall structure by indicating the number of columns, the space between columns, the size of the margins, the placement of objects, and so on.

Layout Guides command Tool that allows you to change margin guides, grid guides, and baseline guides.

Layout Guides dialog box Enables you to change the position of the margin guides, the number of column or row grid guides, and whether you want to create mirrored guides (for publications printed on facing pages).

Lines and borders Boxes around objects, text, and tables.

Margin guides Define the top, bottom, left, and right margins.

Markup codes Also known as tags; when placed before and/or after the text or graphics, they describe how the page should appear when viewed in a browser.

Master page Contains items that you want to show up on every page such as margin guides, clip art, text, and more.

Menu bar Appears immediately below the title bar and contains drop-down menu items, such as the File menu.

Numbered list Sequences and prioritizes items. Publisher automatically updates numbered lists to accommodate additions or deletions.

Objects toolbar Contains commands to insert text boxes, pictures, WordArt, Shapes, and much more.

Page Size A drop-down menu that allows you to choose the page spread.

Popular Publication Types Task Pane Displays a listing of the most used publications.

Predesigned form A template that contains formatting, text, and graphical or financial data placeholders.

Print command Prints a publication.

Public domain Gives everyone the right to freely reproduce and distribute the material.

Publication gallery Offers many different designs.

Publication Types Task Pane Displays a listing of different publication categories.

Publisher Tasks A link that provides commands for previewing your e-mail publication, checking for errors, posting to a Web site, and more.

Pull quote A phrase or sentence taken from a publication to emphasize a key point. It is typically set in larger type, often in a different typeface and/or italics, and may be offset with a border surrounding it.

Purchase Order Used to request services or supplies. This form contains places to list each item, a description of the item, the number of units ordered, any applicable taxes, discounts, and more.

Quote Form Used to bid for jobs or outline how much services or supplies will cost the client.

Recent Publications Task Pane Displays a listing of your most recently saved publications.

Record keeping A procedure that keeps financial records in order. Record keeping may include inventory control, sales quotes, expense reports, purchase orders, statements, and lots more.

Refund Form Used to keep track of any refunds to clients. Contains places to list each item, the date it was purchased, any applicable tax refund, and more.

Reverse Light text on a dark background and is a favorite technique of desktop publishers, commonly used to emphasize a specific element. It is sometimes used in the heading (the identifying information) at the top of a newsletter or flyer and provides a distinctive look to the publication.

Rotating objects Enables you to rotate 90 degrees left or right.

Ruler guides Can be used to position objects that are not repeated on every page.

Sans serif typeface Font without tiny cross lines at the ends of the characters (sans from the French word for without).

Save As command Saves a publication under a different name.

Save command Copies the publication that is currently being edited to disk.

Scroll bars   Used to move up or down and left or right and appear at the right and bottom of the publication window; and the status bar at the bottom of the publication window contains Page Navigation buttons for moving between pages in the publication.

Send Publication as Attachment command   Tool that enables you to send a publication via e-mail.

Serif typeface   Has tiny cross lines at the ends of the characters to help the eye connect one letter with the next.

Software piracy   The unauthorized duplication or use of software products such as Microsoft Office.

Standard toolbar   Contains buttons corresponding to the most basic commands in Publisher, such as saving files or opening a new file, appears below the menu bar.

Statement   Used to itemize invoices for periodic billing.

Status bar   Indicates which page is displayed presently on the screen and shows the position and size of a selected object.

Synchronization   Means that any formatting changes made in a publication will be automatically changed with similar elements on the same publication; this may be turned off in your Publisher options.

Template   A partially completed publication that contains formatting, text, and/or graphics placeholders (dotted-line boxes that show the position of the objects in a publication's design). A template may be as simple as an envelope or as complex as a newsletter or Web site.

Text box   An object used in Publisher to hold text.

Time Billing   Used to bill for time-based services.

Title bar   Displays the application, the name of the publication with which you are working, and the standard window-sizing buttons.

Transparent objects   Enables you to see other text or objects stacked behind or on the master page.

Type size   A vertical measurement that is specified in points (pts). One pt is equal to 1/72 of an inch. The text in most publications is set in 10 or 12 pt type, whereas headings are usually set much larger.

Typeface   Also known as font; a complete set of characters (upper and lowercase letters, numbers, punctuation marks, and special symbols). Typefaces are divided into two general categories, serif and sans serif.

Typography   The process of selecting typefaces, type styles, and type sizes. It is a critical, often subtle, element in the success of a publication.

Web forms   Enable your visitors to place orders, submit information, join a mailing list, or provide feedback.

Web Options command   Allows you to add a title to your Web publication, add sound to your publication, and add Web page descriptors to your Web site.

Web Options dialog box   Allows you to add a title to your Web site, add keywords for search engines, and add a sound file and control the amount of time the sound file plays.

Weekly Record   Used to keep track of employee work hours, both regular and overtime.

Window-sizing buttons   Minimize, maximize or restore, or close your application.

WordArt   A uniquely designed text object.

World Wide Web (WWW)   (Simply, the Web) A very large subset of the Internet, consisting of those computers that store a special type of document known as a Web page.

Zoom command   Displays the publication on the screen at different magnifications; however, it does not affect the size of the text on the printed page.

Multiple Choice Answer Keys

Chapter 1
1. c
2. c
3. d
4. c
5. b
6. d
7. a
8. d
9. d
10. d
11. b
12. b
13. d
14. d
15. d
16. d
17. b
18. b

Chapter 2
1. c
2. d
3. c
4. b
5. d
6. a
7. d
8. d
9. c
10. c
11. b
12. a
13. c
14. c
15. d
16. a
17. d
18. d

Chapter 3
1. c
2. d
3. b
4. b
5. a
6. b
7. c
8. a
9. d
10. d
11. b
12. b
13. c
14. c
15. d
16. b
17. a
18. a

Chapter 4
1. b
2. b
3. d
4. b
5. d
6. c
7. a
8. c
9. d
10. d
11. d
12. d
13. b
14. a
15. d
16. d
17. a
18. d

Index